Making It Happen

DIRECTIONS IN DEVELOPMENT
Public Sector Governance

Making It Happen

Selected Case Studies of Institutional Reforms in South Africa

Asad Alam, Renosi Mokate, and Kathrin A. Plangemann, Editors

WORLD BANK GROUP

Contents

Boxes

Figures

Tables

Foreword

South Africa has achieved a lot on its path of socioeconomic transformation since the end of apartheid in 1994. Although many challenges remain to fostering inclusive growth to address the triple challenges of unemployment, poverty, and inequality, some innovative approaches have been used to build more inclusive public institutions. These have helped to expand service delivery, strengthen quality, and improve the lives of millions of South Africans.

Although much is known about the motivation and nature of the policies and institutional changes that drove this transformation, very little is known of the manner in which they were executed. With this book, *Making It Happen: Selected Case Studies of Institutional Reforms in South Africa*, we offer a selection of twelve case studies to illustrate how policies and institutions were developed and implemented to improve specific public services.

Based on interviews with senior policy makers, the book captures the how-to of designing and executing these policies in a variety of strategic areas, including increasing budget transparency, developing an intergovernmental fiscal system, strengthening tax administration, enhancing the statistical system, developing a modern performance monitoring and evaluation system, expanding HIV/AIDS treatment, reforming the social transfer system, creating a modern national identity system, developing a system for the management of biodiversity, modernizing the national road network management, developing the framework for renewable energy, and formulating the country's much-lauded constitution.

Tracing a twenty-year journey of transformation, this book places particular emphasis on recording the design of these reforms and endeavors to shed some light on the decision-making processes. In particular, it attempts to provide insight on the trade-offs policy makers faced, and the sequencing and complementarities among the various reforms. It finds leadership at different levels, adoption of pragmatic and innovative solutions, and the focus on results as among the key drivers in implementing these changes.

This book is primarily intended to enhance knowledge exchange by exporting South Africa's development experience to the world. It is a product of the country's Knowledge Hub, developed in partnership with the World Bank Group, to provide evidence-based solutions for enhancing service delivery. Many of the lessons identified here have applicability for other countries, with adaptation, of course, to local needs and circumstance. But many of the same lessons have applicability also for the South Africa of today, as the country grapples with many difficult development challenges.

I hope that this book will be equally useful for policy makers, civil society organizations, development practitioners, and all others who are interested in the global imperative to end extreme poverty and boost shared prosperity, and make this world a better place for all.

Makhtar Diop
Regional Vice President for Africa
World Bank

Acknowledgments

Many people have contributed to the development of this book. The initial idea for this book was proposed by World Bank Group President Jim Yong Kim during his 2012 visit to South Africa. The team is very grateful to Mr. Makhtar Diop, Regional Vice President for Africa, for his leadership and support to this work. The team would also like to thank Mr. Jan Walliser, former Director of Strategy for the Africa Region and now Vice President, Equitable Growth, Finance, and Institutions Practice Group, and the current Country Director for South Africa, Guang Zhe Chen, for their continued support.

This book was initiated and completed while Mr. Pravin Gordhan was the Minister of Finance of South Africa. The authors are very grateful for his guidance and support. The authors are also very grateful to Mr. Lungisa Fuzile, Director-General at the National Treasury, for his guidance and encouragement.

The book was written by a team led by Asad Alam, Country Director, who provided strategic leadership and guidance to the team; Kathrin A. Plangemann, Lead Governance Specialist and Cluster Leader for Southern Africa, who as the task manager led the overall preparation of the book; and Renosi Mokate, Executive Director and Chief Executive Officer of the UNISA Graduate School of Business Leadership, who provided invaluable support and insights. The team also included the individual authors Lucilla Maria Bruni, Ben Gericke, David Hausman, Joel Kolker, George Ledec, Phindile Ngwenya, Catriona Purfield, Zandile Ratshitanga, Claudia Sobrevila, Gert van der Linde, Ivan Velev, Chris Warner, Precious Zikhali, and Nonhlahla Zindela (all World Bank staff) as well as Misha V. Belkindas, John Carneson, Neil Cole, Magali Junowicz, and Aarti Shah. Barbara Karni and Charlotte Gauthier provided editorial assistance. Melanie Jaya provided administrative support.

The team would like to thank the internal peer reviewers Kundhavi Kadiresan, Country Director; Junaid Ahmad, Senior Director; and Joel Hellman, Director, for their invaluable contributions. It would also like to thank the individual peer reviewers for each chapter who include Karan Capoor, Michael Engelschalk, Saliem Fakir, Neil Fantom, Ximena Fernandez Ordonez, Alta Fölscher, Peter Freeman, Steven Friedman, Alan Gelb, Matthew Glasser, Felix Junquera-Varela, Barry Kistnasamy, Zoe Kolovou, Lili Liu, Luiz Maurer, Mark Pickering, and Ros Thomas as well as other reviewers who provided comments, including Cem Dener, Verena Fritz, Patrick Kabuya, Sarah Lavin, Maria Njambi Ngarachu,

Vijay Pillai, and David Wachira. The team is indebted to the external reviewers from the Advisory Committee set up for this book for their excellent feedback, including Rashad Cassim, Head of the Research Department at the South African Reserve Bank; Mariam Isa, Economics Journalist and Editor at Business Day; Sibongile Mkhabela, Chief Executive Officer at Nelson Mandela Children's Fund; Joel Netshitenzhe, Executive Director of MISTRA (Mapungugwe Institute for Strategic Reflection); and Professor Wiseman Nkuhlu, Chancellor of the University of Pretoria and Chairman of Rothschild SA.

The book was initiated by Asad Alam, Country Director, under the guidance of Marcelo Guigale, Senior Director, and John Panzer, Director, of the World Bank's Group Macroeconomics and Fiscal Management Global Practice, and finalized under the guidance of Mario Marcel, Senior Director, and James Brumby, Director, of the Global Governance Practice; Guenter Heidenhof, Practice Manager, Public Sector Performance, Africa; and Guang Zhen Chen, Country Director.

The team is very grateful to all who made invaluable contributions and shared rich insights throughout the development of this book, particularly to Tanya Abrahamse, Chief Executive Officer, South African National Biodiversity Institute, SANBI; Tania Ajam, Commissioner, Financial and Fiscal Commission; Ismael Akhalwaya, Head, Management Performance Assessment Tool, MPAT; Nazir Alli, Chief Executive Officer, South African National Road Agency, Limited, SANRAL, and former Chief Director of Roads, Department of Transportation; Ompi Aphane, Deputy Director-General, Energy Policy and Planning, Department of Energy; Mkuseli Apleni, Director General, Department of Home Affairs; Servaas van der Berg, Professor, University of Stellenbosch; Haroon Bhorat, Professor and Director of the Development Policy Research Unit, University of Cape Town; Karen Breytenbach, Head of the Department of Energy's Independent Power Producer Unit; Kay Brown, Chief Director, Expenditure Planning, National Treasury; David Daitz, former Chief Executive Officer, Western Cape Nature Conservation Board and former Manager of Table Mountain National Park; Andrew Dawes, Professor Emeritus, University of Cape Town; Andrew Donaldson, Government Technical Advisory Centre, Acting Head, National Treasury; Dianne Dunkerly, Executive Manager, Grants Administration; Wendy Fanoe, Chief Director, Intergovernmental Policy and Planning, National Treasury; Ian Goldman, Head of Evaluation, Department of Planning, Monitoring and Evaluation, DPME; Pravin Gordhan, Minister of Cooperative Governance and Traditional Affairs, Minister of Finance 2009–14 and from December 2015 to the present, and Commissioner of the South African Revenue Service, SARS 1999–2009; Nolwazi Gasa, former Deputy Director-General, Department of Planning, Monitoring and Evaluation, DPME; Jan Hattingh, Chief Director, Local Government Budget Analysis, National Treasury; Claire Horton, Western Cape Provincial Treasury; Brian Huntley, former Chief Executive Officer, South African National Biodiversity Institute, SANBI; Selwyn Jehoma, former Deputy Director-General, Department of Social Development; Andrew Johnston, former Managing Director, African Infrastructure

Investment Managers (Pty) Limited; Sello Kau, former Deputy Director-General: IT Services, Department of Home Affairs; Sven de Kok, Lead Consultant, FeverTree Consulting; Carin Koster, General Manager, APM and Solution Development, South African Social Security Agency; George Kotsovos, Head, Power and Infrastructure Finance, Corporate and Investment Banking, Standard Bank; Bongani Khumalo, Acting Chairperson/Chief Executive, Financial and Fiscal Commission, Financial and Fiscal Commission; John Kilani, former Director, Occupational Health and Safety, South African Chamber of Mines; Mike Knight, Head of Planning and Development, SANParks; Pali Lehohla, Statistician-General, Statistics South Africa; Bernadette Leon, former Head of Frontline Service Delivery Monitoring, Department of Planning, Monitoring and Evaluation, DPME; Frances Lund, Professor and Senior Research Associate, University of Kwazulu-Natal and Chair of the Lund Committee on Child and Family Support; Justin Ma, Vice President, Investment Banking Division, ABSA Capital; Vusi Madonsela, Director-General of the Department of Cooperative Governance and former Director-General of the Department of Social Development; Thuli Madonsela, Public Protector; Harry Malila, Deputy Director-General, Western Cape Provincial Treasury; Risenga Maluleke, Deputy Director-General of Corporate Relations, Statistics South Africa; Trevor Manuel, Finance Minister 1996–2009 and Minister in the Presidency for the National Planning Commission; Kristal Maze, Chief Director, South African National Biodiversity Institute, SANBI; Mac Maharaj, Minister of Transport, 1994–99, official spokesperson for President Jacob Zuma; Lena Mangondo, Director, Corporate Law, National Treasury; Roelf Meyer, chief National Party negotiator in talks to end apartheid; Vusi Mkhize, Deputy Director-General: Civic Services, Department of Home Affairs; Zaheera Mohamed, Head of Social Development Division, National Treasury; Ismail Momoniat, Deputy Director-General, National Treasury; Euody Mogaswa, Director, Budget Reform, National Treasury; Mvuso Msimang, former Director-General, Department of Home Affairs; Nicolli Nattrass, Professor of Economics and Director of AIDS and Society Research Unit within the Center for Social Science Research at the University of Cape Town; Pathamavathy Naicker, General Manager, Monitoring, Evaluation and Research, South African Social Security Agency; Adius Ncube, Lead Consultant, FeverTree Consulting; Malijeng Ngqaleni, Deputy Director-General, Intergovernmental Affairs, National Treasury; Khungeka Njobe, former Director, South African Biodiversity Institute, SANBI; Stanley Ntakumba, Acting Director-General, Department of Planning, Monitoring and Evaluation, DPME; Vuyo Hlompho Ntoi, Associate Director, African Infrastructure Investment Managers (Pty) Limited; Judy Parfitt, former General Manager for Human Resources of the South African Revenue Service, SARS; Mike Peo, Head, Infrastructure, Energy & Telecommunications, NEDBANK Investment Banking; Virginia Peterson, Chief Executive Officer, South African Social Security Agency; Sean Phillips, former Director-General, Department of Planning, Monitoring and Evaluation, DPME; Alexander Pick, Social Protection and Employment Specialist, National Treasury; Derek Powell, former Deputy General Director, Department of Provincial and

Local Government (DPLG), Multilevel Government Initiative, University of the Western Cape; Itumeleng Rantao, Economist, International Finance, National Treasury; Raphaahle Ramokgopa, Executive Manager, Strategy and Business Development, South African Social Security Agency; Mark Rasmussen, General Manager of Grants Administration, Eastern Cape, South African Social Security Agency; Albie Sachs, Judge, Constitution Court, 1994–2009; Michael Sachs, Deputy Director-General, National Treasury; Tsietsi Sebelemetja, Director, Drafting, Department of Home Affairs legal services; Thomas Sigama, Chief Director, Civic Services, Department of Home Affairs; Zola Skweyiya, former Minister of Social Development; Vivienne Taylor, Professor, University of Cape Town, Chair, Committee of Inquiry into a Comprehensive Social Security System for South Africa; Marcia Sheraton, Western Cape Provincial Treasury; David Tseng, Western Cape Provincial Treasury; Rentia van Tonder, Head, Renewable Energy, Power and Infrastructure Coverage, Standard Bank; Brenton Van Vrede, Chief Director, Social Assistance, Department of Social Development; Shireen de Visser, Western Cape Provincial Treasury; Walter Volker, Chief Executive Officer, Payments Association of South Africa; Gregg Wheelwright, Manager, Distribution, Corporate and Investment Banking, Standard Bank; Andrew Zaloumis, Chief Executive Officer, iSimangaliso, St. Lucia, World Heritage Authority; and Nkosazana Dlamini Zuma, former Minister of Home Affairs. The team also thanks the many others inside and outside the World Bank who provided helpful comments.

Any remaining errors are solely the responsibility of the authors and should not be attributed to the World Bank Group.

Contributors

Asad Alam was the Country Director for Botswana, Lesotho, Namibia, South Africa, and Swaziland at the World Bank Group (2012–15).

Misha V. Belkindas is Cofounder and Managing Director of Open Data Watch, an international NGO working in the area of openness of national statistical systems.

Lucilla Maria Bruni is an Economist in the World Bank's Social Protection and Labor Global Practice.

John Carneson is the Chief Director, Policy and Strategic Management, at the South African Department of Home Affairs.

Neil Cole is the Executive Secretary of the Collaborative Africa Budget Reform Initiative (CABRI), which was housed in the National Treasury between 2004 and 2011.

Ben Gericke is a Program Leader and Lead Transport Specialist in the Africa Region of the World Bank.

David Hausman holds a JD from Stanford Law School and is a PhD candidate in political science at Stanford University.

Joel Kolker is the Lead Water and Sanitation Specialist in the World Bank's Water Global Practice.

George Ledec is a Lead Ecologist in the World Bank's Environment and Natural Resources Global Practice.

Patrick Lumumba Osewe is the Global Lead for Public Health at the World Bank.

Renosi Mokate is the Executive Director and Chief Executive Officer of the UNISA Graduate School of Business Leadership.

Phindile Ngwenya is a former Research Analyst in the World Bank's Macroeconomics and Fiscal Management Global Practice.

Yogan Pillay is the Deputy Director General of the National Department of Health (NDOH), South Africa.

Kathrin A. Plangemann is a Lead Public Sector Governance Specialist and Cluster Leader for Southern Africa in the World Bank's Governance Global Practice.

Catriona Purfield is the former Program Leader for Macroeconomics and Fiscal Management, Finance, Trade, Poverty, and Governance in the South Africa Country Management Unit at the World Bank.

Zandile Ratshitanga is a Senior Communications Officer at the World Bank.

Aarti Shah is an adviser to the executive secretary of the Collaborative Africa Budget Reform Initiative (CABRI).

Claudia Sobrevila is a Senior Environment Specialist in the World Bank's Environment and Natural Resources Global Practice.

Gert van der Linde is a Lead Financial Management Specialist in the World Bank's Global Governance Practice.

Ivan Velev is the Country Program Coordinator for the South Africa Country Management Unit at the World Bank.

Christopher J. Warner is a Senior Technical Specialist in the World Bank's Environment and Natural Resources Global Practice.

Precious Zikhali is an Economist in the World Bank's Poverty Global Practice.

Nonhlahla Zindela is a Senior Operations Officer in the South Africa Country Management Unit at the World Bank.

Abbreviations

AENP	Addo Elephant National Park
ANC	African National Congress
APAI–CRVS	Africa Program on Accelerated Improvement of Civil Registration and Vital Statistics Systems
ART	antiretroviral therapy
ASANRA	Association of Southern African National Roads Agencies
BAKWENA	Bakwena Platinum Concession Consortium
BEE	Black Economic Empowerment
BEMF	Budget and Expenditure Monitoring Forum
CABRI	Collaborative Africa Budget Reform Initiative
CEMIS	Compliance Evaluation and Monitoring Information System
CEO	chief executive officer
CLEAR	Center for Learning on Evaluation and Results
CODESA	Convention for Democratic South Africa
COGTA	Cooperative Governance and Traditional Affairs Department
COP	Conference of Parties
COSATU	Congress of South African Trade Unions
CPI	consumer price index
CRUISE	Center for Regional and Urban Innovation and Statistical Exploration
CSS	Central Statistical Services
DFID	U.K. Department for International Development
DHA	Department of Home Affairs
DIRCO	Department of International Relations and Cooperation
DOE	Department of Energy
DORA	Division of Revenue Act
DOT	Department of Transport
DPLG	Department of Provincial and Local Government

DPME	Department of Planning, Monitoring and Evaluation (formerly Department of Performance Monitoring and Evaluation)
DPSA	Department of Public Service and Administration
DQAF	Data Quality Assessment Framework
DTI	Department of Trade and Industry
EDI	electronic data interchange
EPC	engineering, procurement, and construction
EPMS	Employee Performance Management System
EU	European Union
FFC	Financial and Fiscal Commission
FIT	feed-in tariff
GDP	gross domestic product
GEAR	Growth, Employment and Redistribution Strategy
GEF	Global Environment Facility
GFIP	Gauteng Freeway Improvement Project
GIFT	Global Initiative for Fiscal Transparency
GIZ	German Agency for International Cooperation
GPAA	Government Pensions Administration Agency
GWh	gigawatt-hour
ID	identification
IFP	Inkatha Freedom Party
IGFR	Intergovernmental Fiscal Review
IMF	International Monetary Fund
IPP	independent power producer
IT	information technology
M&E	monitoring and evaluation
MEC	Member of the Executive Council
MFMA	Municipal Finance Management Act
MINCOMBUD	Committee on the Budget
MINMEC	Minister and Executive Council Meeting
MINTECH	Technical Committee to MINMEC
MNDT	Mayibuye Ndlovu Development Trust
MPAT	Management Performance Assessment Tool
MPNF	Multiparty Negotiation Forum
MPNP	Multi-Party Negotiation Process
MTBPS	Medium-Term Budget Policy Statement
MTEF	Medium-Term Expenditure Framework
MTSF	Medium-Term Strategic Framework

MW	megawatt
N3TC	N3 Toll Concession (Pty) Ltd
NACOSA	National AIDS Coordinating Committee of South Africa
NAP	National AIDS Plan
NBI	National Botanical Institute
NERSA	National Energy Regulator of South Africa
NGO	nongovernmental organization
NP	National Party
NPC	National Planning Commission
NPR	National Population Register
OBI	Open Budget Index
OdeTT	Organizational Development Task Team
OECD	Organisation for Economic Co-operation and Development
PAYE	Pay-As-You-Earn
PEFA	Public Expenditure and Financial Accountability
PEPFAR	President's Emergency Plan for AIDS Relief
PFM	public financial management
PFMA	Public Finance Management Act
PIU	Project Implementation Unit
PPP	public-private partnership
RDP	Reconstruction and Development Program
REFIT	renewable energy feed-in tariff
REIPPPP	Renewable Energy Independent Power Producer Procurement Program
RFP	request for proposal
SACFMI	South Africa Corporate Fraud Management Institute
SACP	South African Communist Party
SAFCOL	South African Forestry Company Limited
SALGA	South African Local Government Association
SANAC	South African National AIDS Council
SANBI	South African National Biodiversity Institute
SANParks	South African National Parks
SANRAL	South African National Road Agency, Limited
SARS	South African Revenue Service
SASSA	South African Social Security Agency
SDDS	Standard Data Dissemination Standards
SME	small and medium-sized enterprise
SMS	Short Message Service
Statistics SA	Statistics South Africa

STI	sexually transmitted infection
TAC	Treatment Action Campaign
TB	tuberculosis
TCF	Technical Committee of Finance
TRAC	N4 Trans African Concession
UN	United Nations
VAT	value added tax
WCO	World Customs Organization
WDI	World Development Indicators
WWF	World Wildlife Fund

Note: Unless otherwise noted, U.S. dollar values are based on rand/dollar exchange rates in effect at the time the book was written.

Introduction

South Africa's Lessons in Progress

South Africa's political transformation to democracy has been celebrated around the world. Twenty years after the end of apartheid, economic and social opportunities have expanded for many of the country's citizens. The economy has grown at an average rate of about 3.1 percent a year since 1994. Millions of people who were previously excluded gained access to housing, water, sanitation, power, health care, education, social security, and jobs.

Progress has been extraordinary. But South Africa still faces the triple developmental challenges of high unemployment (24 percent), persistent poverty (37 percent of the population living on less than R 416 a day in 2011 prices), and extreme income inequality (Gini index of 0.65). Growth has slowed, the governance record is mixed, and service delivery is uneven (DPME 2012).

In selected areas, policies, institutions, and delivery mechanisms have been effectively implemented. Intergovernmental fiscal relations, budget transparency, revenue management, performance monitoring and evaluation, and statistical capacity have all improved. Access to HIV/AIDS treatment protocols has expanded, delivery of social grants has increased, and major improvements have been made in the process of obtaining identification documents (a fundamental step for accessing social services). Biodiversity management has been enhanced, national highway construction and maintenance have improved, renewable energy production has increased, and access to electricity has soared. The process by which South Africa's Constitution was drafted is a sui generis case study of how a politically and socially divided country came together to create what is widely recognized as a progressive and unifying constitution.

Little has been written about these successes, especially on the "how-to" of policy making and implementation. Drawing lessons on how policies were made, institutions strengthened, obstacles overcome, and implementation effected is important to inform national and global understanding of the processes of change. These lessons can serve other countries in the region and beyond that may also be struggling to improve many of the same services.

This book is intended to cross-fertilize knowledge under the South Africa Knowledge Hub program by "exporting" South African success stories to other countries. It may also rekindle the spirit of change within South Africa, informing the national debate on many other economic and social challenges. It is thus written for both an international and a national audience.

Other studies have assessed South Africa's economic and social transformation in the 20 years since the end of apartheid (see Presidency of the Republic of South Africa 2014). This book is different. It documents and learns from selected case studies of institutional reforms implemented over the past 20 years. It showcases reforms that worked and draws lessons about why they succeeded. The emphasis is less on what was done and more on the "how-to" of reforms in which significant achievements were made. Each of the 12 case studies is a work in progress; although much has been achieved, more needs to be done to ensure that the institutions created have an impact and the reforms carried out are sustained.

The Landscape in 1994

The inheritance of apartheid was a dismal one for most of the country's citizens. In 1994 South Africa was politically fragmented, with a racially divided governance system. Public services and capacities varied widely across the many Bantustans (self-governing territories) and national and provincial administrations. Service delivery was largely centralized, with race the defining feature for both access and quality. Income and nonincome gaps between blacks and whites were huge. Land, financial, and educational assets were concentrated in the hands of a few. Labor, which had been largely immobile during the apartheid period, suddenly became free to move, leading to mass migrations from rural to urban areas. Concerned about their safety and property rights, large numbers of white people emigrated. Domestic debt was high and the fiscal deficit unsustainable. Foreign exchange reserves had dwindled and domestic savings were very low in the face of foreign sanctions.

South Africa's political transformation took place in the context of epochal world events. The Berlin Wall had come down in 1989, and the Soviet Union had given way to many independent nation-states. The socialist model of economic development was widely seen to have collapsed, and the sway of global capitalism was expanding. Free markets were being promoted around the world. Capital was mobile and seeking countries and investment opportunities with the highest return, as the world was becoming more integrated.

In this global environment, the African National Congress (ANC) took the reins of government. Long a movement of struggle and protest, it found itself in government, adapting to the challenges of running a country and providing for its people. The leaders of the ANC had to develop programs to address the economic and social needs of the country. Most of its leaders came from poor backgrounds, having grown up in the poverty in South Africa's townships, informal settlements, and rural areas. Although some of these leaders received training in renowned institutions of both the East and the West, many were self-schooled, often in prison, using the University of South Africa's unique distance learning program. They lacked experience with governing, even at the local level. In 1994 they were thrust into leadership positions to transform the economic and social environment of their country.

This period was one of unbounded optimism and tremendous impatience. Nelson Mandela had just been released after 28 years in prison. The aspirations of a people long deprived of fundamental human rights and economic opportunities knew no limits. There was a spirit of euphoria for the possibilities that economic freedoms and the inner strength of a "rainbow nation" could provide. There was also impatience for justice and economic and social opportunities after decades of repression. Time was of the essence; people wanted tangible economic and social dividends from the freedoms for which they had fought so hard.

The expectation was for the state to take the lead, deliver services, create jobs, fix problems, and redress the injustices of the past. The end of economic sanctions meant that South Africa would reintegrate with the world and benefit from global trade and investment.

South Africa moved to democracy on its own terms. Democracy meant that the process of change was more and more participatory and inclusive. At the same time as mass revolt against apartheid intensified, discussion fora and think tanks were created on different aspects of the transformation of society, such as the Constitution, education, housing, health, and the economy. They analyzed and discussed the key features of the apartheid system, identified what needed to be changed, considered how the changes might be sequenced, and sought lessons from national and international experience. The think tanks also helped develop a pool of expertise that the new government could draw on.

A key feature of many of the fora was their inclusivity. They included representatives of various political parties, sectors, and liberation movements as well as business, labor, and civil society organizations. Joint secretariats coordinated processes and documented discussions and agreements. Combining evidence-based approaches grounded in research, international experience, and pragmatism to find solutions, these fora were an important feature of the transition period, helping build trust and relationships across the political and racial divide.

In 1993, F. W. de Klerk and Nelson Mandela won the Nobel Peace Prize. In 1994, the first democratic elections were held. In 1995, the Truth and Reconciliation Commission was created. The world was watching how democracy in South Africa was to unfold.

Economic and Social Transformation, 1994–2014

Against this backdrop, democratic South Africa started its economic and social transformation. The first priority was to stabilize the economy. Through adoption of strong institutional arrangements, such as an independent central

Making It Happen • http://dx.doi.org/10.1596/978-1-4648-0768-8

Table I.1 Key Economic Indicators in South Africa, 1992–94, 2005–07, and 2012–14

Indicator	1992–94	2005–07	2012–14
GDP growth (%)	0.8	5.4	1.9
GDP per capita (US$)	3,528	5,720.1	6,999
Inflation (average annual change in CPI)	10.9	3.7	5.8
Government revenues (% of GDP)	25.5	29.8	28.9
Government expenditures (% of GDP)	32.9	38.7	33.0
Budget balance (% of GDP)	−7.3	1.1	−3.9
Public debt (% of GDP)	37.3	30.3	45.1
Gross domestic savings (% of GDP)	17.1	15.5	14.3
Gross domestic investment (% of GDP)	15.8	18.9	19.5
Foreign direct investment (% of GDP)	−0.8	0.4	0.8
International reserves (US$)	3,918	26,414	49,808

Source: World Bank calculations based on official statistics (National Treasury, Statistics South Africa, South African Reserve Bank, Department of Planning and M&E, Department of Basic Education, Department of Higher Education, and Department of Labor.)
Note: CPI = consumer price index; GDP = gross domestic product.

bank, inflation targeting, and market-driven exchange rate policies, South Africa kept inflation under control (table I.1). Conservative monetary policies were complemented by a fiscal stance that sought to increase the tax base and enhance public spending, especially in the social sectors and previously underserved areas, while maintaining tight control of the budget deficit. In 1992–94, the budget deficit was 7.3 percent of gross domestic product (GDP); and a positive budget balance of 1 percent was achieved in the precrisis period of 2005–2007, providing government the fiscal space to respond to the crisis. Postcrisis, fiscal vigilance continues—the budget deficit averaged about 4.3 percent of GDP from 2009 to 2014 and by 2012–14, it had shrunk to about 3.9 percent, as a result of the countercyclical response to the global financial crisis. Public debt was reduced to prudent levels. Foreign reserves were built, a world-class financial sector established, and macroeconomic management capacity enhanced.

The second priority was fighting poverty through job creation and income support programs. Various social programs, in particular the social transfer program, have helped lift millions of people out of extreme poverty. Economic incentives and active industrial policies led to some increase in the employment rate (table I.2), especially among the black population. High and persistent unemployment remains a challenge, and the programs have not boosted investment significantly.

The third priority was service delivery. Basic services, both in the social and the economic sectors needed to be expanded to all citizens. For example, the government undertook a huge program of building schools and doubling university access for previously disadvantaged, particularly black, students. It created housing units for millions of people and expanded access to basic utilities, such as electricity, water, and sanitation.

Table I.2 Key Economic Indicators in South Africa, 1992–94 and 2012–14

Indicator	1992–94	2005–07	2012–14
Poverty headcount rate (% of population living on less than R 501 a day in 2011 prices)	50.5	42.2	37.0
Inequality (Gini index)	0.67	0.67	0.65
Minimum wage (R)	..	..	2,347.0
Shared prosperity (growth of per capita consumption of the bottom 40%)	..	..	3.5
Employment rate (percent)	39.7	44.7	42.8
Unemployment rate (percent)	23.3	22.2	24.3
Black unemployment rate (percent)	30.0	16.2	27.4
School attendance basic education (% of learners)	96.7	97.7	99.3
Access to higher education (% of population)	1.9	4.1	4.1
Access to power (% of population)	50.9	81.2	85.4
Access to state subsidized housing (% of households)		9.0	10.8

Source: World Bank calculations based on official statistics (National Treasury, Statistics South Africa, South African Reserve Bank, Department of Planning and M&E, Department of Basic Education, Department of Higher Education, and Department of Labor.)
Note: .. = negligible; R = South African rand.

Impressive achievements in service delivery notwithstanding, massive challenges remain, largely because of the large numbers of rural to urban migrants, partly a legacy of apartheid. Quality enhancements have lagged, and poor outcomes (in education, for example) have raised questions about the models of service delivery.

Building Inclusive Public Sector Institutions and Implementing Institutional Reforms

Reforms in several areas have been extraordinarily successful. Central to these stories has been the development of inclusive public sector institutions.

The twelve reform areas examined in this book illustrate how the state was able to create inclusive, effective institutions and push through institutional reforms encompassing both policy making and implementation within the existing reform space. The case studies were chosen on the basis of the following criteria:

- The policy challenge had substantial potential economic or social impact.
- Significant institutional reforms were made, from policy making to policy implementation.
- Tangible improvements in outcomes were achieved.
- Other countries expressed interest in the reform, or demand for learning from South Africa is anticipated.
- Policy makers and South African stakeholders are interested in learning about what happened.

Chapters draw on a combination of desk reviews, ongoing World Bank dialogue, and interviews with high-level policy makers and others. This approach provides a unique analysis showcasing how these reforms were designed and carried out. Each chapter starts by providing some context analysis of the key issues in the sector. It then identifies a policy challenge that needed strategic action and analyzes how it was addressed in terms of policy making and implementation. The chapters show how consensus was built, trade-offs were addressed, obstacles were overcome, reforms were sequenced, and international practices were used. They then discuss the results achieved, including their magnitude, sustainability, and impact on stakeholders, before concluding with lessons learned, including success factors, challenges, and the pending reform agenda.

1. *Developing an Intergovernmental Fiscal Framework.* At the advent of democracy in 1994, the government needed to develop a framework that would promote equity, extend services to all, and reduce poverty by redistributing national revenues. The South African Constitution, adopted in 1996, assigned revenue and expenditure responsibility and related functions to newly established subnational governments. It established three separate but interdependent spheres of government, each with specific powers, functions, and responsibilities, along with provisions for revenue assignments. The intergovernmental fiscal framework has evolved over the years. It has proven resilient to major changes, such as the restructuring of local governments. Although much more needs to be done to enhance fiscal management at different levels in order to improve service delivery and strengthen accountability, the system provides a unifying fiscal framework across government.

2. *Increasing Budget Transparency.* In 1994 South Africa had a fragmented and opaque budget, with little public information on resource generation and allocation. Adoption of the Public Financial Management Act showcases how consensus was built to bring about a number of innovations that increased budget transparency. As a result of reforms, South Africa consistently ranks among the top five countries on the Open Budget Index. The performance-based budgeting process, including citizen access to budget information, is a salient feature of the focus on incorporating a performance orientation across sectors in South Africa.

3. *Raising Tax Revenue.* At the end of apartheid, one of South Africa's most pressing challenges was improving the efficiency, efficacy, and adequacy of the tax system and generating income for the reforms in the social and economic sectors. Challenges included a low level of tax compliance (only about 6 percent of South Africans paid income tax); weak, nontransparent, and noninclusive taxpayer services; lack of racial diversity among staff; and a shortage of qualified middle managers. These challenges were addressed by establishing a unified South African Revenue Service (SARS); creating a service culture, through professionalization of staff, process reengineering, and taxpayer service innovations; and transforming the organization so that it could broaden the tax base, raise tax revenues, and reduce tax evasion.

4. *Strengthening Performance Monitoring and Evaluation.* Under apartheid, the welfare of the majority of the population was largely ignored, and little was done to track the quality of service delivery to citizens. Today South Africa is a regional leader in performance monitoring and evaluation (M&E). Since the creation in 2010 of the Department of Performance Monitoring and Evaluation (since 2014, the Department of Planning, Monitoring and Evaluation) (DPME) in the Presidency, the country has instituted a national outcomes system, a management performance assessment system, a national evaluation system, frontline service delivery monitoring, and a national framework for citizens-based monitoring. It is now also working on incorporating the planning function. Although still at an early stage and undergoing changes, efforts to create a culture of performance M&E for the benefit of citizens are laying the foundation for improved government coordination, budget efficiency and effectiveness, and greater transparency and accountability in the use of public funds to ensure quality service delivery to all citizens.

5. *Creating an Inclusive and Credible Statistical System.* South Africa has come a long way from the fragmented, partial, nontransparent, and incomplete statistical system inherited from the apartheid system. Key features include a unified national statistical system, data openness and transparency, and a strong institutional framework that provides for operational independence as well as the ability to hire and retain highly skilled staff. Statistics comply with international standards in many domains. The household survey provides micro-household-level data for policy analysis. Decadal censuses are comprehensive and of a high quality. Administrative data sources complement the data collected through surveys and censuses. As a result of the different reforms carried out, the international statistical community recognizes Statistics South Africa as a strong performer.

6. *Expanding HIV/AIDS Treatment.* After a decade of virtual denial of the HIV/AIDS epidemic, South Africa has addressed the challenge and shown some impressive results. Antiretroviral treatment (ART) has been expanded to millions of people, making South Africa's program the largest in the world. In 2009, with the change of policy, the country launched a massive prevention and education campaign and mobilized public and private funds. It reduced new HIV infections among children by 50 percent. Infant mortality rates fell from 73 per 1,000 live births in 2006 to 42 per 1,000 live births in 2012. Adult mortality rates also fell sharply. As a result, life expectancy, which had declined from 62 years in 1992 to 53 years in 2010, recovered to 60 years in 2012, albeit still low compared with other middle-income countries of similar income levels.

7. *Reforming the Social Assistance System.* Democratic South Africa has established a largely effective basic social transfer system that keeps millions of South Africans out of poverty and reduces inequality. A unified South Africa Social Security Agency (SASSA) integrated nine provincial departments of social development into a single national agency in charge of the delivery of social transfers. Coverage was expanded from 3 million people in

the early 1990s to more than 16 million. To improve service delivery, South Africa adopted new technologies, such as a biometric identification system (which identified and eliminated about 1 million fraudulent recipients), a new payment system, the use of mobile units, and clear service standards and strategic planning systems.

8. *Improving the Delivery of Identification Documents to Facilitate Access to Services.* In the early 2000s, obtaining a South African passport could take months and sometimes required paying bribes. Obtaining a birth registration certificate was even more complicated because of the legacy of apartheid, under which the births of millions of people went unrecorded. The National Population Register was incomplete, unreliable, and fragmented; and integrity and transparency were challenges. These problems were momentous because citizens cannot access social services without identity documents. Over the years, the introduction of new laws and regulations, the development of a service culture, the professionalization of staff, the establishment of modern service delivery systems, and the use of information technology and innovations have enhanced the quality of services, slashed waiting times, and reduced fraud and corruption.

9. *Protecting Biodiversity, Rehabilitating Ecosystems, and Promoting Conservation for Development.* South Africa is one of the world's most biodiverse countries. Despite a very challenging context—that includes private landowner-ship of many high-priority areas for conservation, the need to redress apartheid-era land dispossession, and demands for rapid economic development and job creation—it has created a successful and highly innovative policy and institutional framework to conserve its biodiversity. A rich legal framework sets out the principles and procedures governing biodiversity management. Two important institutions—the South African National Parks (SANParks) and the South African National Biodiversity Institute (SANBI)—have been reformed, and the national parks have been made more accessible to tourists in a sustainable way, ensuring that conservation goes hand in hand with social and economic development in rural areas. Organizational reforms, participatory planning tools, capacity building, and public-private partnerships have helped create jobs and promote inclusive development.

10. *Improving the Management of the National Road Network.* In the post-apartheid era, limited access to roads and the poor quality of the road network were a major challenge to private sector development. The problems were compounded by ineffective and nontransparent management arrangements. In April 1998 an act of Parliament established the South African National Roads Agency (SANRAL) as an independent statutory company operating along commercial lines and at arm's length from government. The purpose of the company—which is registered under the Companies Act, with the minister of transport as the sole shareholder—is to maintain and develop South Africa's expanding national road network. SANRAL has doubled the network, from 7,000 kilometers to nearly 20,000 kilometers,

particularly in the largest urban province (Gauteng). It has reformed organizational structures, upgraded staffing, and introduced new technology. Roads are reportedly built to a high standard, supported by professional staff. SANRAL has also established its creditworthiness, which has enabled it to borrow on capital markets.[1]

11. *Developing Renewable Energy through an Independent Power Producer Procurement Program.* South Africa is the world's fifth-largest coal producer in the world. Not surprisingly, most of its power (70 percent) therefore comes from carbon. In 2009 South Africa was the world's 12th-worst carbon emitter and the largest emitter of carbon dioxide in Africa. To reduce its carbon footprint, the government embarked on a renewable energy program. The program's goal is to generate 20 percent of national capacity from renewable sources. The Renewable Energy Independent Power Producer Procurement Program (REIPPPP) has now completed five rounds of bidding to secure independent power producer agreements. Through the first five rounds,[2] over 90 transactions and private investment exceeding US$20 billion[3] and 6,300MW of power were facilitated, making REIPPPP the largest independent power producer program in Africa. The first projects came on line at the end of 2013. Private sector bidding has increased in each round of bidding, prices have dropped, and transparency and competition have increased. By 2012, South Africa had become one of the top 10 countries in the world investing in renewable energy.

12. *Drafting the Constitution.* The 1996 Constitution of the Republic of South Africa is regarded as one of the most progressive in the world. The inclusive and innovative process through which it was negotiated and adopted is a landmark achievement and a sui generis success story. The process showcases how key factors—commitment to an overarching national goal, leadership, and consensus-building—helped overcome ideological divisions to allow decision makers to agree on technically strong and politically pragmatic solutions. The principles and rights spelled out in the constitution are the legal foundation for implementing many of the reforms analyzed in this book.

Cross-Cutting Lessons and Challenges Ahead

Eight cross-cutting success factors and lessons on policy making and implementation emerge from the analysis:

1. *Unique Reform Momentum: Commitment to a Common National Goal.* The transition to democracy brought with it unique momentum for reform. National goals were clear, creating a shared purpose of building a better future for all citizens. The euphoria of the early post-apartheid days created a sense of mission and commitment to change that infused reform efforts.

2. *Transformational Leadership.* Leadership came from all levels, with a strong emphasis on consensual and collective decision making. Leaders were able to

tap into popular support for transformational change, but they also had to respond to the sense of urgency. Urgency meant that leadership was flexible, with pragmatism often prevailing over ideology to ensure both quick wins and mid- and long-term reforms.

3. *Consensus Building.* Civic engagement and consultation have been hallmarks of successful reforms to build consensus, which some observers have called "policy development under the public gaze." The inclusiveness of processes and the adoption of different participatory approaches—from constitution making to budget transparency to the development of biodiversity frameworks—is a common feature of the institutional development successes.

4. *Learning from International Experiences.* The need to find solutions led South African practitioners to use evidence-based approaches and look to international good practices as part of an evidence-based analysis of options to address each of the key policy challenges. As the case studies show, much thought and effort went into analyzing national and international practices; adapting good international experiences to local conditions; and engaging in regular exchanges to build on, expand, and adjust practices and benchmark South Africa against other countries.

5. *Promoting Inclusive Institution Building.* Professionalization of staff, deracialization of management, and enhancement of skills were integral to inclusive institutional development. Central to this process was the creation of a new culture of public service that put people first. Clear staff incentives, both financial (good remuneration) and nonfinancial (good employment conditions), and clear accountability were instrumental in attracting people from outside the public sector, motivating them, setting performance standards, and offering options for career development.

6. *Creating Virtuous Cycles with "Quick Wins."* Sequencing combined big-bang and gradual approaches. All the case studies bring to the fore the importance of creating virtuous cycles of change, starting with leadership, strategy development, pragmatic and innovative solutions, structured implementation, and quick results. The power of quick results to reinforce political support for change cannot be underestimated.

7. *Adopting Pragmatic, Flexible, and Innovative Approaches.* Most reforms adopted an approach of experimenting and innovating, learning from successes and failures, adapting, applying, and moving on. The focus was on nonideological, practical, pragmatic solutions that could get consensus and, once tested, be scaled up over time.

8. *Strengthening Transparency and Accountability.* Developing processes and systems to promote transparency and accountability along the service delivery chain has been an important factor in the improvement of services documented in this book. Across many sectors, there was an emphasis on making information available to the public. The use of innovation and information and communications technology (ICT) systems simplified the interface between citizens and the state and reduced opportunities for corruption. Transparency

was strengthened, with a view to providing opportunities for greater use of information to hold government accountable and ensure implementation of rules and systems. Much more needs to be done, however, so that the provision of information actually leads to improved accountability.

The transformational challenges before South Africa remain large, especially with regard to implementation. There are many other challenges that are beyond the focus of this book, including inequality, unemployment, and social sector outcomes. But for all challenges it is clear that the process of institution building is a continuously evolving one. South Africa has made enormous progress, as the case studies show. But much still needs to be done to enhance accountability and ensure reform sustainability. At the same time, the permanence of progress attained is not automatically guaranteed—commitment to principle and consistency in implementation are critical to sustaining these successes.

Notes

1. Its creditworthiness suffered in 2013 after it was unable to maintain a strong financial position and implement a controversial e-tolling project in Gauteng.
2. The five rounds include the extended Bid Window 3, held in March 2014, to procure only concentrated solar power technology.
3. The exchange rate for rounds 1 to 3 is based on the dates the agreement was signed while the rate for rounds 4 and 5 is based on the rate at submission.

References

DPME (Department of Performance Monitoring and Evaluation of South Africa). 2012. *South Africa: Development Indicators*. Pretoria: DPME.

Presidency of the Republic of South Africa. 2014. *Twenty Year Review, South Africa 1994–2014*. Pretoria.

CHAPTER 1

Developing an Intergovernmental Fiscal Framework

Catriona Purfield

Introduction

South Africa has a unitary yet highly decentralized system of government with three spheres: the center, 9 provinces, and 278 municipalities (known as local government). The system of intergovernmental relations is not hierarchical. Each sphere is "a distinct government in its own right, each accountable to its own elected legislature or council" (South Africa, National Treasury 2001a). This structure was created at the end of the apartheid era against the backdrop of fundamental political and socioeconomic change.

The new intergovernmental fiscal system would have to help address poverty and inequality and ensure the nonwhite majority gained access to public services.[1] The new intergovernmental framework had to be fused onto the inherited fiscal system, which was highly centralized but racially divided. At the peak of apartheid, in 1975, social spending on whites was approximately 8.5 times greater than spending on blacks (van der Berg and Moses 2012). Public funds and services were administered inefficiently through racially dedicated departments. Oversight and accountability were also inadequate, which contributed to high fiscal deficits and debt. This context set South Africa apart from the many other countries that have sought to decentralize their fiscal systems.

South Africa needed a quick and substantive move to a more decentralized and racially integrated fiscal system. Under the Interim Constitution, a commission was established in 1993 to determine the number and boundaries of a new provincial tier of government.

The transition to the new three-sphere system began in April 1994, when the four provinces and nine black homelands were reorganized into nine new provinces.[2] In November 1995, 1,100 local governments were reorganized

The author is a former Program Leader at the World Bank. This chapter benefited from extensive interviews with current and former government officials as well as from comments by Lili Liu, Lead Economist in the Governance Global Practice of the World Bank.

into 843 transitional municipalities by combining the black and white areas. A final phase of transition occurred in December 2000, when municipalities were consolidated into 286 local government units, comprising 8 single-tiered urban metropolitan governments (Category A Metros) and 232 primary municipalities (Category B Local Municipalities) falling under 46 district municipalities (Category C District Municipalities).

Today the provincial and local government spheres implement more than half of general government spending, up from just under a third two decades ago. This chapter tells the story of how this transformation was achieved.

The Policy Challenge

In the negotiations on the new constitution, the African National Congress (ANC) initially resisted a decentralized system (ANC 1993). It saw centralization as necessary to deracialize the fiscal system and promote redistribution, explains Tania Ajam, a Commissioner at the Financial and Fiscal Commission (FFC). "However, other political parties, especially the National Party (NP) in Western Cape, and the Inkatha Freedom Party (IFP) in Natal pushed for a decentralized system motivated by the prospect that they could control fiscal resources in places where they would likely win the vote," she adds.

In 1993 the multiparty negotiating forum for the Constitution determined that the final Constitution (adopted in 1996) would create provinces with elected assemblies.[3] F. W. De Klerk called the creation of these provinces "one of the Constitution's great compromises. On one hand, [the provinces] were not nearly as strong as the IFP, the NP and the Democratic Party wanted; on the other hand, they provided much greater devolution of power to the regions than the ANC originally advocated" (quoted in Makgetla and Jackson 2012). The decision to create a unitary but highly decentralized system was thus ultimately political. Economic and fiscal considerations were secondary to the political imperative to end apartheid and halt civil unrest.

The key policy challenge was then how best to devolve and democratize power from a highly centralized and racially biased system while expanding service delivery and safeguarding macroeconomic stability. "The policy challenge was to take a system where most powers were vested at center or national level and recast it into one where powers and functions were more devolved," recalls former minister of finance Trevor Manuel.

The 1996 Constitution finalized the intergovernmental framework in a way that sought to address South Africa's unique context. The framework envisaged cooperative intergovernmental relations within a unitary state, to be guided by three core principles:

1. *Cooperation.* All three spheres are envisaged as "distinctive, interdependent, and interrelated" and are obliged to cooperate, negotiate, and assist one another to strengthen capacity. According to Roelf Meyer, an NP negotiator

of the Constitution, the notion of cooperative framework was inspired by Canada's experience.

2. *Equitable revenue sharing.* Revenues are largely raised nationally, but Section 227 of the Constitution entitles the provincial and local spheres to an unconditional equitable share of revenues to provide basic services and perform assigned functions. It requires allocations to be determined annually, taking into consideration the recommendations of the constitutionally independent FFC. The split has to recognize varying fiscal capacity, development needs, and economic disparities.

3. *Transparency and accountability.* Each tier has clearly defined powers and responsibilities, and budgetary processes are constitutionally mandated to promote "transparency accountability, effective and efficient public management." The Constitution grants limited power to the central government (via the National Treasury) to intervene in subnational affairs and stop transfers when there is a serious and persistent failure to carry out executive obligations (South Africa, National Treasury 2011).

The Constitution also created a bill of rights, with profound implications for government spending obligations and responsibilities in the new intergovernmental system. It established citizens' rights to adequate housing, education, health, and social services. Pressure to quickly broaden and scale up access to essential government services was riding high, but fiscal space was very constrained. In 1994 the general government fiscal deficit was 8.3 percent of gross domestic product (GDP), public debt was 41.3 percent of GDP, and South Africa was perceived to be at risk of a fiscal crisis.

The mandate to deliver public services would fall largely to the subnational spheres. Education and health are concurrent responsibilities, shared with the provinces, while basic services such as water and sanitation are shared between all spheres. Policy formulation and funding occur at the center and implementation at the subnational spheres in South Africa's version of the German system of overlapping jurisdictions (Wittenberg 2006).

The government would essentially have to implement the new intergovernmental fiscal system flying blind and to do it immediately with no time to prepare. In the dying years of apartheid, when ANC officials unofficially met their Finance (and State Department[4]) counterparts, "it became abundantly clear that the existing budget system was opaque and fragmented and biased towards racially determined expenditure and not suited to the needs of a democratic system," recalls Ismail Momoniat, deputy director-general of the National Treasury. The government lacked a clear picture of the total budget, actual outlays, service delivery needs, staffing, assets, and pension liabilities. It essentially had to implement two reforms in parallel, the modernization of the opaque budgeting system and the decentralization of the budget system, to meet the new intergovernmental arrangements initially set out in the Interim Constitution and finalized in 1996.

The government was left with little choice but to move ahead with the new intergovernmental fiscal system and prepare the 1994–96 budgets. "Waiting for better information was not an option; any delay in implementation could have led to legal challenges," notes Momoniat. The old national, four provincial, and nine Bantustan budgets were realigned into ten (one national and nine provinces) "using the previous year's estimated outturns plus an increment for inflation and an estimate of what basic service delivery needs could be funded." Functions were inevitability underprovisioned, and policy decisions were made without knowing their true financial implications.

Financial problems began to surface in 1996, when the government agreed with the unions to unify the provincial and national civil service.[5] The 1997/98 budget, in which provinces received their first equitable share, inevitably underestimated their wage costs. With the reporting system unable to detect the large deficits emerging, midyear corrective action was not possible. Provinces such as the Eastern Cape, KwaZulu-Natal, and the Free State went into fiscal crisis (South Africa, National Treasury 2005) as they overspent their budgets on personnel expenditure. At the municipal level, the councils in the Greater Johannesburg Metropolitan Municipality rolled out ambitious spending plans without adequate financing, assuming that the shortfalls would be offset by surpluses of other councils (Brown, Motsoane, and Liu 2013).

Addressing the Challenge

The objective of the reform of the intergovernmental framework was to devolve more fiscal responsibility, in order to promote a democratic, racially integrated, and prosperous society. However, a balance had to be struck. As the experience of 1994–96 showed, central control was needed to safeguard macroeconomic and financial stability. Against the backdrop of great regional variability in poverty and inequality as well as gaps in service delivery, there was also the need to ensure transformation and economic development.

Developing a System for Policy Coordination, Policy Making, and Consensus Building

"Between 1994 (when the Interim Constitution applied) and 1996, when the final Constitution was agreed, the new intergovernmental system had to be implemented almost immediately with little time for the new government to prepare and plan for it. We started with huge asymmetries in expenditure— the bulk of which was racially defined—and the expenditure had to be recompiled and reallocated in order to produce even a baseline budget for the new intergovernmental system," explains Trevor Manuel.

Starting as the new minister of finance in April 1996, Manuel and his staff at the National Treasury prioritized three overarching objectives as they implemented the new intergovernmental fiscal framework, according to Momoniat. The first was to modernize the budgeting system and introduce a multiyear budgeting system to enable better planning. The second was to make the budget a more participatory process where the outcome would be more broadly accepted. To do this Manuel took all major decisions concerning the budget to the Cabinet, set up the Ministers' Committee on the Budget (MINCOMBUD) to involve a committee of ministers, and consulted with provincial Members of the Executive Council (MECs). This was done to ensure that the budget was driven by policy objectives and not a mere bean-counting exercise. This links to their third objective, which was to insist that all policy proposals in the Treasury had to be done via memos, which had to be of the highest quality and finally approved by the deputy general or minister. This helped establish a culture in the Treasury that lives to this day to ensure that all processes have integrity and are properly approved.

To bring this about Manuel quickly reached out to his provincial counterparts. The alliance he formed with them, nicknamed "Team Finance," would be a critical stepping stone in realizing the Constitution's vision of cooperative governance between the different spheres of government. He saw the potential of empowering the MECs—the provincial premier and other provincial line ministers—to become a force for good. While at the Department of Trade and Industry (DTI), he had established the first Minister and Executive Council Meeting (known as a MINMEC), made up of the line minister and the nine provincial MECs, to talk through issues, take joint responsibility, and streamline operations. He sought to replicate this mode of coordination for fiscal policy.

Team Finance would be "apartisan, not about politics but consensus," recalls Cole. Manuel made it clear that "in this we work together." "It was all about sharing problems," explains Jan Hattingh, chief director, Local Government Budget Analysis, at the National Treasury. "It created an environment where ministers and MECs could talk about real fiscal problems and policies."

Officials from the Western Cape Province also recall how provincial policy makers embraced Team Finance. The initial Finance MECs were very committed to it: they respected calls for prudence in spending and backed Minister Manuel's position. Harry Malila, deputy director-general at the Western Cape Provincial Treasury, saw that "Manuel took the provincial MECs very seriously. There was a sense among them that compromises in policy making would have to be reached in the interest of the country."

Looking back we see that, "Manuel was quick to realize that the new system of concurrent functional responsibilities would not work if the Department of Finance just carved off the revenue required by subnational governments to implement their responsibilities," explains Neil Cole, director of the Collaborative Africa Budget Reform Initiative (CABRI). "There needed to be full consultation and coordination between the three spheres in setting policy priorities, designing policies, budgeting, implementation, and reporting given the separation of policy and expenditure implementation responsibilities in the Constitution to make the new system work," recalls Derek Powell, former deputy director-general of the Department of Provincial and Local Government (DPLG), which later became the Cooperative Governance and Traditional Affairs Department (COGTA).

The fact that Team Finance was operating before the 1997 Intergovernmental Fiscal Relations Act (IFRA) suggests that finding informal mechanisms that build institutional effectiveness matters as much as the formal legal framework. The IFRA formalized Team Finance as the Budget Council for the Provinces. The act thus gave powers beyond informal consultation to the gatherings of the minister and the nine MECs, and this had an important persuasive effect on participation and decision making. The IFRA specified who would sit on the council, what it would discuss, and how often it would meet. The IFRA also sought to mimic the Team Finance process at the local government level where it created the Budget Forum, a coordination mechanism between the Budget Council and the municipal sphere via their formal representative organization, the South African Local Government Association (SALGA).

Promoting Common Purpose and Evidence-Based Decision Making as a Means of Overcoming Political Obstacles

Regular meetings, open discussion, consultation grounded in data, and a focus on problem solving fostered "common purpose and trust, helping overcome potential political obstacles," according to Manuel. The Finance MINMEC, which only later became colloquially known as "Team Finance" and subsequently the Budget Council, held at least four meetings a year. In his thirteen years as minister of finance, Manuel never missed a meeting, signaling strong commitment to the process. The Finance MINMEC/Budget Council set aside three days a year to drill down and understand fiscal trends.

Manuel's idea was that, instead of forming alliances along party political lines (with, for example, an ANC caucus), it would be better to operate as a governmental structure and be open—an approach emphasized under the Mandela government of National Unity but that continued even after the NP had left it. To avoid relying solely on the "political will" of opposition MECs from KwaZulu-Natal (IFP) and the Western Cape (NP), it was important to establish the importance of institutions with evidence-based policy and data as a reference point for discussions. It was not enough just to bring together political heads; there was also a need for technical staff to collaborate. Manuel understood the interface between the political and administrative layers of government, and the critical role that both had to play in the budget and treasury processes.

Reflecting his understanding of this interface, Manuel empowered National Treasury staff to form a Technical Committee of Finance (TCF) to prepare inputs ahead of these high-level meetings. At the sector level, MINMECs (also called Joint MINMECs because they brought MECs of finance together with the ministers of the relevant sector) and supporting 10×10s (technical committees that comprised nine provincial and one national sector expert, plus their finance counterparts) were created. Andrew Donaldson, who joined the new Fiscal Analysis Unit of the Department of Finance in 1993, explains that there was "real commitment on the part of finance officials to work with provincial counterparts." Manuel also created space for his own senior managers to put issues on the table every two weeks.

The TCF used actual budget outcomes to promote evidence-based discussions. In preparing the 1997/98 budget, Team Finance and the TCF visited each province to compile data on expenditure outturns and forecasts. Each visit covered three provinces and lasted three days, and the process was repeated three times. Discussions could be robust. "The competent National Treasury team often clashed with provinces, which did not want the center to know what they were up to," explains Manuel. Still, at the end of each visit, Manuel made a point of personally briefing the provincial premier. Manuel and the Treasury officials visited provinces with weaker capacity more frequently.

"The sense of consultation throughout this process was important to give the intergovernmental process impetus," notes Manuel. In October of every year, before the budget was finalized, the Cabinet invited the premiers of the nine provinces to an extended Cabinet meeting at the Union Buildings, where the allocations for the following year were shared with them so that they could begin their budget processes. This extended meeting at the level of Cabinet was the only arrangement for a sense of national or collective decision. According to Malila, this process "afforded the provincial premiers and treasuries an opportunity to raise their concerns and to achieve greater balance and certainty in their allocations." The data gathering and consultative processes "signaled strong commitment to consultation; it also provided opportunity to share wisdom, develop understanding of constraints, and troubleshoot emerging problems," according to Cole. "It also established the view that the province's function was respected."

Having anchored issues in data and evidence, "when the MECs of Finance got together, the sense was that they needed to respond to the evidence before them and not to speak a particular party's political code," notes Manuel. During these meetings, there was often convergence between the largely urban provinces of Gauteng (ANC) and the Western Cape (governed by the opposition NP) and the rural provinces of the Eastern Cape (ANC) and KwaZulu-Natal (governed by the opposition IFP) on issues. "This meant the ANC and an opposition party would argue from the same perspective. This allowed for a calm to settle, and this calm was an important precursor to the trust" that helped overcome opposition.

As a result of adopting inclusive consultation and use of evidence, "faced with a united front in the form of 'Team Finance,' the new macroeconomic stabilization program proposed in 1996, the Growth, Employment And Redistribution (GEAR) strategy, that envisaged the reduction in the overall budget deficit and debt burden through measures to constrain spending including by downsizing of the central provincial civil services, faced little resistance in the national cabinet," Donaldson recalls.

Promoting Mutual Accountability in Intergovernmental Fiscal Policy Making

One mechanism that helped foster mutual accountability for prudent policy decisions across the spheres was the subnational revenue, or "equitable" share. Every year the Cabinet determines the vertical share of national revenue that is delegated to the subnational spheres, after statutory items such as debt service are deducted. As a result, when Manuel engaged in national-level Cabinet discussions on the budget, he was held in check by the provincial MECs, who looked to him to fight for their share. Once the equitable share was determined, MECs were accountable to one another because expenditure overruns were generally funded out of this envelope, implying less for other provinces (common pool problem). This mechanism worked to make each MEC accountable to his or her eight peers as much as to the National Treasury.

Manuel points to social assistance, initially the responsibility of the provinces, to illustrate. Some provinces faced large expenditure overruns as they expanded access to social assistance payments too rapidly (unfunded mandates). Manuel recalls the MEC for Social Protection in one province taking the stance that fiscal responsibility was not its obligation. This stance created enormous tension, and the issue was brought to Team Finance to solve. Manuel convened a "bilateral Joint MINMEC," where Team Finance and the TCF met with the national and provincial departments of social development. The meeting was an opportunity to export Team Finance's sense of shared fiscal responsibility to a line department function. The deliberations and the recommendation of the FFC to establish a national-level social security agency resulted in the decision to make social assistance a national competence (see chapter 7).

Integrating the Subnational Spheres into Budget Processes

The new subnational spheres had to be integrated into the budget process, which itself needed fundamental overhaul. Between 1994 and the creation of the National Treasury in 2000/01, fiscal policy was divided between the Department of Finance (charged with revenue collection and the macro framework) and the Department of State Expenditure. The budget was an annual input-based exercise with inconsistent accounting practices. It was compiled with little consultation outside the two departments. There was no in-year reporting; outcomes were available with lags of years.

Minister Manuel took bold action. Momoniat recalls Manuel saying that his first budget would be a three-year budget, and it was: "He did not accept excuses, and in some sense he created an unrealistic target that was music to the ears of those who were new to the department and wanting to reform the budget process." It also helped that the multiyear budget was a key reform proposal forwarded by the ANC as it prepared to take power, championed by Manuel and the Treasury, and the three-year Medium-Term Expenditure Framework (MTEF) was first piloted in Gauteng a year before it was rolled out. The MTEF exemplifies how strong political will, a "clean slate" of officials with no vested interest in the old processes, and strong support created the conditions for bold reform.

The MTEF brought an unprecedented degree of predictability to the revenue sharing and spending allocations for the new spheres, recalls Malila. According to Cole, "From its initiation the MTEF promised things that were able to be delivered, it never promised what it couldn't afford." The MTEF was based on cautious assumptions, which meant that there was little deviation between forecast and actual revenues shares going to the subnational spheres. The marked-over expenditure of 1997/98 was reversed and stabilized with an overrun of less than 2 percent in 1998/99, the first year of the MTEF (Fölscher and Cole 2004).

However, in its first year of full implementation, the MTEF faced a crucial test. The Asian crisis struck, and budget revenues underperformed relative to targets. The shortfall could have killed the new MTEF, according to Donaldson: "A decision was taken to use the contingency allocation and move the impact of the shock on expenditures to the outer years of the MTEF rather than cut allocations." This measure preserved the spending allocations to provinces and cemented the credibility of the MTEF. "It demonstrated to the subnational tiers that they could plan on the basis of their projected allocations. It established trust," said Donaldson. Also critical were the facts that macroeconomic stability was preserved and the reforms implemented as the South African Revenue Service (SARS) consolidated and broadened the tax base (see chapter 3), allowing the budget and expenditure reforms to take place. But the centralization of revenue collection at SARs was also a practical acknowledgment that the national government would be more efficient in collecting taxes given the large gaps in capacity and income levels across the provinces.

"It was also possible with the MTEF to show how the rollout of new policies, such as the child care grant, would proceed—first covering all children under the age of six and progressively older children," explains Cole. Delivery on these funding promises "established the budget process and MTEF as one; there was no other game in town," said Cole. The 2003 Division of Revenue Act extended the three-year MTEF framework to the municipal sphere. It published the allocations per municipality for the following three years and required that municipalities prepare three-year budgets (South Africa, National Treasury 2003).

In retrospect, the MTEF did not fully support greater allocative spending efficiency toward nationally agreed priorities and better service delivery by the subnational spheres. Momoniat attributes this shortcoming to the unwillingness to grant implementing units the same degree of predictability. Annual budgets leave frontline staff without the predictability or flexibility to allocate resources to address challenges on the ground.

At least in the Western Cape, implementing units' budgets are prepared on a three-year basis, according to Malila, but "ultimately the decision on how to allocate transfers is, as set out in the Constitution, an executive one. Provinces have the right to redirect funds to meet their priorities and needs."

Promoting Accountability and Transparency in Budget Implementation across the Three Spheres of Government

A key challenge of any intergovernmental system was ensuring accountability throughout the three-sphere system, as required by the Constitution. "It would not be enough to reserve accountability in the end to just the parliament and provincial legislatures. By the time problems are heard in these bodies, they would have festered too long," explains Momoniat. "We also needed a more proactive or ex ante system, with earlier points of accountability to enable the government to deal with problems as early as possible. Hence an early warning system was introduced with monthly reporting and in-year monitoring and accountability mechanisms."

"The Public Finance Management Act (PFMA) of 1999 was a huge step forward and a massive undertaking given the evolving intergovernmental system," argues Momoniat. Its premise was to "let managers in all departments and entities manage but to hold them to account." The PFMA focused on outputs that managers had to commit to achieving with their budgetary resources. It also articulated the link between budget reform and the intergovernmental system. It shifted responsibility for the management and use of resources from the center to managers in spending departments and agencies of each sphere. At the same time, it expected their minister or political head to monitor and hold them to account for their performance, and for the legislature to hold the minister and department accountable for the output they promised in their budgets. In 2003 these reforms were extended to the local government sphere under the Municipal Finance Management Act (MFMA).

The PFMA also had strong teeth to promote accountability. In the early days "people were initially scared of the sanctions and took them very seriously," Momoniat recalls. In terms of the law, accounting officers could be found guilty of financial misconduct and have disciplinary or criminal proceedings brought against them. But in the absence of actual sanctions these clauses became less effective in constraining behavior as the years passed. Equally important was the role of the parliamentary committees. These committees were seen at the time to be very demanding in ensuring performance by government officials and cabinet ministers; there was a real sense that "if you did not deliver, there was trouble."

Holding managers to account would require better data on budget implementation. Following the subnational fiscal crisis in 1997/98, the Cabinet instructed the National Treasury to establish an early warning system on budget implementation. This reform was championed by Velile Mbete at National Treasury. Hattingh recalls initially visiting the provincial treasuries to compile a simple one-page summary of budget outturns—such was the extent of the data available. Monthly reporting on budget implementation was initially met with strong resistance. However, once it was insisted on, subnational governments quickly fell in line. This practice was then formalized in the PFMA, which required that monthly revenue and spending information also be made public within 30 days after the month end, so that all participants in the budget process, including legislatures, could assess implementation performance during the year, not only after the year end.

The Division of Revenue Act (DORA) and Intergovernmental Fiscal Review (IGFR) were innovations that strengthened the monitoring of subnational finances. The DORA, first prepared in 1998/99, fulfilled the constitutional requirement that the division of revenue among the three spheres be equitable, justifiable, and transparent and show how allocations compare with the FFC's recommendations. The IGFR was "a pathbreaker that changed the budget negotiation dynamic between the spheres," according to Momoniat. "Provinces would demand greater allocations for key functions like schools and hospitals, and the production of comparable statistics facilitated benchmarking and helped identify costs drivers," explains Malijeng Ngqaleni, deputy director-general of Intergovernmental Affairs at National Treasury. Western Cape officials agree that the IGFR allowed the National Treasury to exert greater influence and resulted in improved policy design and implementation. In 2002 the IGFR expanded to include municipal finances, and in 2008 the IGFR was split into a provincial review and a separate Local Government Budgets and Expenditure Review (South Africa, National Treasury 2008).

Looking back, did the new public financial management framework aim too high? As the annual reports of the auditor general show, most entities failed to attain the standards. In retrospect, Momoniat believes, "we acted in good faith and assumed all actors would be committed to improving service delivery.... We thought it would suffice that if problems were brought to light via this modern process, pressure via the legislatures or media and from the electorate would bring correction." In the last decade or so, however, the ability of Parliamentary Committees to provide effective oversight has weakened, in part reflecting party political pressures, which has made the committees less effective in holding the executive to account. Wendy Fanoe, chief director, Intergovernmental Policy and Planning, National Treasury, argues that, "ultimately in a system with concurrent expenditure responsibilities, accountability blurs."

South Africa's electoral list system makes it difficult for citizens to hold politicians to account, as the intervention by the National Treasury in Limpopo Province in 2011 shows. Ajam and Fourie (2014) describe how, against a backdrop of inadequate provincial legislature oversight, the unstable political-administrative interface in Limpopo resulted in political appointments that created capacity problems and undermined incentives for corrective action. This challenge also occurs at the parliamentary levels, where members of parliament (MPs) are elected from a party list system that makes it difficult for their constituencies to hold them to account, as assumed in the PFMA.

Funding the New Intergovernmental System to Foster Incentives for Fiscal Discipline

The 1993 Interim Constitution anticipated that the provinces would be funded largely through unconditional transfers. The spatial skewedness of the tax base made it impossible to decentralize revenue-raising powers without exacerbating inequality. However, as Ajam recalls, "there was huge uncertainty and lack of information to design the funding apparatus.... So instead of detailed intergovernmental fiscal design codified inflexibly in the [final] constitution, a process and an independent consultative institution, the FFC, were created."

Inspired by India's Finance Commission, the ANC's 1993 Regional Policy Document envisaged an independent commission staffed by a full-time secretariat.[6] The Interim Constitution conceptualized the FFC as a consultative body of technical experts to advise the executive and legislatures on the revenue-sharing process. Each province nominated a public finance expert to represent its interests, and the national government nominated nine experts. In 2001 the FFC was transformed into an independent expert commission (Ajam 2014).

The exchanges between the FFC and the National Treasury show how tensions between the desire to devolve more responsibility and sustain fiscal discipline were resolved. The FFC's first report recommended that the vertical split of revenue keep the national share constant while allowing the provincial share to grow over time (Financial and Fiscal Commission 1996). Donaldson explains why this proposal was rejected. "International experience clearly showed that centrally determining the pool of resources to be shared in line funding constraints was the best way to preserve macro stability." The FFC and the National Treasury agreed that debt service and a contingency reserve should be "taken off the top," but the vertical revenue split among the three spheres remained a "political judgment" made by the Cabinet but informed by the MINCOMBUD and the Budget Council to reflect policy priorities. This view prevailed, reflecting the desire to retain fiscal discipline.

Turning to the division of revenues within each sphere, the FFC advocated a formula-driven costed-norm approach to replace the system of ad hoc transfers and meet the requirements of the Constitution.[7] The 1998 and 2001 FFC reports recommended a division based on a transparent formula that would incorporate provincial demographics to approximate need and tax capacity (Financial and Fiscal Commission 1998, 2000). In 2000 it recommended that the revenue-sharing formula be based on nationally mandated norms and standards linked to the delivery of basic public services (Financial and Fiscal Commission 2000). For the municipal sphere, an equitable share formula was introduced in 1998/99. The formula largely reflected the poverty profile of localities, as it aimed to ensure that low-income households in all municipal jurisdictions received access to basic municipal services (South Africa, National Treasury 2000).

A transparent formula that uses demographic and economic profiles of the provinces to allocate revenues between the provinces and a formula that aims to reflect the costs of the provision of basic services by the municipal sphere are now detailed annually in the DORA. However, the National Treasury rejected a costed norms approach, lest it create incentives to escalate costs and reduce efficiency. "The consequence of this decision was all too predictable," notes Ajam. "In the absence of norms, provinces could not be held to account for how they delivered their functions." Perhaps more important, argue Momoniat and officials from the Western Cape, is the fact that national line ministries did not establish norms and standards for their service delivery, missing the opportunity to use their monitoring powers to force change.

The taxation power of the subnational spheres was another area of diverging views. The Constitution limited the taxation powers of the provinces to a flat surcharge on personal income. To strengthen the link between provincial tax and expenditure decisions, the FFC recommended phasing in this surcharge, coupled with an offsetting reduction in the national share. Momoniat describes the trade-offs the center saw: "Making additional own-resources available to the provinces that had yet to develop the capacity to budget and spend efficiently would have led to waste and could have delayed vital public finance management reforms: expenditure management and accountability needed to precede tax assignment.... Provinces would have first to demonstrate their ability to deliver efficiently, but already in 1998/99 many were underspending their budgets and not collecting their existing service fees."

The Budget Council sought a second opinion from the Katz Tax Commission. This commission cautioned against such a move, citing weak and uneven tax capacity and weakness in national tax administration. Subsequently, the government developed the Provincial Tax Regulation Process Act (2001), by which provinces can apply to the minister of finance to levy taxes. After considering the input of the FFC, the minister of finance can approve or disapprove the tax. If approved, other provinces need only pass legislation. As of 2015, only the Western Cape had applied (to levy a fuel tax, in 2005); its application was rejected.

The 1997 fiscal crisis in the provinces provided an opportunity to demonstrate the center's commitment to enforcing hard budget constraints. The Eastern Cape was unable to pay pensions, but the center did not provide funds (Wittenberg 2006).[8] In 1997 the MECs agreed that provinces would not borrow until a borrowing framework was developed (South Africa, National Treasury 2001a). This informal rule remained until the 2004 borrowing guidelines were issued (see South Africa, National Treasury 2005, which describes these guidelines).

Another principle established by Manuel was to insist that provinces pay over all their national taxes due, as governments must lead by example and pay all taxes due. Some provinces had not paid the pay-as-you-earn (PAYE) tax[9] withheld from their employees; Manuel insisted that they pay all money owed, and he established a system where provinces could not renege on their tax payments to SARS. However nontax payments continue to be an area of contention between the three spheres.

In the local government sphere, the national and provincial Gauteng governments forced a tough restructuring without a bailout on the greater Johannesburg metropolitan municipality.[10] In light of this experience, the 1998 *White Paper on Local Government* recognized the need for a municipal borrowing framework (Department for Provincial Affairs and Constitutional Development 1998). In 2000 the Framework for Municipal Borrowing and Financial Emergencies explicitly ruled out central government guarantees and the powers of provinces to intervene. The MFMA (2003) elaborated the framework. In line with the Constitution, it explicitly restricted long-term borrowing by municipalities to capital expenditure, defined debt broadly to include contingent liabilities as well as explicit debt, and clarified the roles of the three spheres and the courts in intervening in municipalities that are in financial stress, which was clearly defined as failing to pay creditors or provide basic services (Brown, Motsoane, and Liu 2013).

The Challenge of Creating New Administrations

New administrations had to be forged from the old apartheid structures, and the workforce had to be racially transformed. Provinces such as the Western Cape, KwaZulu-Natal, and Gauteng were formed from the four old provinces and inherited their old administrations. Other provinces, such as the Eastern Cape and Limpopo, were pieced together from various homelands.

To illustrate the challenge the creation of these new administrations posed, Momoniat takes the example of education in the Eastern Cape. "The new province merged the staff, assets, and administrative processes from part of the Department of Education of the erstwhile Cape Province (a white-only education system), the education departments of the Coloured and Indian communities, the African departments of education from the Transkei and Ciskei Bantustans, and the Bantu education department for townships like Port Elizabeth." The homeland bureaucracies had been run along systems of patronage under apartheid. Merging the different cultures while trying to retain and build skills and make the workforce more diverse was to prove an enormous challenge.

In the transition, the old bureaucracies demanded and received time-bound employment guarantees. In 1996 the unions and government agreed to unify the civil services of the national and provincial level under the Public Service Employment Framework.[11] Backlogs of promotions were addressed through automatic promotion; and wage scales, which had differed by race across the different administrations, were merged. To give just one example of how large the wage gap could be (which also varied by location), Manuel recalls that an African female teacher in the Transkei earned only 45 percent of the salary of a white male teacher. The differentiation in pay scales by gender and race was clearly untenable in the context of equal pay for equal work. At the same time wage scales were merged, employment in the health and education sectors also expanded, to try to address service delivery backlogs.

The wage bill exploded. Overall personnel spending rose by 11.3 percent in real terms in 1996/97 (South Africa, National Treasury 2001a), "but even this is likely to be an underestimate, given the absence of any detailed retrospective accounting of the actual cost," notes Momoniat. Faced with the need to demonstrate progress in the racial transformation of the civil service and restore fiscal finances to a more sustainable trajectory, in 1998 the government offered generous buyouts and pension plans to reduce the workforce after the employment guarantees had reached sunset or expired. In 1999 the Western Cape shed about 8,000 teachers; it was only in 2014 that the number of teachers returned to 1998 levels.

This restructuring of the civil service compounded capacity problems at the subnational level. Although the 1998 package facilitated the transition to a more deracialized workforce, it hollowed out midlevel management, particularly at the provincial level, according to Donaldson. The problems of weak capacity were particularly severe in provinces created from the old homelands, where the exodus of experienced staff was greater. These capacity constraints have had long-lasting implications on the quality of public service delivery in these provinces.

Sequencing Reforms in Order to Build on and Learn from Experience
The development of the intergovernmental system was more a process than an event that ended with the agreement on the Constitution (South Africa, National Treasury 1999). South Africa did not enjoy the luxury of carefully designing

and sequencing the devolution of fiscal powers to subnational governments. Constitutional requirements held the process to a very tight timeline. Policy makers had to move on many parallel fronts.

The Constitution created the broad scaffolding of the new intergovernmental system, but its construction moved in smaller steps, often prompted by the need to find solutions to emerging problems. Legislation was designed in light of such experience and then rolled out progressively to the different spheres. Figure 1.1 presents the key mileposts along this journey. Many initiatives, such as the Budget Council, and monthly budget implementation reporting, started informally or on an experimental basis before becoming formalized. When experience revealed problems, as in the case of social assistance, changes were made.

Such an incremental approach to reforms provides scope for solutions and improvements to develop to country contexts over time in the light of actual experience, as Andrews (2013) emphasizes. The PFMA was enacted in 1999, and implementation was phased in over five years. It applied only to the center and the provinces. The appointment of chief financial officers, internal audit committees, and monthly reporting were prioritized. Measurable program objectives were introduced later.

At the local government level, the MFMA marked the culmination of learning from the PFMA process and extensive consultation to ensure the right balance between the municipal autonomy granted by the Constitution and the central government's obligation to ensure fiscal sustainability. It took two years to develop the basic financial management framework (1998–2000), a year for Cabinet approval (2001), and an additional two years of parliamentary debate, including 41 committee hearings and three versions of the bill, before the necessary constitutional amendments and the final MFMA were enacted in 2003 (Brown, Motsoane, and Liu 2013). Since then, the National Treasury has focused on strengthening municipal budgeting and reporting practices (through, for example, the 2009 Municipal Budget and Reporting Regulations) and treasury and cash management.[12]

Results Achieved

By 2000 the provincial and local spheres began implementing a rising share of the budget, which itself saw an increasing share of spending devoted to education, health, and social assistance. Today the intergovernmental fiscal system is characterized by a high degree of decentralization in spending functions. The two subnational spheres implement more than half of total general government expenditure (table 1.1).

This transformation was achieved while safeguarding fiscal stability. The overall budget shifted from a deficit of 8.3 percent of GDP in 1994 to a surplus of 1.3 percent of GDP by 2008. The gross debt burden of the general government fell from just shy of 40 percent of GDP in 1993 to a low of just over 25 percent of GDP in 2008. The 2008/09 global financial crisis, the subsequent slowdown

Figure 1.1 Key Milestones and Evolution of Subnational Spending Share In Total Spending

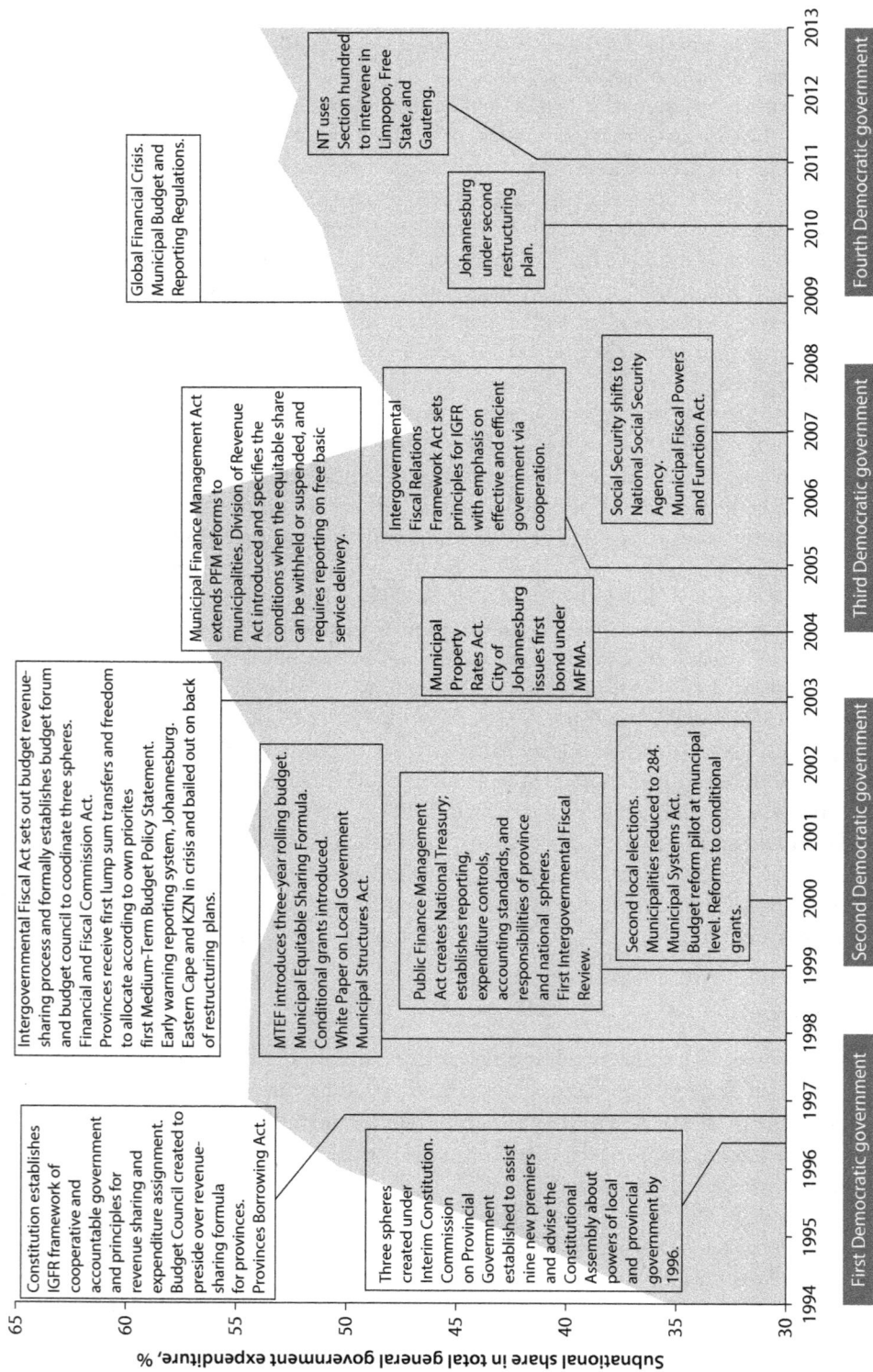

Y-axis: **Subnational share in total general government expenditure, %** (30 to 65)

X-axis: 1994 to 2013

Government periods: First Democratic government | Second Democratic government | Third Democratic government | Fourth Democratic government

Constitution establishes IGFR framework of cooperative and accountable government and principles for revenue sharing and expenditure assignment. Budget Council created to preside over revenue-sharing formula for provinces. Provinces Borrowing Act.

Intergovernmental Fiscal Act sets out budget revenue-sharing process and formally establishes budget forum and budget council to coodinate three spheres. Financial and Fiscal Commission Act. Provinces receive first lump sum transfers and freedom to allocate according to own priorites first Medium-Term Budget Policy Statement. Early warning reporting system, Johannesburg. Eastern Cape and KZN in crisis and bailed out on back of restructuring plans.

Three spheres created under Interim Constitution. Commission on Provincial Government established to assist nine new premiers and advise the Constitutional Assembly about powers of local and provincial government by 1996.

MTEF introduces three-year rolling budget. Municipal Equitable Sharing Formula. Conditional grants introduced. White Paper on Local Government Municipal Structures Act.

Public Finance Management Act creates National Treasury; establishes reporting, expenditure controls, accounting standards, and responsibilities of province and national spheres. First Intergovernmental Fiscal Review.

Second local elections. Municipalities reduced to 284. Municipal Systems Act. Budget reform pilot at municpal level. Reforms to conditional grants.

Municipal Finance Management Act extends PFM reforms to municipalities. Division of Revenue Act introduced and specifies the conditions when the equitable share can be withheld or suspended, and requires reporting on free basic service delivery.

Municipal Property Rates Act. City of Johannesburg issues first bond under MFMA.

Intergovernmental Fiscal Relations Framework Act sets principles for IGFR with emphasis on effective and efficient government via cooperation.

Social Security shifts to National Social Security Agency. Municipal Fiscal Powers and Function Act.

Global Financial Crisis. Municipal Budget and Reporting Regulations.

Johannesburg under second restructuring plan.

NT uses Section hundred to intervene in Limpopo, Free State, and Gauteng.

Note: EC = Eastern Cape; IGFR = Intergovernmental Finance Review; KZN = KwaZulu-Natal; MFMA = Municipal Finance Management Act; MTEF = Medium-Term Expenditure Framework; NT = National Treasury; PFM = Public Finance Management.

Table 1.1 Intergovernmental Budget Relations, 1994 and 2013

	1994		2013	
Item	General government revenue/ consolidated expenditure	Percent of GDP	General government revenue/ consolidated expenditure	Percent of GDP
Revenue	100.0	25.5	100.0	32.7
Center	84.6	21.6	82.4	26.9
Provincial	4.8	1.2	1.2	0.4
Local	10.7	2.7	16.5	5.4
Expenditure	100.0	33.9	100.0	35.8
Center	64.6	21.9	46.0	16.5
Provincial	25.4	8.6	32.1	11.5
Local	10.0	3.4	22.0	7.9
Balance	–	–8.3	–	–3.1
Gross debt	–	39.4	–	40.3

Source: 2013 Government Finance Statistics compiled by the South African Reserve Bank.
Note: GDP = gross domestic product; – = negligible.

in growth, and the use of countercyclical fiscal policies to support the economy caused the overall deficit and debt burden to rise subsequently. The slowdown in revenue growth also placed pressure on the finances of all three spheres. Nevertheless, many of the people interviewed for this chapter maintain that retaining macroeconomic and fiscal stability while creating the new intergovernmental fiscal framework was perhaps the greatest achievement of the reform of the intergovernmental framework. The implementation of GEAR and the establishment of macroeconomic stability even while the intergovernmental system was evolving illustrated that when necessary the government was able to implement difficult measures even if its actions were not popular.

Moving from the challenge of designing an intergovernmental architecture to delivering public services through it would prove a more complex problem. On the one hand, access to power, water and sanitation, health, and education services has expanded. Between 1994/95 and 2011/12, the proportion of households with access to basic sanitation increased from just over 50 percent to 83 percent, and access to a basic level of water supply rose from just over 60 percent to more than 95 percent of households (Presidency, Republic of South Africa 2014). Electricity connections rose from about 50 percent to about 86 percent of households by 2013/14. On the other hand, the quality of services remains problematic, and several of these services are provided via state-owned enterprises that are outside the intergovernmental system and are themselves facing financial difficulties. The number of service delivery protests ballooned, reflecting growing dissatisfaction with the quality of services and perceptions of corruption and inefficiency.[13]

In the context of slower revenue growth after the 2008/09 financial crisis, it is important to ensure appropriate spending prioritization, effective and efficient service delivery, and good governance. As a whole, the local government sphere is less fiscally dependent on the center for transfers than is the provincial sphere. Just over two-thirds of municipal expenditure is covered by own-revenues from power, water charges, and property tax. Local governments thus have greater scope than the provinces to allocate resources to nonpriority items. In this context, the sharing of responsibility for the local government sphere between the National Treasury, COGTA, and the provinces has created coordination and accountability challenges.

South Africa's local governments face divergent challenges when it comes to service delivery. Rural municipalities, which are home to the majority of South Africa's poor, have higher dependency ratios and a weaker economic base than their urban counterparts. They face large imbalances between their limited revenue capacity and high expenditure needs that reflect large service delivery backlogs in water, sanitation, and power. But this picture is rapidly changing. By 2030 more than 70 percent of South Africans will live in cities, up from just over half today (South Africa, National Treasury 2011). As the proportion of poor people living in South Africa's 8 metros and 21 secondary cities grows, urban municipalities will face increased pressure to provide free basic services and housing while expanding and refurbishing infrastructure (transport, schools) to support economic activity. Urban municipalities generally have a poor record in collecting user fees to cover the cost of the services they provide, and they face massive spatial planning challenges, given the legacy of townships that housed most of the population on the fringes of cities.

Joint accountability and a changing political dynamic also explain why some problematic aspects of the intergovernmental system, such as inefficiency and corruption, proved difficult to address. "The prevalence of joint or mutual accountability within the intergovernmental with the TCF and Budget Council at its pinnacle often makes it challenging to implement reforms," explains Manuel. He uses the example of procurement to show these challenges. Initially all procurement was centrally controlled under the State Tender Board. However, under the new PFMA and Public Services Act, the emphasis shifted to allowing "managers control over their resources." Supply chain management was released on a pilot basis, but departments at the national and provincial level seized full control; Treasury tried in vain to try to take control back, but at that time political considerations dominated. By the time the centralized compliance office for procurement was eventually created, it was "closing the stable door truly after the horse had bolted," according to Manuel. Powell in turn sees the creation of the Department of Planning and Monitoring at the Presidency and new medium-term strategic frameworks as exacerbating the "joint decision-making trap," further undermining accountability.

The intergovernmental consultative process also struggles to develop solutions to address the problems of service delivery and governance. There is a sense that although the process was immensely successful in the formative years, political commitment to it diminished over time. Cole believes an opportunity was missed for the Budget Council, the Budget Forum, and the TCF to evolve into systems that could warn of emerging financial problems, such as the problems in Limpopo. "In many respects, these fora were the ideal place by which to gauge whether policies and services were working on the ground and what follow-up would be required to address problems." Legislative oversight via the various parliamentary committees also weakened with time.

Hattingh shares his insight as to why commitment to the consultative process weakened over time. "The third national election saw a complete turnover in provincial MECs and key officials in national and provincial treasuries. It was like a death." Incoming politicians did not understand the "battles and chaos" that gave rise to these mechanisms, and handovers were poor. In some sense, the system was also a victim of its own success, offers Hattingh. "As public finances became less restrained in the 2000s, focus shifted from consulting on problems to how to divide additional revenue resources."

At the municipal level, the fact that the Budget Forum has struggled to gain traction was to some extent to be expected, reflects Fanoe. "It is more difficult for very diverse municipalities to forge a common stance in SALGA, especially against the backdrop of weak capacity. Likewise the MINMECs, which were charged with coordinating functions like health and education, lacked the same legal backing of the Budget Council and as a result often struggled to arrive at decisions, particularly when sector ministers would get divergent orders from national and provincial governments."

Conclusions: Success Factors, Challenges, and Lessons Learned

At the end of apartheid, South Africa was in a unique reform space. Many countries that seek to decentralize fiscal structures often fail, because of the far-reaching political, financial, and administrative requirements. The end of apartheid, the backdrop of civil unrest, and South Africa's new Constitution generated conditions conducive to a high degree of change.

Several factors contributed to the success of the new intergovernmental system in meeting its objective to decentralize fiscal functions while safeguarding fiscal stability. The following four factors offer lessons to other countries that are seeking to reform their intergovernmental systems. They can both guide the reform agenda going forward and help policy makers in other countries considering similar reforms.

First, leadership was strong but inclusive and broad based. Trevor Manuel's leadership was consultative, inclusive, and empowering; and it was critically backed by two presidents who gave him authority and who supported the clear differentiation between the roles of the administration that needs to govern and those of politics and political parties. Manuel reached out to the new provincial leaders, treating them as equals and earning their trust; and these leaders in turn championed reforms in their own spheres and also held the line with their ministerial peers, helping maintain fiscal discipline. This approach created immense buy-in to the new system, across spheres. Manuel lent considerable political authority to the reform process, making bold decisions, such as the decision to adopt the MTEF; and he used his position to champion the reforms needed to cement the system. But there was also space for officials in National Treasury to lead, experiment, and learn through implementation. Mindful of constraints in capacity and lack of information, policy makers often proceeded in small steps. They remained open to local, as well as international, expertise. This approach created space for policy makers to develop their own solutions, as witnessed with the MTEF, budget monitoring systems, and changes in social security assignment and the revenue-sharing formulas. Creating new institutional arrangements also facilitated change. The FFC, Team Finance, and the TCF were new institutional mechanisms that helped build institutional effectiveness. These mechanisms empowered and connected experts across all levels, breaking down boundaries and silos and allowing officials in all spheres to liaise, share knowledge, and troubleshoot problems.

Second, leaders understood the interface between the political and administrative spheres and ensured that policy was shaped by evidence by focusing on data and emphasizing problem solving to find practical solutions. Rather than rigidly adhering to a doctrine of "federalism for the sake of federalism," or to political mantras, leaders were practical, as demonstrated by the decision by the MECs to self-impose an informal ban on provincial borrowing. Reforms, such as those in public finance management, were sequenced to give priority to measures that ensured timely access to comprehensive data on budget implementation to help support policy decisions. Substantial human resources were allocated to the TCF. In the initial years, strong legislative oversight was provided by the various parliamentary budgetary committees, in particular the Standing Committee on Public Accounts.

Third, reforms need to take account of differences in administrative and economic capacity, both across and within spheres. In many ways South Africa was really two countries in one: some provinces and municipalities had greater capacity and ability to function in a more decentralized system than others. This divergence called for a more differentiated approach to reform than the symmetric one adopted where reforms were applied to all provinces or all municipalities at once. Better-equipped provinces or municipalities could have proceeded more quickly in taking on greater responsibilities or bolder reforms, while weaker ones required more intensive handholding and more simplified reforms. By not taking account of the differences, policy makers failed to anticipate how some reforms, which entailed greater autonomy, made situations in some municipalities worse.

Fourth, incentives were created to promote cooperation and coordination. The fiscal crisis in Johannesburg and some provinces was used to demonstrate that the central government would not provide bailouts. Incentives were tilted toward fiscal discipline, minimizing the risk of "moral hazard," whereby subnational players try to offload the costs of their spending and borrowing on others through bailouts. The "top slicing" of the subnational vertical share of revenue also created incentives against free-riding by subnational players on the common pool of national revenues. The three-year MTEF gave funding predictability to the provincial and local government spheres, but the quid pro quo was higher-frequency reporting. However, the experiences also show that different elements of the institutional framework need to be aligned and provide incentives in order to foster accountability. Overlapping or concurrent expenditure responsibilities, the electoral list system, and reliance on transfers rather than own-revenue and the existence of state-owned enterprises outside the system make it difficult to enforce accountability. Greater clarity on the issue of concurrent responsibilities is badly needed to clarify which sphere is responsible for policy design, implementation, and monitoring in each function so to be better able to hold that sphere to account.

Some 20 years on, the intergovernmental system has not completely settled; several challenges remain.

- First, although the new intergovernmental system contributed to broadening access to public services, the quality of these services remains highly problematic. While the auditor general has played a critical role in highlighting shortcomings in financial management, a key weakness in the current system is that it does not assess nonfinancial performance of sector ministries where sector experts, for example in education, would be better placed to assess the actual quality of the public services delivered.

- Second, despite a strong legal framework, public financial management remains weak, especially at the subnational level, where many entities fail to receive a clean or even a qualified audit from the auditor general. In reality, it is difficult if not virtually impossible to sanction nonperformance by officials. Few players are sanctioned for breaking the law. Thus, stabilizing public financial systems is not enough because these systems also need to find underpinnings in strong mechanisms that ensure accountability as well as more medium-term strategic planning.

- Third, inefficiency and corruption in public spending remain challenges in part because the divide between administration and the political system has weakened. Political appointments to the administration have become more common, often overriding considerations of expertise. On the political front, it is difficult to hold elected officials to account given the electoral system while legislative oversight via the parliamentary oversight committees has weakened and needs strengthening to become an effective check on budget implementation. All of this has undermined the public's faith in the intergovernmental system, leading to calls for greater centralization.

- Fourth, continued political commitment to consultation, cooperation, and learning are needed to ensure continuity in reforms. The gradual erosion of consultative processes and the production of data that occurred as the economic and political landscape changed point to the need for continuous effort to explain and justify reforms and to take steps to ensure effective documentation and handover as staffing and administrations change. The learning and evolution of institutions to changing circumstances cannot stop if success is to be sustained.

In one respect South Africa's experience may be less applicable to other settings. The wide acceptance of the new intergovernmental system reflected the fact that incoming officials were "clean slates," highly committed to doing the right thing, lacking exposure or vested interest in the old system. However, the successes, challenges, and lessons from South Africa show that it is possible to reform an intergovernmental system under very difficult circumstances but that such reform is complex. It involves many players, demanding high levels of coordination and cooperation. It requires addressing issues of fiscal policy design, public financial management, transparency and accountability, capacity building, and, perhaps most critically, service delivery to citizens.

Twenty years is a short time in which to build a new democratic intergovernmental system from old apartheid structures. Tensions remain between the short-term expediency of relying on the central government to fix service delivery and governance problems and the long-term need to build subnational capacity by allowing local governments to develop their own solutions. Resolving them will require recapturing the spirit of broad engagement and problem solving to develop practical solutions.

Notes

1. The poorest 40 percent of the population accounted for only 11 percent of national income, the wealthiest 10 percent for 40 percent (Momoniat 2001).

2. The apartheid structure consisted of four provinces: the Cape of Good Hope and Natal (former British colonies) and the Orange Free State and Transvaal (former Boer republics). The racially segregated homelands comprised Transkei, Bophuthatswana, Venda, and Ciskei (autonomous) as well as Gazankulu, KaNgwane, KwaNdebele, KwaZulu, Lebowa, and QwaQwa (partially autonomous). See Makgetla and Jackson (2012) for information on how the new provinces were formed.

3. In 1993 South Africa adopted an interim constitution, which outlined the principles to which the final constitution had to adhere. For more information on the constitution-making process, please refer to chapter 12 of this book.

4. The treasury function was initially shared between two departments in the national government. The Department of Finance was responsible for the macroeconomic framework, taxation, and financing. The State Department was responsible for allocating and controlling expenditure.

5. This implied that the government was required to pay uniform salaries at the higher white civil service salaries, which resulted in a massive increase in personnel expenditure.

6. The author thanks Philip van Ryneveld for this insight.

7. Sections 227 and 229 of the Constitution require that transfers to subnational tiers take into account disparities in fiscal capacity and needs across provinces, but the center cannot impose conditions on these transfers.

8. Between 1996 and 1998, the Eastern Cape, KwaZulu-Natal, and the Free State were subject to Section 100 Constitutional interventions and Mpumalanga in 2001 (South Africa, National Treasury 2005).

9. A pay-as-you-earn tax (PAYE) is a tax on employees' income, usually withheld at source.

10. Section 139 of the Constitution requires the provincial government to intervene in cases where a municipality fails to fulfill its obligations. See Woldemariam, Widner, and Bacoon (2012) on the resolution of the Johannesburg financial crisis.

11. Municipalities were still in the process of being amalgamated, so their staffs were not incorporated.

12. Examples include the Municipal Systems Improvement Grant to fund and build capacity on financial management (Layman 2003); the National Treasury guidelines on budgeting planning and measurement of service delivery (South Africa, National Treasury 2000, 2001b); and strategic and annual performance plans (South Africa, National Treasury 2010).

13. According to the Multi-Level Governance Initiative (2013), complaints reached an all-time high in the first eight months of 2012, with more than 225 protests.

References

Ajam, Tania. 2014. "The Financial and Fiscal Commission: Two Decades of Institutional Evolution." Paper prepared for the Financial and Fiscal Commission 20th Anniversary Conference, Cape Town, August.

Ajam, Tania, and D. J. Fourie. 2014. "The Role of the Provincial Treasury in Driving Budget Reform in South Africa's Decentralized Fiscal System." *Administratio Publica* 22 (3): 43–61.

ANC (African National Congress). 1993. Regional Policy Document. Pretoria.

Andrews, Matt. 2013. *The Limits of Institutional Reform in Development: Changing Rules for Realistic Solutions.* New York: Cambridge University Press.

Brown, Kenneth, Tebogo Motsoane, and Lili Liu. 2013. "South Africa: Leveraging Private Financing for Infrastructure." In *Until Debt Do Us Part: Subnational Debt, Insolvency, and Markets*, edited by Otaviano Canuto and Lili Liu. Washington, DC: World Bank. https://openknowledge.worldbank.org/handle/10986/12597 License: CC BY 3.0 IGO.

Department for Provincial Affairs and Constitutional Development. 1998. *The White Paper on Local Government.* Pretoria: Department for Provincial Affairs and Constitutional Development.

Financial and Fiscal Commission. 1996. *The Financial and Fiscal Commission's Recommendations for the Allocation of Financial Resources to the National and Provincial Governments for the 1997/98 Financial Year.* Pretoria: Financial and Fiscal Commission.

————. 1998. *The Financial and Fiscal Commission's Recommendations and Comments: The Allocation of Financial Resources to the National, Provincial and Local Governments for the 1998/99 Fiscal Year.* Pretoria: Financial and Fiscal Commission.

————. 2000. "Preliminary Recommendations for 2001: A Costed Norms Approach for the Division of Revenue." Consultation Document, Financial and Fiscal Commission, Pretoria.

Fölscher, Alta, and Neil Cole. 2004. "South Africa: Transition to Democracy Offers Opportunity for Whole System Reform." In *Budget Reform Seminar: Country Case Studies.* Pretoria: Collaborative Africa Budget Reform Initiative (CABRI).

Layman, Timothy. 2003. *Intergovernmental Relations and Service Delivery in South Africa: A Ten Year Review.* Report commissioned by the Presidency of South Africa.

Makgetla, Tumi, and Rachel Jackson. 2012. "Negotiating Divisions in a Divided Land: Creating Provinces for a New South Africa, 1993." Policy Note, Princeton University, Princeton, NJ. http://www.princeton.edu/successfulsocieties/countries/africa/country .xml?id=12.

Momoniat, Ismail. 2001. "Fiscal Decentralization in South Africa: A Practitioners Perspective." Policy Paper, World Bank, Washington, DC.

Multi-Level Governance Initiative. 2013. *Service Delivery Protest Barometer*. http://mlgi .org.za/barometers/service-delivery-protest-barometer.

Presidency, Republic of South Africa. 2014. *Twenty Year Review 2014*. Pretoria.

South Africa, National Treasury. 1999. *Intergovernmental Fiscal Review*. Pretoria.

———. 2000. "Best Practice Guide 2000." In *Year Management Monitoring and Reporting*. Pretoria.

———. 2001a. *Intergovernmental Fiscal Review*. Pretoria.

———. 2001b. *Treasury Guidelines on Budgeting, Planning and Measuring Service Delivery*. Pretoria.

———. 2003. *Intergovernmental Fiscal Review*. Pretoria.

———. 2005. *Intergovernmental Fiscal Review*. Pretoria.

———. 2008. *Local Government Budgets and Expenditure Review*. Pretoria.

———. 2010. *Framework for Strategic Plans and Annual Performance Plans*. Pretoria.

———. 2011. *Local Government Budgets and Expenditure Review*. Pretoria.

van der Berg, Servaas, and Eldridge Moses. 2012. "How Better Targeting of Social Spending Affects Social Delivery in South Africa." *Development South Africa* 29 (1): 127–39. https://nicspaull.files.wordpress.com/2011/04/svdb-moses-2012 -how-better-targetting-of-social-spending-affects-social-delivery-in-sa2.pdf.

Wittenberg, Martin. 2006. "Decentralization in South Africa." In *Decentralization and Local Governance in Developing Countries*, edited by Pranab Bardhan and Dilip Mookherjee, 329–55. Cambridge, MA: MIT Press.

Woldemariam, Michael, Jennifer Widner, and Laura Bacoon. 2012. "Restructuring Service Delivery: Johannesburg, South Africa, 1996–2001," Case Study, Princeton University, Princeton, NJ. http://www.princeton.edu/successfulsocieties/countries/africa/country .xml?id=12.

CHAPTER 2

Increasing Budget Transparency

Neil Cole, Aarti Shah, and Gert van der Linde

Introduction

The transition to democracy in 1994 ushered in a new constitutional dispensation that changed the structure and distribution of power of the South African state, with implications for the way in which public resources are managed. In addition to integrating the formerly fragmented public finances of the apartheid state and adapting to the new national, provincial, and local fiscal framework, enhanced transparency and accountability have been central to the new dispensation and its public finance management reforms.

South Africa's public financial management (PFM) system has undergone substantial reforms since the mid-1990s. Early reforms shaped macroeconomic stability, improved revenue collection, realigned public spending, and sought to improve the efficiency of resource allocations and effective service delivery. More recently, the reform program has focused on strengthening governance and the performance orientation of the entire PFM system.

The PFM reform program rolled out a new intergovernmental system that requires all three levels of government to formulate and approve their own budgets. It introduced three-year spending plans for national and provincial departments under a Medium-Term Expenditure Framework (MTEF). It created new formats for budget documentation that include a strong focus on service delivery information. It moved toward functional budgeting and required departments to produce and table in Parliament timely annual reports that disclose performance information. It also improved auditing and oversight practices. Changes to the budget process have allowed stakeholders to deliberate on key policy choices and on matching resources to plans rather than item-by-item cost estimates (Fölscher and Cole 2005).

Neil Cole is the Executive Secretary of the Collaborative Africa Budget Reform Initiative (CABRI), which was housed in the National Treasury between 2004 and 2011; Aarti Shah is an adviser to Mr. Cole at CABRI; and Gert van der Linde is a Lead Financial Management Specialist in the World Bank's Global Governance Practice. This chapter benefited from extensive interviews with current and former government officials as well as from comments by peer reviewer Alta Fölscher, consultant).

Underpinning these reforms has been a commitment to improve the timeliness, quality, and usefulness of information in the allocation and use of funds at the national, provincial, and local levels of government. Equally important has been the commitment to build and strengthen a public service that adheres to a high level of accountability.

South Africa's budgeting system went from being highly fragmented, with opaque budget information, to being robust and credible, a world leader in terms of provision of budget information. In 2010 South Africa was placed first on the Open Budget Index (OBI), which is a ranking that is determined by the International Budget Partnership, based on substantial reforms of the budget process and publications, alongside commitments to equitable and sustainable financing of the new government's Reconstruction and Development Program (RDP). In 2012 South Africa was placed second on this list.

Notwithstanding the Treasury's impressive budget modernization program, complementary policy coordination and management reforms across government have been less impressive, making it difficult to assess the overall impact of the budget reforms. Value for money is not as high as expected, and corruption is increasingly presenting a problem.

This chapter traces how the improvements in budget transparency were achieved over the 20-year period by examining the substance, intent, and implementation of budget reforms. It examines the results from improved transparency and the extent to which transparency has provided a basis for accountability. The chapter concludes by exploring why, despite a much more transparent budget system, the links between budgeting and policy implementation, including management responsibility, are yet to be fully developed. Lessons are highlighted and reform priorities are identified.

The Policy Challenge: The Institutional Restructuring of the Budget

Since the advent of democracy, the context and impetus for budget and broader public service reform in South Africa have been driven by the policy challenge of providing more and better public services for all within a constrained fiscal framework. The apartheid state delivered generous social benefits to white people, at significant cost. The challenge the new government faced was to deliver services of a similar standard to all South Africans, without dramatically increasing fiscal resources through higher taxes or borrowing. It decided to equalize a range of public service benefits and salary structures, while at the same time adopting an economic stabilization package aiming at increasing tax revenues and reducing public debt.[1]

In the 1994/95 fiscal year, public debt rose to about 47 percent of gross domestic product (GDP), leaving very little room for the state to improve the equity of public services (Fölscher and Cole 2005). The only way the government could achieve greater equity in spending was to understand the minute details of all aspects of public spending, with two aims in mind. The first was to identify the levers for moving resources from one service or area to another. The second was to improve the quality and efficiency of spending.

Transparency was a much-needed means to an end. Budget reform was about shining a bright light on the spending record, in order to reform the pattern and effect of public spending, for political ends. If, for example, the government wanted to equalize resources across schools, it had to know how much was spent on schools, what the money was spent on, and what the consequences of shifting spending would be. Getting better value for money from every rand spent would be important in improving the quality of services. Without information, without transparency in the PFM system, these shifts would not be possible.

The new government inherited an annual budgeting system that was highly fragmented, with few links between policy, budgeting, and implementation. Under the previous dispensation, public finances were organized into 14 separate racial or territorial budgets.

The existence of homelands and self-governing territories inside South Africa as well as racially divided service delivery departments complicated and obscured spending patterns. The homeland of Bophuthatswana, for example, received a block allocation from the budget of the Department of Foreign Affairs, some of which it spent on education. Aggregating actual spending on education was a time-consuming task because of different budget practices, large differences between budgeted and actual spending, inconsistent accounting practices, and fragmented financial management systems.

Another problem was that in the context of poor expenditure control and high inflation under apartheid, deviations from budgeted expenditures were often large. It often took years to ascertain how much was actually spent on a service. In many respects, the public finance system was designed to hide rather than show where resources were allocated.

The consolidation of the separate budgets for health or education or police to correspond with the organizational restructuring of the state was therefore a substantial undertaking. This could only be done through greater transparency and a thorough analysis of the cost accounts.

To address the policy challenge of providing more and better public services by changing the patterns and efficiency of expenditure, improvements in transparency needed to achieve four objectives:

1. Open up the budget in terms of both information and decision making, in order to create a legitimate process in which funds could by allocated horizontally across sectors and vertically across spheres of government to deliver services to all, with buy-in both within government and by external stakeholders.
2. Make the budget more comprehensive and broaden its coverage, in order to facilitate management of the fiscal situation and change the pattern of expenditure. Achieving this objective required modernizing the way in which public funds were managed.
3. Produce information in a meaningful manner for intelligent consumption and analysis within and outside government, in order to facilitate better management and accountability of public funds. Achieving this objective

would be an important input in driving performance and improving the quality of public spending.

4. Use transparency as a means to increase fiscal prudence. During the late 1990s, provinces massively overspent their budgets (Friedman 2103). Clear budget formats and in-year financial reports became tools to impose fiscal discipline on the provinces.

As part of the transition to a post-apartheid society, South Africa quickly moved from a fairly closed state to a more open democracy. During this period, there was a global trend toward transparent budgets, new public management approaches, and greater accountability. When former political activists entered the Department of Finance after the transition, they lacked experience and knowledge of the budget process and the numbers behind the budget. Getting a better understanding of the numbers was part of the learning process.

Addressing the Policy Challenge

The principles of transparency and accountability are enshrined in South Africa's Constitution. They have guided the National Treasury in formulating the laws, practices, and procedures that govern the management of public finances. As the preface of the 1994/95 Budget Review notes, "More than ever before, there appears to be an urge for expanded and detailed information on the Budget and the processes that lead to budgetary and fiscal decisions, as well as an account of the progress which the Government has made in achieving its goals of recon-struction and development" (South Africa, National Treasury 1995).

Context of Reforms

Understanding the changing economic and political context since 1994 provides depth to analysis of why transparency has been a critical feature of the PFM reforms South Africa has undertaken.

Changes in the economic context. The economic context can be divided into three periods (Naidoo 2014). During the first period (1994–2000), immediately after the end of apartheid, growth was slow. Fiscal consolidation was a necessity, both because growth was modest and because the apartheid government had been fiscally profligate in its final years. Extending budget coverage and expendi-ture reporting were tools to help increase fiscal prudence. The second period (2001–08) was characterized by rapid growth (fueled by a commodity boom) and significant increases in public spending, making allocation decisions easier. The third period (2009–14) included the global financial crisis and significantly slower economic growth. This period—coinciding with changes in the political context—was characterized by a tighter fiscal envelope and greater contestation over scarce resources. The contestation over resources necessitated even greater transparency and more collective decision making.

Changes in the powers of and relationship between national, provincial, and local levels of government. In the first few years after 1994, the government tried to build a system of cooperative governance among the three spheres. Although national government always dominated the decision-making process, provinces and local government were integrated into the process through intergovernmental fora such as the Budget Council and the Budget Forum, and parallel intergovernmental structures were established in education, health, social security, and housing. In more recent years, the cooperative governance institutions through which there was engagement between national, provincial, and local governments have weakened and the national government's confidence in provincial and municipal administrations has waned.

Substance of Reform

Commitment to the principle of budget transparency has not faced major obstacles. It remained robust under the leadership of three successive ministers of finance—Trevor Manuel, Pravin Gordhan, and Nhlanhla Nene. Various reforms improved transparency.

The Early Years: Fiscal Consolidation and the Boom Period

Former minister of finance, Trevor Manuel, recalls how budgeting was conducted in the early days:

> In 1994 the Department of State Expenditure, where much of the number crunching took place, was fairly uniform in race and gender terms. It was an archaic institution that operated without (excel) spreadsheets, and at that time the Internet was not well utilized. These guys used to sit around a table with square paper, and they'd add down and across, all in pencil and each with an eraser until the numbers added up. There was a manual vote register that they entered everything into, because the old Exchequer Act required high levels of control and it was three meters long. What we needed to do was modernize the process.

As it embarked on the modernization process, the new administration recognized that it had inherited fairly robust financial management and payroll systems, and a reliable capacity to maintain these systems and adapt them to the changes in budgeting, chart of accounts, and the reporting requirements that were implemented.

The opportunity to equalize service provision and reduce inequality deepened public interest in fiscal management. The institutional changes to establish three interdependent but distinctive spheres of government (national, provincial, and local) were to have a major impact on the way public finances were managed. The complex transition process required systematic explanation of the changes and their effects on public finances, as well as the development and presentation of comparable databases for the purposes of analysis and consistent policy making. The shaping of the intergovernmental fiscal system was one of the first instances in which policy and institutional changes provided strong impetus to collect comprehensive and comparable budget information and to make this information public. The preface to the 1994/95 Budget

Review stated, "The annual presentation of a Budget is fundamentally an exercise in public accountability" (South Africa, National Treasury 1995).

Among the very formal commitments the first African National Congress (ANC) minister of finance, Trevor Manuel (1996–2009), made was to adopt the spirit of the Constitution and the RDP regarding transparency in the budget process and to break down secrecy. "I sought to decolonize the process. I didn't have in classic Westminster style a locked Gladstone briefcase and the ritual of unlocking the briefcase to deliver the budget in Parliament that had been a complete secret to that point, as they do in many other countries."

The first budget Manuel delivered, in March 1997, changed the way in which the budget was communicated to the public. The budget speech became popular because of the use of poetry, imagery, more accessible language, and local African languages. "We wanted the budget to be owned by people," says Manuel. For that to happen, the National Treasury and Parliament needed to publish more comprehensive budget documentation, and analysts and the media needed to pore over this information. Space also needed to be created for a consultative and legitimate budget process.

In October 1997, Manuel tabled the first Medium-Term Budget Policy Statement (MTBPS) in Parliament; it was a midyear statement on the policy intention of government over a medium-term horizon. The budget tabled in February 1998 was therefore the first Medium Term Expenditure Framework (MTEF) that contained not just a broad top-down fiscal framework but also a complete set of program breakdowns in a three-year framework, together with a contingency reserve and macrofiscal projections. The enactment of the Public Finance Management Act (PFMA) in 1999, and requirements for several new budget documents, was a significant step in increasing transparency, openness, and cooperative government.

In the 1997 statement, Manuel wrote, "For too long, budgets have been made behind closed doors. These are important decisions, which affect all our futures. We are publishing today the same information that is before Government as we finalize the Budget. Every citizen, every stakeholder will be able to read this Statement and see what we are trying to achieve, and the resources we have available."

By tabling the MTBPS about four months before the budget, the department gave Parliament and civil society the opportunity to engage with the budget. It was also in this budget year that budget documents were placed on the Internet for the first time. The principles of transparency and accountability were mentioned repeatedly in budget reviews from 1995 to 2002. Over the period 1997–99, budget reviews laid out the reform challenges and approaches informing the content of the PFMA, which was enacted in 1999. A "People's Guide to the Budget" was introduced in 2000, followed by an "Estimates of National Expenditure" document in 2002. The "People's Guide" is published in five South African languages in order to reach a wide audience. From about 2000, when the budget reforms initiated since 1997 were being embedded, greater emphasis was also placed on the production of revenue and tax information.

Transparency was not just about producing the numbers; it was also about the decision-making process. Many important changes to the budget process were introduced early on to enable transparent decision making and consensus building between key stakeholders.

The Ministers' Committee on the Budget (MinComBud) was established to empower a subset of Cabinet ministers to take off their sector hats and become part of a collective and transparent decision-making process. It opened up the budget process and gave greater legitimacy to the allocation process. Similarly, the Budget Council provided a forum for the intense exchange of information on the allocation of public finances between the minister of finance and the nine provincial members of executive committees, provincial cabinet ministers. In addition, the constitutional requirement of an iterative exchange between the National Treasury and the Financial and Fiscal Commission (FFC) meant that information could not be hidden from the public as it had been in the past. The caliber of participants in these structures was very high, often consisting of seasoned anti-apartheid activists who were committed to breaking with the past, according to Manuel.

The international trend toward greater accountability helped give substance to what it meant to be more transparent, according to Andrew Donaldson, the former deputy director-general of the Budget Office and Public Finance at the National Treasury. The substance related to using outputs and more service delivery–oriented information in the budget process, making coverage more comprehensive, and shifting to three-year budgeting, which is what much of the work focused on. The MTEF (introduced in 1997 for the 1998 fiscal year) provided information on policy and program outcomes, outputs, and financial performance rather than just input-based resource requirements. The three-year budget projections were first steps in a wider overhaul of the budgetary process, emphasizing transparency, output-driven program budgeting, and political prioritization. By signaling the policy priorities for a three-year period upfront, the Treasury gives Parliament and civil society the opportunity to participate in discussions on the second and third years of the MTEF, which helps shape future spending patterns.

The new MTEF came under stress in 1999 when economic growth slowed sharply and the forward estimates had to be revised down. The slowdown was short-lived though, and the downward revisions were more than reversed in 2000. This was followed by a period of seven years in which it was possible to make substantial additions to budgets, until the global financial crisis of 2008.

Early budget reforms as well as key principles—ensuring transparency, increasing comprehensiveness, providing political oversight of policy priorities, using information strategically, and changing behavior through changed incentives—were embodied in the Public Financial Management Act No. 1 of 1999, which Parliament passed following a two-year engagement with the legislatures and civil society. The act set outs a strong regulatory framework for financial management. It requires the publication of monthly, quarterly, and annual budgetary information; the submission of timely annual financial statements to the auditor-general; and the presentation of annual reports to Parliament. These measures are based on a philosophy of "let managers manage but hold them accountable through reporting" (South Africa, National Treasury 2000). They enhanced the authority for better internal financial management and served as a basis for accountability.

Reporting formats were modernized in accordance with the International Monetary Fund's Government Finance Statistics system, with some modifications. South Africa also better linked its budget to its transaction-processing system through a modernized chart of accounts. As a result of these reforms, budgets could be analyzed for information within programs that were relevant for both policy makers and the public. Improved classification also supported the extension of budget coverage to include social security funds, provinces, and public entities, yielding a clearer picture of taxes and spending of the entire government sector. Such breadth of coverage is almost unique in public finance.

The Later Years: The Financial Crisis and the Smaller Fiscal Envelope

In the earlier period, budgets grew rapidly, baselines were guaranteed, and the whole resource allocation process was geared toward additional resources. There was less pressure to interrogate the baselines. "In this environment, the budget is a beauty contest about which department gets additional funds. This puts Treasury in a powerful position, because we get to decide. Over time, this leads to changes in the pattern of spending," explains Michael Sachs, the deputy director-general of the Budget Office at the National Treasury.

Since 2011 the expenditure framework has been cast as a ceiling; no additional resources have been available. "In this environment, with no additional resources, the budget becomes a zero-sum game. The politics of the process is different and the role of the Treasury is different," notes Sachs. Once trade-offs have been made to determine the expenditure ceilings, Treasury has to step back and allow departments to make decisions within the budget constraint. Treasury's role is more about enforcing the constraint and promoting value for money decisions within the constraint.

Over time, generating and publishing information that would allow the measurement of performance beyond spending data became important in order to hold departments and government in general to account. The sharper focus on performance was driven in part by the pressure to improve effectiveness and efficiency given the tight fiscal situation, which the global financial crisis exacerbated. According to former minister of finance Pravin Gordhan, strengthening monitoring and evaluation, using available information to track service delivery, and closing the feedback loop will help promote change and strengthen accountability.

A defining feature of this period was the creation, in 2010, of the Department of Performance Monitoring and Evaluation (DPME) and the National Planning Commission (NPC). One could read their establishment as a signal that the coordinating role of the National Treasury in terms of policy priorities was being reduced. There was a sense, according to Donaldson, that the Treasury had perhaps overreached by attempting to do too much to bring together strategic planning and performance information in the budget process.

Increased government expenditure and a focus on outputs did not always lead to the expected improvements in outcomes. As a means of improving performance and accountability in the public service, in 2009/10 DPME attempted to shift the mind-set of government departments away from producing outputs to delivering outcomes (The Presidency, South Africa 2010). By working backward from outcomes, departments would be able to better design outputs and activities to achieve results. Connecting resources to real improvements in people's lives would also strengthen accountability.

The South African government identified 12 national outcomes that would provide strategic focus on priority areas. Each minister signed a performance agreement with the president identifying his or her contribution to achieving these outcomes. This outcomes-based approach was also designed to improve coordination between spending agencies delivering outputs related to a common outcome.

To complement this shift to focusing on outcomes, the National Treasury introduced function budgeting or portfolio budgeting by function) in 2010. This approach implies that each outcome is achieved by the combined contributions of different government institutions in the various functions or sub-function groups (South Africa, National Treasury 2013). Resources are allocated to the function group, and trade-offs are made within the group in order to best achieve the outcome. "This approach provides more transparency and better coordination in the budgeting process" (South Africa, National Treasury 2011). To bridge the interface between policy and budgeting, Treasury is structuring more policy engagement with functional groups throughout the budget process.

Fiscal tightness in an arena of decentralized authority, greater budget contestation, and the absence of a powerful arbitrator have prompted additional changes to the budget process. Once again, the principle of transparency in decision making has been drawn upon to create a greater sense of legitimacy around the budget process. Budget rules, timeframes, and processes have been made much more explicit at a political level through Cabinet memoranda early on in the budget calendar.

Structures that no longer worked well in the new political context were reformed. MinComBud was formally established as a committee of the Cabinet with a clear mandate, and the number of members was reduced. Terms of reference were defined for the Medium-Term Expenditure Committee, and its composition and mandate were made clearer. The Budget Council and Technical Committee on Finance were reinvigorated. Clarity and transparency about the budget process were particularly important in 2014, when the whole process was redesigned. These changes should facilitate better-quality information and earlier decision making and provide more time to produce publications, all of which should increase public transparency.

Over the past 20 years, South Africa instituted a series of reforms to institutions, rules, and practices, including introduction of the MTEF; a new chart of accounts; monthly, quarterly, and annual departmental reporting; and local and provincial government expenditure surveys. The reforms resulted in better-quality and more comprehensive, timely, and comparable budget information with a performance orientation and more transparent decision making. The reforms were tailored to address specific problems and introduced incrementally. "I don't think it's possible to go faster than the institutional change allows you to go. There's a balance between trying to push the boundaries and knowing that these are boundaries that can be pushed," notes Manuel.

Implementation of Reforms

Planning and implementing such an ambitious reform agenda would not have been possible without the reformist zeal of the first generation of officials across government serving a new democracy. Trevor Manuel was considered a strong proponent of establishing and sustaining the transparency regime (Friedman 2013). The administration needed a cadre of officials who would inculcate the principles of transparency and accountability and at the same time establish a stable public service in the period following the 1994 elections.

A major consideration in this regard was ensuring that public servants were willing and able to serve the new administration. In 1994 most public servants had served the apartheid government. It was therefore incumbent on the new government to fill or match senior positions in the administration with veterans or sympathizers of the fight against apartheid who were eager to democratize government. Twenty years later, many of those officials are still at the Treasury and remain strongly committed to maintaining transparency and accountability (Friedman 2013).

Bringing together people who worked for the apartheid administration with a young cadre of people who looked to create a dynamic and innovative Treasury environment in that early period was challenging, according to Manuel. As part of the process of modernizing, the Department of Finance and the Department of State Expenditure were merged to create the National Treasury. The budget examiners from State Expenditure were retained to continue the close working relationship with line departments. They had a deep understanding of depart-mental budgets and were vital in ensuring that the Treasury had a handle on the numbers, especially before reforms were implemented.

For example, around 1997, at a time when the fiscal position was tight, then-minister Manuel sat down with the budget examiners in an attempt to find money. The examiners suggested that money could be taken from the Department of Defense. The Department of Defense claimed there was not a cent to spare. With the backing of former president Thabo Mbeki to continue interrogating the defense budget, Manuel met with Joe Modise (the defense minister), Ronnie Kasrils (the deputy defense minister), and the generals. They had come prepared with a trolley of dot matrix paper. "'So, Minister, you think you can take money? There are all our line items. We've gone through it. You're not going to find any money.' Hannes Smit [the Director-General of State Expenditure] had prepared me for this, you see, because you can play this game and pretend that you are transparent, but in fact, it isn't even translucency, it's just opacity in the way in which you conduct yourself." The examiners' knowledge and experience of departmental budgets was such that they knew exactly where funds could be cut. "We sent this off to Thabo Mbeki and he convened Joe Modise and me and said, 'Well done.' And Joe said, 'But how did you do that?'"

Several elements were important to building up the capacity of the National Treasury:

- Insiders who had knowledge of how this opaque system worked, especially people who had a long relationship with the line ministries, were valued.
- Trevor Manuel drew in trusted people with whom he had worked at the ANC who were outside government, some from administration, and others from development banks or the private sector.
- Advisers seconded from the U.K. and U.S. treasuries brought in ideas and experiences that were adapted to the South African context.
- Manuel played a catalytic role in the reform process. He provided the authority to lead the process, and he convened and motivated his staff. Although he may not have had the same technical depth as his staff, he notes, he was able to push ideas forward, count on support ("air cover") from the president and the Cabinet, and be part of a team when necessary. One of his take-aways from being minister of finance for 13 years is that "if you are not populating the rest of government with the same style and the same kind of commitment, you have uneven development."

Under ministers Gordhan and Nene, the Treasury has continued with the MTEF and strengthening functional and program budgeting, while reinforcing oversight over provinces and municipalities, in a context of sluggish growth and difficult public finance trends. As a result, greater effort was made by the Treasury to consult more broadly, also including the views of civil society organizations, when making budget decisions. This approach required even more comprehensive and accurate knowledge and information about the spending patterns and plans of departments. It is too early to tell whether it will succeed in both driving key budget reforms and raising the quality of government spending decisions.

International initiatives influenced transparency reforms to some extent. South Africa is a member of the Collaborative Africa Budget Reform Initiative (CABRI), which is committed to the promotion of transparency and accountability across Africa. It also participates in the Global Initiative for Fiscal Transparency (GIFT) and the Open Government Partnership. The Treasury absorbs the spirit of these initiatives and gains technical knowledge from them, which it applies to the South African context rather than dogmatically doing what the standards say. For example, GIFT promotes public participation at every step of the process. "We have heavy consultations with departments bilaterally, with function groups, with Parliament and civil society at strategic points in our process. To consult throughout the process is impossible. Each country has a different system and a different set of weaknesses. You can only evolve from where you are and where you need to be. We draw on and contribute to the spirit of the initiatives but do not necessarily follow them to the letter," notes Kay Brown (chief director, Budget Office, National Treasury). Improved budget transparency has been the result of a series of budget reforms that have built on one another, driven by need and context.

Results Achieved

Over the past 20 years, the South African government has progressively improved the extent of budget information available to Parliament and the public. Since 2010 it has been recognized as a global leader. Reforms to the budget process have enabled a more inclusive and transparent decision-making process. This section examines whether this strong improvement in budget information has led to improvements in linking budgets with planning and service delivery, and holding managers and elected officials accountable.

Opening up the Budget Process

South Africa has built a transparent and credible budget process. It scored As on all the Public Expenditure and Financial Accountability (PEFA) indicators that measure budget transparency and credibility (Jacobs, Bennett, and Hegbor 2014). Budget reforms to improve transparency of information and transparency in decision making have worked well for the most part. Some budget-making structures, such as the MinComBud and the Budget Council, have struggled in the new political context, but recent changes to make their roles and the rules of the budget process explicit should improve their effectiveness.

The National Treasury produces a wealth of information, publishing eight budget documents every year. The 2012 Open Budget Index South Africa report makes recommendations on improving the quality of the citizens' budget, providing a more comprehensive picture of fiscal risk in the Budget Review and adding more information on the variance between forecast and actual macroeconomic indicators at the Year-End Report (IBP 2012). The budget team is clear that any further reforms should be driven by need rather than simply to improve scores on an international survey.

The big issue, however, is the lack of transparency in the procurement process. South Africa scored a D on the PEFA indicator on public access to complete, reliable, and timely procurement information. "When speaking about transparency in procurement, I think we are behind the curve," notes Andrew Donaldson. Several controversial, high-profile procurement issues have made it into the public domain.

The extent of nondisclosure of information for the purposes of commercial confidentiality is unwarranted. The procurement policy framework has very complex overlapping objectives, including increasing cost efficiency and addressing other price-related issues, improving the quality of services and products, empowering black South Africans economically, increasing industrial participation, and localization. All of these outcomes are difficult to measure. Donaldson argues that the complexity interferes with competition and raises questions about whether things are being done well. Nondisclosure of information raises the risk of corruption and bad decisions.

"Transparency from the start of procurement process is the best antidote to corruption, flawed processes, or just the risks associated with complexity," says Donaldson. "In the modern information age you have the option not just of taking advantage of greater disclosure and transparency; you also can systematize tender processes using modern information technology, as opposed to documents submitted in envelopes, in ways that are good for accountability and good for post facto auditing." The National Treasury is starting to make progress on these issues. It has created the Office of the Chief Procurement Officer, whose role will be to enhance value for money in procurement decisions.

Achieving Fiscal Outcomes and Reprioritizing Spending

South Africa has largely met the objectives of the early years: to improve budget information, get a good handle on the numbers, and extend budget coverage in order to make important fiscal and public policy decisions that would redress the inequalities of the past. The economic, budget, and public finance reforms put in place after 1994 led to substantial improvement in the fiscal position. Tax revenue increased, enabling significant reductions in tax rates; spending growth was in line with budgeted objectives; deficits came down; and the debt-to-GDP ratio fell sharply before the financial crisis. The budget, which had registered a deficit of about 7 percent of GDP in 1993, showed a surplus of about 1.3 percent of GDP in 2007. Over this period, debt levels fell from more than 50 percent of GDP to a low of 22 percent, creating significant fiscal space in which to respond to the global financial crisis. Over this period, but especially between 2001 and 2008, public spending increased by more than 7 percent a year in real terms. Since the financial crisis, there has been a deterioration in the fiscal position, as a result of lower revenues, more investment in infrastructure, and a rising public sector wage bill.

During the first decade of democracy, there was significant reprioritization of spending toward education, social grants, cash transfers, and health and away from defense and economic subsidies to industry. During the second decade of democracy, spending on urban services such as housing, water, sanitation, electricity, and public transport increased sharply. These shifts enabled the government to raise the social wage (a package of services targeted largely at the poor), which raised living standards. Better information, broader budget coverage, and transparent decision-making processes made these shifts possible.

A report by the World Bank (2014) notes that South Africa's highly redistributive fiscal system has significantly reduced poverty and inequality. Cash grants and free basic services have lifted the incomes of some 3.6 million people above $2.50 a day (purchasing power parity). The rate of extreme poverty— measured as the share of the population living on $1.25 per day or less—fell by half, from 34.4 percent to 16.5 percent. The child support grant and old-age pension have had the largest impact on poverty.

South Africa has had more success than peer countries—including Argentina, Brazil, Ethiopia, Indonesia, and Mexico—in using fiscal policy to tackle inequality and poverty. However, because the income gap was very high to begin with, the level of inequality is still much higher than in most other countries.

Service delivery improved when budget transparency increased. Outcomes, however, have lagged spending allocations, reflecting a weak public sector and significant incapacity throughout the state but especially in regions where the poorest live.

Improving Performance

Producing credible performance information is still at the early stages. Influencing budget policy decisions through the use of performance information and using this information as a tool for accountability is still a long way away. Defining the coordination of planning and performance management, embedding the outcomes approach, and implementing function budgeting constitutes work in progress. These reforms have not been without challenges and resistance, especially from some government departments. The various processes still appear somewhat disparate, and there is an ongoing tension between how much is measured and evaluated by the center of government and what takes place in line departments. The next step is to continue to build an effective set of institutions that use information to hold people accountable.

An unanswered question is whether the emphasis on in-year monitoring has overburdened departments and municipalities. There is a constant need for up-to-date information. "Is there an expectation that goes too far?" asks Manuel. "Are we asking too much of ministers who on top of having to manage their complex portfolios need to have the time and headspace to know just as much about the financials?"

The lack of comprehensive, up-to-date, quality performance information is still an issue. Administrative data is not readily available and annual reports in practice fall short of what they were intended to be. They are glossy publications that emphasize what went well, with inconsistent performance information across years. The information is difficult to interrogate without inside knowledge of the department.

Increasing Accountability

"What is missing in our system is accountability," notes Michael Sachs. "We have a lot of really good information out there that is not used. The reason it is not used has more to do with society, Parliament, the state of journalism, and the state of civil society organizations. In the United Kingdom there is a layer of policy institutions that absorbs the information that the Treasury puts out and with integrity communicates to the public and civil society. It exists in South Africa in a few instances." South Africa lacks the plethora of think tanks and intellectual centers that analyze information in many Western countries. Civil society organizations largely mirror the major power centers in the country, with few people speaking on behalf of poor, rural, unemployed, and marginalized constituencies, according to former finance minister Pravin Gordhan.

In contrast, the South African financial sector is well developed and produces deep analysis on the budget, which to some extent fills the vacuum left by the limited discourse within civil society. The National Treasury has proactively engaged with civil society to support these stakeholders in translating messages from government to society. The goal is to make budget information more accessible, so that it is not just a privilege of middle-class households with Internet access, as claimed by Friedman (2013).

After the 2014 budget, senior officials from the National Treasury presented aspects of the budget to the economics departments of half a dozen universities, in sessions that were open to the public. It also organized a workshop with selected civil society organizations. For the first time, the Budget and Expenditure Monitoring Forum (BEMF) and the Congress of South African Trade Unions (COSATU) were invited to the MTBPS lock-up for analysts. "You get a sense from the COSATU statement that the drafter has read every bit of the MTBPS, which was probably not the case in previous years," observes Sachs. The Treasury also supported BEMF in producing a citizens' adjustments budget. Over time organizations like the BEMF will continue to strengthen their analytical capacity to examine value for money and to contest rather than just translate budget issues. Such capacity is healthy for democracy.

Weaknesses within the committees themselves and in the analytical and research support Parliament is able to provide make up the capacity of Parliament's committees to engage with the detail of the budget. As a result, legislative oversight is ineffective and resources scarce. The Money Bills Amendment Procedure and Related Matters Act No. 9 of 2009 created a Parliamentary Budget Office. Getting this office off the ground has been slow; in effect, the act produced another center where analytical capacity has to be built. But the office is clearly needed. Donaldson believes that a better outcome would have been to locate the FFC in Cape Town and for the FFC to have become the embryonic analytical support to Parliament and its appropriations and finance committees. "We missed an opportunity to build the FFC into an expert and advisory capacity that might have had a closer relationship to Parliament if that had been the way it have been structured and setup in the 1990s," he notes. In an effort to address weak parliamentary committees, the National Treasury and DPME also held workshops with parliamentary committees and content advisers. Officials from the National Treasury explained where to find relevant information, how to analyze the information, and how to engage with departments on issues of value for money.

The media is another important interlocutor. Media coverage of the budget puts budget issues under the spotlight for a week. "What we don't have enough of is ongoing analysis and coverage of service delivery challenges and budget implementation. I think our media has a long way to go," says Donaldson. Friedman (2013) argues that the failure of the media to use information appropriately may say more about the state of journalism in South Africa than it does about transparency.

The other important stakeholder in holding the government to account is the auditor general. South Africa has a long history of steady development in audit capacity. By international comparisons, its audit institutions are well established and strong; they have considerable independence and are taken seriously. Having audited annual financial statements and regulatory and performance audit reports covering most aspects of public spending is an important aspect of the transparency story, in part because of extended budget coverage. Twenty years ago, budgeting was based on incomplete information about the previous years' expenditure. The improved timeliness of audits and financial statements was an important reform commitment of the 1990s. By September or October of each year, the National Treasury is able to provisionally budget on audited financial statements (or those in the process of being audited) for the previous financial year.

Conclusions: Success Factors, Challenges, and Lessons Learned

The South African story on budget transparency is a positive one. The government fully used the reform space it had at the beginning of the democratic era to design and implement a range of reforms that opened up the budget allocation process. The reform space began to narrow as the democracy matured until the country faced a tight fiscal situation, which again spurred a series of reforms.

Greater transparency has enabled the government to improve the fiscal situation while redirecting spending to where it was needed most. However, by the mid-2000s it was clear that despite significant reforms increased resources did not necessarily lead to better service delivery. As a result, more care was taken to promote external accountability. Citizen concerns and public opinion began to influence the presentation of information on public finances.

Transparency has provided the basis for better accountability. However, much work still needs to be done to generate performance information, evaluate it, and use it to improve internal management and enhance external accountability. The strengthening of the accountability chain remains a key objective in the decade ahead.

Five factors accounted for the success of reform. First, improved transparency went from being championed by one minister of finance to becoming the strategic imperative of the National Treasury and embedded in the ethos and values of government. Transparency was more than a guiding principle; it became a tool to manage the political and economic environment. Creating an inclusive and transparent decision-making mechanism was as critical as being transparent about the numbers.

Second, people were an important part of the success. The Treasury retained important reformers while bringing in a fresh injection of energy, people with an astute understanding of both the political and economic challenges. Because it understood and was able to respond to the changing political and economic context, the Treasury was able to craft and implement reforms that took advantage of opportunities as they arose.

Making It Happen • http://dx.doi.org/10.1596/978-1-4648-0768-8

Third, the reform process was largely incremental, driven by need, with space for experimentation and learning from mistakes. Reforms responded to practical needs. International practices were a guiding influence on what was important to consider, but the reform path was uniquely South African.

Fourth, authority for reforms came from the public finance legislation, which was used strategically to embed policy reform principles.

Fifth, major improvements in transparency would not have been possible without related improvements in technology. Data are now collected, collated, analyzed, and disseminated in ways that were not previously possible. Technological change clearly aided the transparency agenda.

Five key challenges remain. First, transparency is lacking in procurement, increasing the risk of corruption and raising the probability of poor procurement decisions.

Second, the production of performance information and its use in influencing budget policy have not been deeply embedded.

Third, flaws in the accountability chain have led to suboptimal service delivery outcomes, despite a high degree of budget transparency. Parliament has been weak in holding the executive accountable for performance, and the intergovernmental system has blurred the lines of accountability. Parliament would have benefited from having a policy support function early on.

Fourth, public debate on budget policy is limited. It might have been stronger if expertise from universities and other centers had been brought into the budget formulation process to improve policy advice. Using such expertise would also have helped these institutions strengthen their own policy advisory capacity.

Fifth, unlike the Treasury, many sectors of the government have not necessarily retained and recruited highly capable individuals. There is significant unevenness in the capacity of government across spheres and sectors, resulting in major gaps in performance.

The agenda going forward will continue to focus on deepening function budgeting and making the budget process more explicit. The link between managing performance and accountability will be strengthened. Transparency on its own cannot make a government more accountable. Complementary institutions and a broader commitment are required to hold government accountable for the resources it spends. The National Treasury will continue to work with Parliament and civil society organizations to facilitate their use of budget information, so that public debate on budget policy issues and performance is better informed. Parliament and civil society need to play a stronger role in helping society hold elected representatives accountable for their actions—ultimately what democracy is about.

Note

1. The Reconstruction and Development Program (RDP), the government's program of action at the time of the 1994 elections, set out targets and priorities for the first term in office. It had a strongly redistributive theme, stating, "We can only achieve our

economic objectives if we establish transparent, participatory and accountable policy-making procedures in both the public and private sectors" (ANC 1994). Adoption of the Growth, Employment and Redistribution Strategy (GEAR), in 1996, was aimed at achieving macroeconomic stability, partly by constraining public spending in the short term. Budget reform was critical to achieving the objectives of both the RDP and the deficit reduction policies of the GEAR.

References

African National Congress. 1994. *The Reconstruction and Development Programme: Policy Framework*. Braamfontein: Umanyano.

Andrews, M. 2013. *The Limits to Institutional Reform in Development: Changing Rules for Realistic Solutions*. Cambridge University Press.

CABRI (Collaborative Africa Budget Reform Initiative). 2014. *Exploring the Missing Links in Public Financial Management Reforms*. Pretoria: CABRI.

Constitution of the Republic of South Africa. 1996. http://www.gov.za/documents /constitution/constitution-republic-south-africa-1996-1.

Fölscher, Alta, and Neil Cole. 2004. "South Africa: Transition to Democracy Offers Opportunity for Whole System Reform." In *Budget Reform Seminar: Country Case Studies*. Pretoria: CABRI.

Friedman, S. 2013. *Budget Transparency in South Africa: Its Origins, Sources of Sustenance and Survival Prospects in Open Budgets—The Political Economy of Transparency, Participation, and Accountability*. Washington: Brookings Institution.

IBP (International Budget Partnership). 2012. "Open Budget Survey 2012." IBP, Washington, DC.

Jacobs, Davina F., Tony Bennett, and Charles K. Hegbor. 2014. *Public Expenditure and Financial Accountability 'Repeat' Assessment for the Republic of South Africa, 2014*. Rotterdam: ECORYS Nederland BV.

Naidoo, K. 2014. "Fiscal Policy Since the Transition: A Significant Success Story." Report prepared for the 20-Year Review by The Presidency. Unpublished.

South Africa, National Treasury. 1993/94–2014/15. *Budget Reviews*. Pretoria: National Treasury.

———. 2000. Guide for Accounting Officers: Public Finance Management Act. Pretoria: National Treasury.

———. 2011. Estimates of Expenditure. Pretoria: National Treasury.

———. 2013. "A Discussion on Function Budgeting: International Experience and the Case of South Africa." Internal document Pretoria: National Treasury.

The Presidency, South Africa. 2010. *Guide to the Outcomes Approach*. Pretoria: The Presidency.

World Bank. 2014. *Fiscal Policy and Redistribution in an Unequal Society*. Vol. 6 of *South Africa Economic Update*. Washington: World Bank.

CHAPTER 3

Raising Tax Revenue

David Hausman and Precious Zikhali

Introduction

The South African Revenue Service Act of 1997 merged the former Inland Revenue with the Customs and Excise Directorates in the Department of Finance (now the National Treasury) to form the South African Revenue Service (SARS).[1] The new agency was made autonomous from many of the country's civil service rules to allow it more flexibility.[2]

In 1994, the year of South Africa's first democratic elections, national government tax revenue accounted for 22.9 percent of gross domestic product (GDP) (SARS Annual Report, 2014). This relatively high revenue reflected the apartheid structure of South Africa's economy, which included a large formal sector. Revenue and tax compliance were low relative to their potential, however. More effective and inclusive revenue collection was essential for the new government to deliver on its promises to citizens. In 1998, with an unemployment rate of 30 percent (World Development Indicators database [WDI][3]), South Africa faced massive service delivery challenges: poverty and inequality were high, structural unemployment was a problem, and backlogs of infrastructure needed to be cleared. There was an imperative to extend water, electricity, health care, and housing opportunities to people previously unserved. At the same time, the government wanted to keep taxes low enough to prevent investors from pulling their money out of the country.

SARS helped confront these challenges by reforming tax administration and raising significantly more revenue. Between 1998 and 2014, it increased the

This chapter draws heavily on a case study written by David Hausman (2013) for Princeton's Innovations for Successful Societies project (http://www.princeton.edu/successfulsocieties/content/data/policy_note /PN_id125/Policy_Note_ID125.pdf). That case study was first published in 2010; for this chapter, David Hausman, JD (Stanford Law School) and PhD candidate (Stanford University), provided only the analysis up to 2007. Precious Zikhali, an economist at the World Bank, is the author of the other sections of this chapter and responsible for the analysis post-2007. This chapter benefited from extensive interviews with current and former government officials as well as from comments by peer reviewers Felix Junquera-Varela (Lead Public Sector Specialist, GGODR) and Michael Engelschalk (Senior Private Sector Development Specialist, GTCDR).

number of income tax payers from 2.6 million to 16.8 million. Tax revenue rose from 22.9 percent of GDP in 1994 to 26.1 percent by 2014—well above the average for all upper-middle-income countries of about 14 percent (WDI). By 2008, before a dip during the recession, revenue had reached 27 percent of GDP, despite tax cuts in 2002/03 (South Africa, National Treasury 2002).

Behind the growth in tax revenue were a series of institutional reforms that helped persuade more South Africans to pay their taxes.[4] This chapter tells the story of two of those changes. First, the organization rebuilt the ranks of upper and middle management, transforming the racial makeup of the organization while improving performance. Second, in order to improve service for taxpayers, broaden the narrow tax base, and strengthen tax compliance, a team of managers and consultants separated back and front offices and introduced an annual filing season in which employees of the revenue service left their offices to help taxpayers file their returns. The processes and structure of the agency were redesigned to improve their efficiency, and communication channels between SARS and businesses, tax practitioners, banks, and taxpayers were opened. In each of these changes, Pravin Gordhan, former head of SARS and later former minister of finance, played a central role, both determining policy and overseeing the details of implementation.

The Policy Challenge

By 1998 SARS had been made autonomous and management had the freedom to hire, pay, and reorganize. The reform team nonetheless had to contend with several internal problems: a lack of qualified middle managers, underrepresentation of black employees and managers, and low standards of service. Pravin Gordhan found himself in charge of an organization that could not collect sufficient revenue because its legitimacy had been eroded. This policy challenge reflected two main obstacles. First, a culture of tax avoidance had developed in South Africa. Under apartheid, tax evasion was a form of protest by people who sought racial equality. Only about 6 percent of South Africans paid income tax.[5] Businesses were selective on compliance and often underpaid. Although most citizens earned too little to be liable for tax, most people who did owe taxes did not pay them. The tax base was narrow, with a disproportionate reliance on income tax. About 37 percent of total capital formation in South Africa was moved offshore between 1980 and 2000, resulting in a R 238 billion loss in tax revenue (Mohamed and Finnoff 2005).

Second, management was weak, unrepresentative, and in some cases corrupt. Line officers sometimes turned a blind eye to underpayments. "In SARS 1998 you could walk in with a bottle of whiskey and just give it to [the officer]... and it was accepted over the counter," recalls Gordhan. "You could say 'Come, let me take you to lunch.' That was accepted."

For Gordhan the challenge was to make the institution more diverse while retaining staff with skills and experience. "I had to recognize that knowledge was vested in a team of people who were coming from the white community and who, in 1998, constituted, if I'm not mistaken, 65 percent of the organization," Gordhan said. "So part of the organizational challenge was also to transform the demographics of the organization and give black South Africans an opportunity to both enter the organization and grow within it." Gordhan had two obvious policy options: he could have simply laid off many white employees, or he could have sacrificed diversity for experience, retaining white employees in the short term. Partly because of guarantees made during the political transition from apartheid, layoffs were not an option in the short term. Moreover, Gordhan and his management team hoped to retain experienced employees, who were mostly white, while transforming the organization racially and instituting dramatic changes in customer service policies.

The solution, he decided, was to ask workers to sacrifice job security in exchange for employment security—in other words, to promise staff a position but not necessarily the position currently held. This solution allowed him to retain the support of current staff. The new policy, which reflected the reality that management could not transform the organization by firing staff, involved dramatic reorganization. Officials centralized administrative functions and decentralized customer service functions to branch offices. But this broad description of the reforms does not capture the details that managers believe led to success. The smaller acts described in the next section—acts such as offering queuing taxpayers tea and biscuits on a cold day—should not get lost in a summary of the reforms.

Addressing the Policy Challenge

Reform began with reorganization and outreach within the agency. The formal objectives of reform included raising revenue and increasing diversity. More fundamentally, restoring legitimacy was essential to convincing the citizens and businesses who paid a large share of the taxes to comply—and more broadly to persuading South Africans that they had a social obligation to support the services they used. In a sense, the democratic transition as a whole laid the foundation for the success of this campaign. Therefore, in addition to improving management and diversifying the ranks, Gordhan's team sought to build better relationships with citizens and businesses. Service had received little attention in the past. The new leadership had to find ways to inspire the organization's line officers to make the experience for taxpayers friendlier and easier, as well as more understandable.

Transforming Processes and People

The initial focus was on processes and people. The finance minister, Trevor Manuel, had insisted that no one would be laid off in the short term, a stipulation partly associated with agreements that underpinned the country's transition to majority rule. "Together with Judy Parfitt [the general manager for human resources at SARS], we worked out an approach which said, 'We don't want to fire anybody in SARS in this process of transforming the organization. We want to keep them on board,'" Gordhan said. "'We want their skills to be available to us, but at the same time there will be change.' There wouldn't be paralysis as a result of taking this approach." As a first step toward transforming the racial makeup of the agency, Gordhan brought several hundred black employees into informal management positions. "I created a management team below the existing executive team which would allow for more participation by black managers, not with formal power but at least with some informal influence," he said. "We convened senior managers representing each of the SARS offices, both the customs and revenue business, but instructed each of them that they had to come with a black individual—which was unheard of—to ensure that there would be a more diverse set of people representing the offices. That's when we first talked about transformation in the broad sense and began to get people to buy in."

According to Gordhan, the early meetings laid the foundation for reforms that combined racial transformation with a new conception of the role of a revenue agency in a fully democratic South Africa. "[Senior managers] participated and they heard the message, which said we're going to make this into a different organization. We're going to start a change process," Gordhan said of the initial meeting. "To their credit, there were several senior white managers who had bought into my approach by then and openly supported the need to transform the organization, even at that meeting, in the early days. I can't say we got buy-in, but we started an awareness that we were going to begin to move differently. It took another probably six to nine months if not more, to experiment with setting up a transformation unit, generating ideas about how transformation could begin."

These early transformation efforts metamorphosed into a human resources plan, according to Gordhan. "At the same time a new colleague had also come in on the HR [human resources] side of the business and began to set up for the first time formal HR processes and systems and so on which played an important foundational role," he said. "So those sorts of business initiatives— the HR system, the early notion that we need to change the organization—all of this came together some time in 1999." The new colleague, Judy Parfitt, "became a key ally in bringing black managers into the organization, as did some of the other white managers," Gordhan said. The plan for large internal reforms—including racial transformation, recruitment of new managers, and a new service orientation—became formal during Gordhan's second year as commissioner. The internal reform team engaged the help of private sector consultants to assist with the reorganization. The consultants assumed responsibility for some of the work of overhauling the organization, lifting burdens from the shoulders of the people who had to oversee the agency's daily operations. "That then formalized the process," explains Gordhan. "It was late 1999, early 2000, then we began to kick off the Siyakha process. Siyakha in Zulu means 'We are building.'" The Siyakha program developed out of a diagnostic study of SARS's operations, conducted between 1997 and 2000, meant to identify problems and ways to improve performance.[6] It focused on improving processes, taxpayer services, and staff professionalism and integrity. Its implementation began in 2000 and stretched until 2006.

Overhauling Management

As a first step, Gordhan launched an informal but systematic search for top managers to staff a process engineering unit. "Together with the consultants, we developed our own process team.... One of the things that we did as far as our people were concerned ... we took huge bets on them—meaning we couldn't wait for 10 years for somebody to get 10 years' experience and then say 'Now you can take on this one simple position,'" Gordhan said. "So taking bets meant judging a person's character, level of commitment, and capability and placing them in a completely new position, which they might not have been adequately trained for. Most of them did marvelously; some didn't. But we learned by actually doing."

Much of this management search took the form of recruiting, both inside and outside the organization. "You have to walk the floor and talk to people and observe processes," Gordhan said. "That's how I learned. Then you'll also begin to identify enthusiastic people, and you'll spot them in different parts of the country, in different roles. Then you take your chances and pull them in and constitute the team, give them a clear mission." The management team discovered many people with talents the organization needed and encouraged them to apply.

Gordhan also looked for candidates in other government institutions and in business. "Over time people from the private sector were willing to come and work with us as well, partly because we're outside of government, partly because there were huge advantages in being part of the change processes, but also to contribute to the country," he said. SARS made a special effort to identify talented and skilled black applicants. It identified black teachers who had accounting skills and would consider jobs with the agency. SARS's ability to attract qualified people with integrity was critical to the organization's turnaround.

In tandem with the search for managerial talent, Gordhan and Parfitt negotiated with the unions to restructure the organization. The program, formalized in the Siyakha People Placement Protocol, was meant to both facilitate racial transformation and promote managerial talent and people with special skills. Formal negotiations with the union allowed the process to advance. The Siyakha protocol was "a change protocol, negotiated with the unions and cosigned with them," Gordhan said. About 20 percent of SARS employees were required to reapply for newly created positions, competing with applicants from outside the organization. Employees who did not receive one of the new positions were retained at SARS; their pay was frozen, though not reduced.

People who reapplied took three tests: a psychometric test (Potential Index Batteries/Situation-Specific Evaluation Expert), developed by a South African company and intended to measure basic capabilities such as memory, mental alertness, and self-acceptance; a functional proficiency test; and the Lee Moral test, which Johan du Toit, a consultant who worked with Parfitt at SARS for six years, recalls as "a traditional, extensive, psychometric-centric intervention (hence expensive, but robust) for determining managerial competency."

Making It Happen • http://dx.doi.org/10.1596/978-1-4648-0768-8

Gordhan described the process of reshuffling as a foundational reform that enabled transformation and later customer service improvements. "Any managers who were technically competent but not managerially competent became specialists," he said. "That opened up spaces for people—black people with even master's degrees and so on—to come in from the outside and begin to occupy those spaces and learn the business and so on."

Broadening the Tax Base and Fostering Tax Compliance through Improved Customer Service

In 2005 SARS adopted a three-pronged compliance model: education, service, and enforcement. Emphasis was placed on education and service; enforcement was used only as a last resort. This model entailed education awareness campaigns and outreach initiatives, including visibility campaigns, workplace visits, a mobile tax unit, and road shows and exhibitions of SARS services. SARS drew lessons from the experiences of the Australian Tax Office, the Australian Customs Service, the Canadian Customs and Revenue Agency, Chile's National Customs, the United Kingdom's Her Majesty's Revenue & Customs (previously Inland Revenue), and the U.S. Internal Revenue Service. These experiences supported concentration of processing, enforcement, and service functions into specific centers.

Gordhan adopted a simple approach to the problem of how to create a service mentality. He and his team improved customer service by separating front and back offices, taking SARS staff to taxpayers during an annual filing season, recognizing staff who provided good service, and publicizing the mission of SARS.

By centralizing core administrative functions, such as accounting and human resources, in a few national offices and reorienting branches toward customer service, Gordhan hoped to achieve several goals. Segregating the back office support functions from front office contact with citizens could theoretically ensure consistency and reduce the chances of favoritism.

"One of the things that South Africans pre-1998 were used to was coming into an office and saying, 'I know Adrian. Can I speak to Adrian please?'" Gordhan said. "This design—to change the way branch office staff interact with taxpayers—was deliberate in the sense that it didn't want that kind of contact to continue." The separation of front and back offices made such informal dealings more difficult.

Durban, South Africa's third-largest city, was chosen as the pilot site for the front office/back office split. Because the pilot would set an example for SARS offices throughout the country, top management paid close attention to details. Displaying his hands-on approach, Gordhan himself went to Durban for the launch. "There was obviously a lot of apprehension. People didn't know where the hell we were going," Gordhan said. "I was in Durban on the first day. The staff didn't have a clue of what to do. One or two senior managers were with me. We were on a floor above, but we could see what was happening on the service floor. So we said, 'Ah, let's go.' So we went down. We showed them exactly how to arrange tables, chairs, how to arrange queues, how to service people, how to make sure that they don't wait too long in the queue. No sooner had we done that and set that as an example, that example spread throughout the country. People began to innovate in their own way."

SARS then used the Durban example to help other regional offices transform themselves. "You can just change one section, make it work, and then others can come and see it," Gordhan said. "So when we started, from KwaZulu-Natal we went to the Western Cape. If I'm not mistaken, at the early stages we probably brought 50 people over from the Western Cape to come and have a look and say, 'This is what your future is going to look like. Participate in it and make it happen on your side.' It worked."

As the pilot project expanded, customer service improved, often purely as a result of independent initiatives of branch managers. "At the Belville office in Cape Town, the manager decided it was a cold morning and people were still in the queue outside, so what we're going to do is give biscuits, tea, and coffee," Gordhan said. "Of their own accord—no head office instruction. So part of it, you drive from the top in terms of intent and example. Most organizations will have activists if you give them the space to pick up that and add their own variations."

The new division of responsibilities between the front office and the back office established a more formal relationship with citizens and limited the space for favoritism, but it could also make service seem less approachable. "It has a flip side to it," Gordhan said, "because people are used to the personal contact with an individual they know. So it took a little while for the public to get used to the fact that we're working differently."

To help give the service a friendlier face, a public relations campaign accompanied the rollout of the new front office concept and inaugurated an annual filing season outreach initiative. The campaign included not only advertising but also sending staff to taxpayers at their workplaces. Gordhan said: "Today that has become a very institutionalized thing, where you will go to big companies, set up computers, and help the staff of, say, 4,000 in a particular building to fill out their tax returns." SARS staff also reached people outside big offices, setting up operations in libraries and city centers.

This tactic of making tax offices more accessible was a new phenomenon in South Africa. "We've generated a lot of enthusiasm and awareness among the South African public as a result of reaching out to them, not just sitting in our offices and waiting for them," Gordhan said.

The program reached out not only to citizens and firms but also to tax advisers and banks. Establishing partnerships with the private sector was meant to get them to commit to higher levels of examination and compliance. Gordhan described the tax advisers as a particularly difficult group to persuade. "They tend to be laggards in this process and don't like change, which would narrow their space to maneuver around either tax or customs administration," he said. In 2009 SARS and the Banking Association of South Africa signed an accord that articulated a framework for cooperation between the two parties. It sought to improve tax compliance and address low effective taxes on banks by promoting ethical tax practice by banks while ensuring tax certainty and efficient servicing by SARS. The new SARS management opened up channels of communication and responded quickly to complaints.

Gordhan stresses the importance of responsiveness. "So there would be times people would phone my office, I would take a call," he said. "On one occasion I can remember clearly a guy said, 'In your Durban office X, Y, Z isn't working and the managers aren't fixing that up.' That afternoon I put a team of five or six people together and I said, 'Go to Durban. Go and meet this gentleman first and listen to what he is saying. Then go to the office and go to check; are the things he is saying true?' Sixty percent of it was true."

To improve staff morale, the reform team made sure that relatively few people had to move to new cities or locations as a result of the internal reorganization. It also started to recognize strong employee performance, offering bonuses to teams and divisions that performed well not just in raising more taxes but also in improving service and efficiency. A grading and rewards system—the Employee Performance Management System (EPMS)—was put in place. It marked a shift away from the old bonus system toward a system under which promotion was based on performance and competence. The new system helped align salaries to the market, making it easier for SARS to employ and deploy skilled personnel. The system was later replaced by an electronic performance assessment system (the scorecard system) under George "Oupa" Magashula, who took over as head of HR in 2006.

A strict policy on corruption was a corollary of the new model. "Within, I think, six months, we banned all gifts," Gordhan said. "We banned all acceptance of dinners and lunches. Initially it was like a blanket ban: You accept nothing. Then slowly we sort of loosened things up. But in that way we established integrity as a key value. If we caught you, you knew you would be dealt with." This strict policy meant not only certain and harsh punishment for corruption but also publicity for those punishments. "Any behavior that was dishonest—and obviously especially fraud and theft—it was 'name and shame' in a very public way," Parfitt said. This tough approach to corruption was meant to protect the reputation of the organization and thus improve compliance. Sanctions for corruption included prosecution, arrests, and dismissal.

In terms of enforcement to promote compliance, some early high-profile and aggressive tax collection initiatives helped build momentum for reform. In one high-profile case, for example, SARS seized shares of an insurance company in order to force shareholders to pay their taxes.

As SARS pursued more aggressive enforcement, it benefited from the strong backing of the finance minister and indeed the government as a whole. "The political backing was a crucial part of ensuring that when you get pushback—as we did in some instances from, say, the private sector and so on—we would have both the legitimacy and the political backing and our own institutional strength to be able to cope with that," Gordhan said.

But enforcement was expensive in terms of staff time and goodwill. Therefore, the reform team worked hard to change hearts and minds, first deepening and formalizing some of the personnel changes it had launched experimentally and then altering the relationship to South African citizens.

Reforms After 2007

The Modernization Program introduced in 2007 enabled SARS to build on improvements made between 1997 and 2006, particularly in terms of improved customer service. Reforms include the shift from multipage static forms to single-page dynamic forms, from basic call to integrated contact handling, from manual paper channels to digital/self-service channels, from manual to automated processes, from gatekeeping (that is, a one-size-fits-all compliance approach with a focus on control and enforcement) to risk management (that is, a focus on high-risk areas), and from limited to third-party validation. An improved pay-as-you-earn (PAYE) system was rolled out, and everyone in formal employment was required to register with SARS. SARS made available a platform and free software through which PAYE data were submitted electronically. This system helped reduce taxpayer errors on returns and improved compliance by employers. In 2004 SARS introduced an electronic filing (e-filing) system that replaced manually submitted taxes with a secure, online facility. In 2013, 22.5 million returns (98 percent of all returns) were filed electronically, up from 1.6 million in 2006. According to SARS annual reports, the average turnaround time for processing a personal income tax return fell from about 55 working days in 2006 to just 0.26 working days in 2013.

Overall, modernization reforms allowed SARS to shift human resources away from routine tasks toward education, service, and enforcement. The Compliance Evaluation and Monitoring Information System (CEMIS) was set up in 2011 and was aimed at enhancing the agency's understanding of taxpayer compliance levels. CEMIS would measure taxpayer compliance levels across different segments of taxpayers and taxes. These reforms strengthened enforcement capacity and resulted in increased ease of compliance for taxpayers. The Tax Administration Act of 2012 was a step toward modernizing and harmonizing various administrative provisions that were duplicated in various tax acts.

In a bid to reduce the tax administrative burden of small business, SARS launched the Turnover Tax in 2009, an innovative system aimed at assisting small businesses to streamline their tax obligations. It targets businesses with an annual turnover of up to R 1 million. A sliding tax rate is applied to the taxable turnover of the business. The Turnover Tax is a substitute for value added tax (VAT), income tax, provisional tax, capital gains tax, and secondary tax on companies. It thus significantly reduces the time and cost of submitting tax returns. In 2013 the minister of finance appointed South Africa's first tax ombudsman (Judge Bernard Ngoepe), who was tasked with providing taxpayers with low-cost mechanisms to deal with administrative complications that could not be resolved by SARS.

Improving customs administration was also an integral part of broadening the tax base and tackling tax compliance issues. Customs faces unique challenges, including corruption, poor security management, porous borders, and noncompliance with legislation. Processes were largely paper based and labor intensive. Between 2001 and 2006, Gordhan held the position of elected chairperson of the World Customs Organization (WCO), increasing his interest in modernizing customs. In 2009 a customs modernization program was launched to integrate various information technology (IT) systems with the broad goal of easing trade across borders.

The reforms at customs were done under the guidance of international consultants, particularly retirees from Her Majesty's Customs and Excise from the United Kingdom. The reforms included introducing an electronic data interchange (EDI) system in 2005, which resulted in significant reduction in paperwork. The electronification of SARS's customs process was announced in 2010. It was pitched as a system that made it easier for SARS to identify illegal and illicit trade. The capacity of customs was increased through a strong recruitment exercise, particularly to augment its audit function. An antismuggling unit was put in place to improve border control. The focus on the behavior of criminals helped shape antismuggling efforts. It changed potential tax evaders' mind-sets by showing that increased enforcement efforts increased the risks of noncompliance.

The role of SARS's autonomy in the success of reforms cannot be overemphasized. Prior to the establishment of SARS as a semiautonomous agency, tax administration was driven by procedures and controls. Implementing change would have been slower because the process would have had to go through the bureaucratic processes in the National Treasury. Thus, flexibility gained through autonomy made it easier to institute and implement reforms.

Autonomy over personnel management facilitated modernization of SARS's personnel system. The introduction of its own personnel system enabled SARS to adopt a system of competitive, market-referenced remuneration thereby attracting and retaining qualified professional staff. The agency was able to creatively respond to the problem of retaining its highly skilled professionals, particularly auditors and tax lawyers. In addition, autonomy gave SARS flexibility to outsource services, for example IT staff, and offer its employees many training opportunities. Autonomy meant SARS could manage its tendering processes more closely, which helped reduce corruption (Taliercio 2004). Owing to its autonomy, SARS could decentralize its operations to regional offices, institute special prosecution and revenue initiatives, and offer its staff special incentives.

Overcoming Resistance to Change

More than 80 percent of the agency's workforce was unionized at the time of the reforms. The unions could have blocked efforts to change job descriptions, move people to new locations, and create a more efficient organization, but they did not. Participants in the change process attributed union cooperation to Pravin Gordhan's leadership style as well as to the way the new job structure was designed.

Initially, many unions represented workers and managers in the tax service. The apartheid government had encouraged a kind of "divide-and-rule" approach that fragmented union membership. After transition, new rules required that each union be at least minimally representative of employees of different ethnic or racial backgrounds. The number of unions fell to two, which eased negotiation. For their part, agency directors were careful not to play the unions—one still majority white and the other majority black—against each other, in order to build a commitment to a nonracial workplace.

The directors and the unions sat together for eight months to craft an agreement. They developed a shared strategy and principles for resolving disagreements. The agreement included two-year pay protection in addition to a ban on retrenchments. The pay protection covered people who were moved into positions with lower remuneration than the posts they had left or failed to retain. During a two-year grace period, these employees could obtain additional training and try to win promotions or move to other jobs that paid more.

The resulting Siyakha protocol made it possible to overhaul the agency. Unions and agency directors held a joint "road show" at the agency's regional offices to make sure employees and managers understood the details of the changes they had agreed to. Without the protocol and the effort to communicate its terms, resistance to change could easily have resulted in thousands of labor disputes.

Although there was substantial internal resistance to the changes—many employees did not want to change jobs, even if they maintained employment security—a strong culture of negotiation allowed reform to move forward following the pay and employment security concessions made to the unions. In particular, the grading and remuneration system, along with a flatter organizational structure, created tensions among staff. Centralizing decision making was unpopular with managers, some of whom resigned rather than accept redeployment. "Resistance would probably have been unmanageable without [the collective agreements]," Parfitt said. "That's not to say that management and the unions held hands and walked into the sunset. There were some bitter disagreements and a couple of disputes and one or two narrowly averted strikes. But I think a deep trust and this very powerful shared commitment to creating a better life for all—it was a wonderfully mobilizing concept." Overall, this effort is probably best described as a gradual rather than a big-bang approach to internal change, but the key was not speed but rather the degree of consultation and buy-in.

Of course, the challenges were not only internal: citizens are rarely eager to pay taxes. Building a service culture within the organization required not only creating incentives for performance but also changing the culture. Doing so required employees to face customers—literally. Before the reforms, "a lot of the people who found themselves in service jobs had worked in dark, windowless offices," Parfitt said. The new branch offices created direct contact with taxpayers. The result has been easier tax filing.

Making It Happen · http://dx.doi.org/10.1596/978-1-4648-0768-8

Results Achieved

Measured by the size of the tax base, the organizational reforms were a success: the tax register grew about 129 percent between 2009 and 2014. In March 2009, it stood at 9.3 million—including individuals, companies, trusts, employers, VAT vendors, importers, and exporters, of which 59 percent were individual taxpayers. The register rose to about 21.4 million by March 2014. Tax revenue levels rose from R 114 billion in 1995 to R 900 billion in 2014, thanks in part to important efficiency gains in collecting taxes.[7] The number of taxpayers filing their taxes electronically rose from 6,150 in March 2002 to 4.5 million in 2012, when e-filing accounted for 10.2 percent of all tax revenues (SARS 2013).

Consequently, as a share of GDP, South Africa's tax revenue grew from 22.9 percent in 1994 to 27.2 percent in 2009, as shown by figure 3.1. By March 2014 the share of total tax revenue had fallen slightly, to 26.1 percent of GDP. Revenues remained strong despite the global financial crisis and the end of Gordhan's tenure, however.

SARS received a generous budget early on. From 1999 to 2000, for example, its budget increased 25 percent, from R 1.75 billion to R 2.197 billion. Its budget by March 2014 was almost R 10 billion (SARS 2014). As a middle-income country, South Africa could afford to put money into revenue collection—an investment that paid for itself in new revenue generated. More important, efficiency of collection has generally been improving over time: by March 2014, the operating cost as a percentage of total tax revenue was 0.97 percent, a clear improvement from 1.17 percent in 2010 (SARS 2014).

Figure 3.1 Tax Revenue in South Africa as a Percent of GDP, 1994/95–2013/14

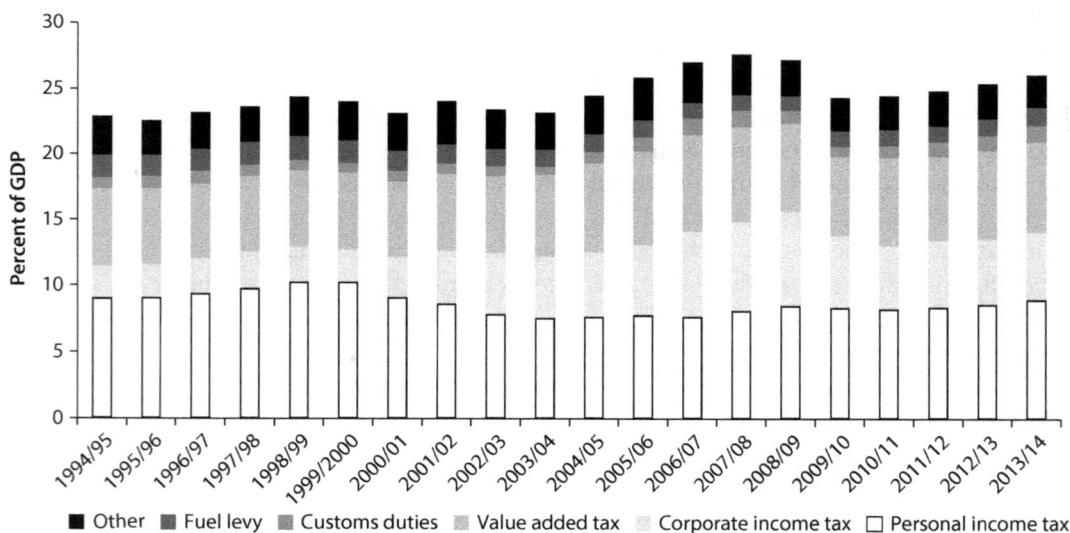

Source: SARS tax statistics (various years from 1994 to 2014).
Note: GDP = gross domestic product.

Making It Happen • http://dx.doi.org/10.1596/978-1-4648-0768-8

Reforms succeeded in changing the racial makeup of SARS. The task was facilitated by the fact that it was given the resources to expand its staff. The number of permanent SARS employees increased from about 12,500 in 1998 to 15,307 in March 2009 and fell to 14,137 in 2014. In 2014 almost 71 percent of SARS's permanent workforce was black. Women occupied 62 percent of all positions and 41 percent of management positions (SARS 2014).

Reforms also dramatically changed citizens' perceptions of SARS (and of its head, Pravin Gordhan).[8] In 2009 SARS received the grand prix platinum award in the inaugural Public Service Excellence Awards for best reputation of all government departments and state-owned enterprises.[9] SARS also received four gold awards (for overall effectiveness, service orientation, service orientation in rural areas, and best reputation in the financial services category) and two bronze awards (for internal effectiveness and community engagement).

The organization's success has attracted international recognition. In 2010 the World Bank ranked South Africa 24th of 189 countries on ease of paying taxes, but only 41st on overall ease of doing business (World Bank and PricewaterhouseCoopers 2010). In 2015 the country's ranking had improved to 19th of 189 economies with respect to ease of paying taxes for a medium-size case-study company (World Bank and PricewaterhouseCoopers 2015). Its professionalism and working conditions made SARS an employer of choice, with annual staff turnover of only about 2.5–3.5 percent.

Other public institutions have shown interest in learning from SARS's experiences. SARS is providing technical support in the modernization of the Government Pensions Administration Agency (GPAA). In 2010 it began collaborating with the Department of Home Affairs to develop and implement a system to control movement by correctly identifying people entering and leaving the country.

Moving forward, there is interest in further tax reform. In his 2013/14 budget speech, Minister of Finance Gordhan announced plans to initiate a tax review "to assess our tax policy framework and its role in supporting the objectives of inclusive growth, employment, development, and fiscal sustainability." In July 2013 he announced the members of the Tax Review Committee (known as the Davis Tax Committee) and its terms of reference. Among other tasks, the committee will consider the overall tax base and tax burden.

Conclusions: Success Factors, Challenges, and Lessons Learned

The SARS experience holds a number of success factors and lessons learned for reformers elsewhere. First, autonomy meant SARS could be more proactive, innovative, and flexible. Autonomy allowed the agency to carry out reforms faster than it would have had the agency not been autonomous.

Second, strong and continued leadership was key. Continuity of leadership with a shared vision and value system helped push the transformation agenda. SARS had one commissioner for 10 years, as well as one finance minister (Trevor Manuel). Stability at both political and management levels gave SARS the legitimacy to take risks. Effective leadership and management by Pravin Gordhan, who had strong organizational and political experience, helped create change and defuse resistance. By attracting people with organizational skills from other government departments and the private sector, SARS created a group of dynamic managers. Reshuffling management and technical personnel allowed SARS to retain technical skills while making its management more diverse and more competent. Through organizational reforms, such as separating front and back offices, and providing incentives, such as rewarding individual initiative, Gordhan and his team created an organization with a reputation for excellent customer service. Management had a hands-on approach that involved going out to the field to communicate changes to staff in the field. Informal interactions, both between management and employees and between employees and taxpayers, built goodwill.

Perhaps the most important lessons were how to gather support within the agency through a contentious but respectful process of negotiation and ensure that agency staff cooperated with the changes. Change required serious consultation and real concessions to organized interests. Eight months of talks with unions led to a no-firing guarantee and a two-year pay protection promise. This consultation and negotiation allowed informal norms to change in step with formal rules. This also implied forging a strong and effective partnership with stakeholders, particularly the private sector, to improve compliance. SARS's success was thus a people story, not a technology story. "Part of our broader strategy was that this would be a nontechnology change," Gordhan said. "So although there will be adaptations to some of our existing legacy systems, we would not focus on technological investment at this point in time. It was more about processes and people and changing the service approach and ultimately also changing the enforcement approach of SARS. That is what we worked with for five or six years." Activism provided crucial preparation. In Gordhan's view, the experience of the anti-apartheid struggle helped develop strategic and tactical skills and made people understand the importance of engaging with people to build support.

Third, adopting a strong anticorruption approach in the early years helped improve the credibility of the agency. For example, separating front and back offices reduced opportunities for corruption. Strong early sanctions for fraud also deterred further corruption.

These successes should not hide the challenges that remain. First, although SARS greatly increased revenue collection in the formal sector, collecting taxes in the informal sector remains a challenge.

Second, SARS also has to ensure that training and knowledge transfer keep pace with changes in tax laws and the way the organization interacts with clients. In particular, increases in the number of staff that deal with the public in the call center placed greater emphasis on training of staff not only in tax matters but also in information technology skills. Because tax laws constantly change, SARS has to ensure that training and knowledge transfer keep pace with these changes.

Third, SARS faces challenges in detecting tax evasion by international businesses. To avoid paying taxes, multinational corporations often use sophisticated financial schemes, including transfer pricing and the use of tax havens. SARS launched a compliance program in 2012 that identified seven areas where compliance can be improved: wealthy South Africans and their trusts, large businesses and transfer pricing, construction, cigarettes, clothing and textiles, tax practitioners, and trade intermediaries and small businesses (SARS Annual Report, 2012). Tackling these areas will require new skills—for example, better monitoring of transfer pricing—as well as closer cooperation with the international community. The illicit economy also reduces revenue collection. SARS estimates that R 2.0–R 4.5 billion is lost as a result of smuggling and consumption of contraband cigarettes (SARS 2013). Detection systems need to be improved to deal with these challenges.

Fourth, since the end of Gordhan's term in 2009, SARS has lacked continuity in leadership and reform sustainability. This has resulted in challenges in further maintaining the initial reform commitment and ensuring continued reform drive. Recently, a number of senior managers have resigned; others were suspended or faced disciplinary action. The agency also grapples with alleged incidents of corruption, which might undermine the sustainability of reforms and pose a risk to the credibility and reputation of the agency.[10]

Depending on how these developments are managed going forward, they may have adverse effects on taxpayers' perceptions of the agency and could undo the gains SARS has made in building a relationship of mutual respect and trust with taxpayers.

Notes

1. SARS is mandated to collect all revenue due, ensure maximum compliance with tax and customs legislation, and provide a customs service that maximizes revenue collection, protects South African borders, and facilitates trade.

2. No. 34 of 1997: South African Revenue Service Act (Part I, Section 2) www.gov.za /documents/download.php?f=70780.

3. World Development Indicators (database), World Bank, Washington, DC (accessed December 15, 2014), http://data.worldbank.org/data-catalog/world-development -indicators.

4. The tax administration reforms at SARS were closely guided by the report by the Katz Commission set up in 1994 by the minister of finance to examine and make recommendations on the tax structure. The establishment of SARS—an independent tax and customs administration—came out of the recommendations of the commission. It recommended that, to raise revenue collection, the tax burden had to be reduced rather than increased, a measure that could be achieved by reducing marginal tax rates. Raising revenue would thus be achieved mainly by broadening of the tax base.

5. Although only 6 percent paid income tax, they (the rich white population) paid a disproportionately high share of taxes, explaining the high tax revenue/GDP ratio in 1994.

6. Implementation of the Siyakha program was sequenced by province. The program was put on hold in December 2001, following a review of the program in KwaZulu-Natal that highlighted a lack of skills, particularly in service and enforcement, and the need to integrate technology and information technology (IT) enhancements in accordance with the new organizational structure. A year later, Siyakha 2 was rolled out in the Western Cape, focusing largely on training and change management. Siyakha 2 benefited from lessons learned in implementing Siyakha 1, which underscored SARS's approach of experimenting, learning, applying, and moving on.

7. As expected, tax collection varies significantly depending on the type of tax.

8. By 2010 Gordhan was the minister of finance. He was one of only two cabinet ministers to receive an A grade in the *Mail & Guardian*'s annual Cabinet report card (*Mail & Guardian* 2010).

9. The Public Sector Excellence Awards, established by an independent organization (the Brand Leadership Academy), are aimed at honoring excellence in the public sector. A representative national sample is used to select citizens who are asked to provide feedback with respect to the performance of government departments and parastatals.

10. Examples of cases of corruption can be found on SARS's media releases Internet page, http://www.sars.gov.za/Media/MediaReleases/Pages/default.aspx.

References

Hausman, David. 2013. "Reworking the Revenue Service: Tax Collection in South Africa, 1999–2009." Innovations for Successful Societies Case Study, Princeton University, Princeton, NJ. http://successfulsocieties.princeton.edu/sites/successfulsocieties/files /Policy_Note_ID125.pdf.

Mail & Guardian. 2010. "Cabinet Report Cards 2010: Part 2" December 23. http://mg.co .za/article/2010-12-23-cabinet-report-cards-2010-part-2.

Mohamed, S., and K. Finnoff. 2005. "Capital Flight from South Africa, 1980–2000." In *Capital Flight and Capital Controls in Developing Countries*, edited by Gerald A. Epstein, 85–115. Northampton, MA: Edward Elgar Publishing.

South Africa, National Treasury. 2002. 2002 Budget Review. Pretoria.

SARS (South African Revenue Service). Various years. Tax Statistics. Pretoria.

———. Various years. *Annual Reports*. Pretoria.

———. 2013. *Annual Performance Plan 2012/13*. Pretoria.

Taliercio, R. J. 2004. "Designing Performance: The Semiautonomous Revenue Authority Model in Africa and Latin America." Policy Research Working Paper No. 3423, World Bank, Washington, DC.

World Bank and PricewaterhouseCoopers. 2010. *Paying Taxes 2010*. Washington, DC: World Bank and PricewaterhouseCoopers. https://www.pwc.com/gx/en/paying-taxes /assets/paying-taxes-2010.pdf.

———. 2015. *Paying Taxes 2015*. Washington, DC: World Bank and PricewaterhouseCoopers. http://www.pwc.com/gx/en/paying-taxes/pdf/pwc-paying-taxes-2015-high -resolution.pdf.

CHAPTER 4

Strengthening Performance Monitoring and Evaluation

Kathrin A. Plangemann

Introduction

The performance agenda, and performance monitoring and evaluation (M&E), has been a core driver of public sector reform in South Africa. Since the end of apartheid and the start of democracy, South Africa has undertaken important steps toward greater performance to enhance service delivery outcomes. Performance management has taken place along the public sector performance value chain, from results-based planning to performance-based budgeting and performance management in the civil service.

Performance M&E is the most recent piece of the performance agenda, constituting the fourth corner of the performance square. A performance M&E system can be defined as an integrated, results-oriented, government wide framework based on a combination of tools and incentives that ensure greater effectiveness, efficiency, transparency, and accountability of policies, programs, and projects to enhance service delivery, fiscal management, and improve government focus and capacity to achieve overall government outcomes.

A new Department of Performance Monitoring and Evaluation (DPME) was created in the South African Presidency in 2010 to strengthen performance M&E in order to improve service delivery. In the relatively short time since its creation, compared to other M&E systems world wide, the South African system has made impressive steps toward anchoring a greater performance approach across sectors and levels of government.

DPME is strategically located within the Presidency, and has its own minister. DPME has an annual budget of about US$20 million and a staff of

The author is the Lead Public Sector Governance Specialist and Cluster Leader for Southern Africa in the Governance Global Practice of the World Bank. This chapter draws heavily on the work done by the South African Department of Planning, Monitoring and Evaluation (formerly Department of Performance Monitoring and Evaluation) (DPME), including Phillips et al. (2014), World Bank (2012), and other publications and work by DPME as cited in the references. This chapter also benefited from extensive interviews with current and former government officials.

about 240.[1] Together with the Cabinet, it has been a powerful driver of reforms, adopting and pushing the implementation of policies, products, and tools on performance M&E.

DPME works together with other key stakeholders on the other parts of the performance square, both horizontally across sectors and vertically across levels of government. A key partner is the National Treasury, which has been an important driver of performance reforms, following the 1999 National Public Financial Management Act, performance-based budgeting, and its monitoring through strategic plans and annual performance plans (see chapter 2). Other partners include the Auditor General, who has recently started performance audits; the Department of Public Service and Administration (DPSA), which is engaged in performance management for the public service; Statistics South Africa (see chapter 5), working on the quality of data available for planning and M&E; and Parliament, strengthening parliamentary oversight through greater use of performance information. DPME is also engaged with civil society and academia, science councils, and the private sector (management consulting firms and specialized evaluation companies). It has also been able to position itself within the international M&E community and coordinates a large and diverse community of development partners, which support different parts of DPME.

Setting up a comprehensive, government wide system to change the performance culture in an environment that was still marked by the legacy of apartheid was a major challenge. The transition to democracy confirmed the vital role of the state in mediating social and economic relations in a highly unequal society. The public administration was geared toward a traditional approach, focusing on inputs and activities. There was limited inclusiveness of the policies, programs, and projects to be designed, implemented, and monitored as well as limited diversity in the civil servants in charge of doing so. Overcoming the legacy of apartheid required providing opportunities for all citizens, by ensuring that government policies, programs, and projects actually reach all intended citizens and had the intended impacts.

Key initiatives include the following: (i) the Outcomes Approach that focuses on 14 government priority outcomes; (ii) the Management Performance Assessment Tool (MPAT) to assess the quality of management performance of national and provincial departments and a similar tool for municipalities; (iii) a system of monitoring front-line services, including a presidential hotline and a citizen-based monitoring framework; and (iv) a comprehensive national evaluation system that promotes the use of research evidence.

These initiatives have generated extensive evidence for policy making and achieved relatively large institutional and expenditure coverage. They have started to produce a sharper government focus, influencing policy making and implementation toward greater efficiency and effectiveness and helping the public sector move toward a greater culture of results. The system will need to mature in its design; expand coverage, use, and impact; and become more integrated with planning and performance-based budgeting so that it can fully influence policy making and budget decision making for improved service delivery. An important step in this direction arose after the 2014 presidential elections with the incorporation of the planning function and the merger with the National Planning Commission when DPME became the Department of Planning, Monitoring and Evaluation.

The Policy Challenge

Triggered by high poverty and inequality, widespread service delivery protests, the loss of support in the 2009 elections, and criticism of the overall performance of the African National Congress (ANC), the President and top officials realized that they needed to take bold action. For example, in health and education, despite high investments, outcomes were quite limited. These pressures increased willingness in government to be frank about the quality of public services, corruption, and other governance challenges and helped develop a political consensus to improve government performance. It became clear that the government needed to demonstrate improvements in service delivery to citizens and improve its image, nationally and internationally. As Ian Goldman, head of evaluation at DPME and one of the witnesses of the early stages of DPME, notes, "Something needed to be done quickly; otherwise there was a risk of even greater erosion of ANC's credibility." The main challenge was how to improve government effectiveness and efficiency as well as accountability and transparency through a greater focus on public sector performance to improve service delivery for all citizens.

One of the key riddles for public sector management to undertake service delivery reforms was the question of how to achieve horizontal and vertical coordination across levels of government. At the central level, different, sometimes overlapping responsibilities have created coordination challenges for both the center of government and departments, producing inefficiencies and suboptimal service delivery outcomes. Across levels of government, responsibilities have been either at one level or shared (for example, education and health). The implications of central-level challenges and different delivery models in and across sectors and levels of government further created inefficiencies and compounded service delivery challenges. As Sean Phillips, former DPME director-general and one of the founding fathers of DPME, emphasizes, "The problem was that there has been insufficient value for money: for example, education and health results versus expenditure per capita." The initial environment of limited strategic direction, efficiency, and transparency challenges; weak upward and downward accountability; and lack of effective oversight limited the reform space and called for a targeted, gradual approach to achieve lasting results.

To address these challenges, different pieces of the performance puzzle have been developed since 1994. Building on the Constitution (see chapter 12), the democratic government embarked on a sustained public sector reform program. A civil service performance management and development system was developed. Budget reforms spearheaded by the National Treasury initially focused on the financial dimensions of public expenditure management and gradually also on nonfinancial information, in pursuit of greater value for money spent in service delivery (see chapter 2). The 1995 *White Paper on Transformation of the Public Service* (DPSA 1995) introduced initial M&E concepts. The 1997 *White Paper on Transforming Public Service Delivery* (DPSA 1997) brought in the new public management approach, including targets and results, delegation and accountability for results, and the Batho Pele (People First) principles around transparency, service standards, and so forth.

With the focus between 1994 and 2005 on major policy reforms, monitoring was not yet a priority. This was even more the case because in the early years of democracy the policy focus was naturally more on expanding access to service delivery and a greater focus on quality only came in over time. Monitoring and very little real evaluation were generally conducted in a fragmented manner, driven largely by departments (Engela and Ajam 2010). From 2000 onward, pressure mounted to introduce a more comprehensive approach, driven by the need to report on the promises made by the President in his annual state of the nation address. This approach developed into a Program of Action, in which key priorities were identified and progress reported. In 2009 an advisory body, the National Planning Commission, was established to develop a long-term 2030 Vision and National Development Plan, which was also perceived as a way to move the planning function out of the National Treasury into the Presidency.

In 2005 the Cabinet approved a plan for the development of a government wide M&E system. It envisaged a "system of systems" in which each department would have its own monitoring system. In 2007 the Presidency published a strategic policy framework to guide the government wide M&E system (Presidency, Republic of South Africa 2007). This framework was an important step in developing the system and provided a conceptual anchor. It included the need for specific policy frameworks for program performance information, quality of statistical data, and evaluation and sought to strengthen the linkages among the Presidency, the National Treasury, and Statistics South Africa yet also increased the administrative burden on departments, which faced a multitude of reporting systems.

In light of the service delivery protests and the conceptual progress made over time, the creation of a performance M&E system in the Presidency was seen as a powerful way to enhance performance on the ground while also signaling ANC's public commitment to performance. The design of the system had to combine technical and political objectives. The system needed to be strong enough technically to achieve its objectives yet politically feasible, aligned with ANC's conceptualization of the role of government and other political economy objectives. Initially, the President, who had previously been involved in ANC intelligence work, thought the M&E system would be very useful for gathering information on government that would help control government action. But it was soon realized that the system could also achieve broader technical and political objectives.

For the design of the system, several options were explored. The first was to set up an early warning system, with a multitude of local offices of the Presidency, to find out what was going on at the local level in order to be able to take action.

This option was ruled out because of feasibility questions and its cost implications, and it was decided that a more strategic approach was needed.

Creating a cutting-edge, government wide performance M&E system was seen as the best way for the Presidency to improve service delivery, hold departments accountable, and portray itself as a modern, sophisticated public sector reformer. As thinking about the performance M&E system matured, the initial preferred option for the creation of the new unit in the Presidency was to take on the role of a delivery unit as a rapid-response type of mechanism for taking action on service delivery issues.[2] This was the initial focus of DPME, and its team was engaged in quite a bit of troubleshooting. A study tour to the United Kingdom was undertaken to explore this option, but it was felt that the Presidency should not only be a troubleshooter but also take on a more comprehensive and strategic role, in line with its mandate.

After careful review of options, it was then decided to create a more comprehensive performance M&E system, to be set up in the Presidency under the new DPME. The Presidency was seen as the ideal place for the new system, as the President and his team could closely control it and use the information created. Locating the DPME in the Presidency was also meant for it to be a counterweight to the powerful National Treasury.

The Presidency published a position paper on M&E in 2009, setting the basis for the outcomes approach, the first mandate for DPME. The outcomes approach aims at strengthening the strategic focus of government, improving interdepartmental and intergovernmental coordination, and focusing on key areas such as education, health, and security. From a political perspective, it showed that the government was actively pursuing better performance, focusing on key outcomes relevant to citizens. From a technical perspective, it was a mechanism holding departments accountable to the Presidency to ensure improved performance. In 2010 the Cabinet adopted the 12 priority outcomes building on the five priorities in the ANC manifesto. The first pillar of the new system had been erected.

Addressing the Policy Challenge

The new performance M&E system mainly aimed at strengthening government effectiveness and accountability through improved policy, program, and project performance, with the ultimate goal of improving service delivery. Efficiency was also an important objective, to be pursued through the outcomes approach, MPAT, and the evaluation system; but it was pursued less vigorously than in other countries, such as Chile, where it was the main reform driver. The focus on accountability, particularly internal accountability, helped the Presidency get a better grasp of departments and enhance both its coordination and control functions. The system was meant to be responsive, showing citizens that the government was listening to their concerns and taking action to improve service delivery, particularly through the presidential hotline and other front-line service delivery tools. Transparency was also an objective, although less so than in other countries, such as Mexico. For South Africa, the focus was more on making information widely available than on the system's potential use as an anticorruption tool, which would have reduced buy-in from different stakeholders. In terms of incentives, the system was meant to have a political effect and counter criticism, both from citizens and from the international community, helping to maintain and increase the power and popularity of government. While the system has developed much further from the original focus on the outcomes approach, the key underlying formal and informal objectives remained largely in place.

While there was keen political interest in setting up the system, a strong drive for the design of the new system came from the technical level. Under the overall political leadership, the technical team was given the mandate, resources, and technical space to design the system, and was encouraged to do so. "Political leadership came in to help when needed but otherwise let us do the work the way we wanted to do it, as long as we stayed within the official line," recalls a senior DPME official. Proactive leadership by the director-general, the deputy director-generals, and the heads of programs to constantly design, refine, expand, and promote the use of the system was a fundamental factor in paving the ground for the system's use. Top politicians provided leadership. Delegation from the political to the technical team was strong, as shown by the high level of trust displayed, the design flexibility, and the unusually high levels of delegated spending authority.

The technical team took a pragmatic approach to the design and implementation of the system. The initial approach was selective, focusing on strategic outcomes rather than tackling the whole system at once. Instead of starting with a legal mandate or comprehensive strategies, the system was built up starting small, using pilots, testing, learning, adjusting, and then gradually moving to a rollout, readjusting, and refining. Its initial creation might have been a bit more of a top-down approach, building on the location in the Presidency; but as new systems developed there was a lot of horizontal and vertical collaboration and consultation. In subsequent design stages, the bottom-up approach became more important, and the focus moved toward stimulating effective demand by stakeholders, including departments, subnational governments, and civil society for the citizen-based monitoring framework. Management arrangements within DPME were set up in a flexible way, which allowed further evolution of thematic areas, effective collaboration between units, staff mobility between units, and the creation of new units and tools as the need emerged. Such a strategic yet gradual approach in system design can be characterized as an approach of strategic incrementalism. There were clear objectives, expected results, and a strategy; yet, it was flexible and built up gradually over time. This made a big difference in helping build up greater buy-in and support over time. This was not done at the expense of speed: within five years the system has been designed and rolled out at a very fast pace, compared to peer countries.

Designing and managing such a comprehensive and innovative system required sufficient capacity, which needed to be built up. To design the system, a group of very strong technical individuals, with some national and international exposure on performance M&E, was asked to lead the initial effort. The team that designed the system was one of "pragmatic doers as well as visionaries," according to Ian Goldman, one of the founding fathers of the system. DPME recruited strong technical staff, who were often trained on the job. It also provided leadership positions, such as at the director level, to help build a new cadre of management from in-house positions. Strong performance expectations, technical rigor, and an institutional commitment to excellence permeated all levels of staff. It was made clear that the system needed to be credible to have any chance of success and that failure was not an option. Staff were encouraged to further develop their skills by pursuing further education or training. Staff faced both performance incentives (financial and nonfinancial) and disincentives (perform or move, a soft application of the "up-or-out" principle). A culture of continuous learning and feedback was created, with regular requests for feedback from stakeholders and national and international experts.

A specialized unit was set up for capacity-building purposes, which designed a capacity-building strategy. It conducts national and international workshops and created a national M&E community of practice by mobilizing support from capacity-building service providers, such as the technical assistance unit in the National Treasury, and external stakeholders, including universities, private companies, and the multi-donor-funded Center for Learning on Evaluation and Results (CLEAR).[3]

International good practices strongly influenced the way the system was designed. Instead of reinventing the wheel, the DPME team wanted to learn as much as possible from other countries. The DPME team visited Australia, Brazil, Canada, Colombia, India, Indonesia, the Republic of Korea, Malaysia, Mexico, the United Kingdom, and the United States to analyze their M&E systems and to learn from both their successes and their failures. Although the study tours required significant funding, mostly from donors, together with desk studies, they helped South Africa learn from others' experiences and enable rapid development of systems as well as avoid expensive mistakes in design and implementation—and thus proved to be a strategic investment. In building on what others had done, DPME was able to access good practices, adjusted international best practices to the local context, and proceeded rapidly in the design of its own systems. Although the replication and adjustment of good practices often required more in-depth dialogue and analysis, it was an important step to design a system inspired by the best parts of different systems.

The development of the new performance M&E faced several important obstacles. They included the lack of previous experience with performance M&E systems, inadequate capacity to design and manage it, lack of a performance culture in government, horizontal and vertical coordination challenges, data issues, a difficult reform environment, a multitude of service delivery challenges, and resistance from stakeholders. Addressing these obstacles required political will, technical know-how, a strategic focus, selectivity, and a gradual approach.

Breaking down resistance, building consensus, and creating demand from stakeholders for the system were possibly the most daunting challenges. Pockets of vested interests across government opposed to any sort of performance control made it difficult to find broad-based support for rolling out the system. For example on the MPAT, while there was interest in its use, the initial self-assessments were often not very realistic. This resulted in a disconnect between overly positive departmental reports and public experiences of service delivery. Departments thus missed the opportunity to use their monitoring processes as a way of improving service delivery. This was also reflected in a tendency to produce and report on process indicators, rather than indicators measuring improvements in outputs, outcomes, or impact. Overcoming resistance in some departments to conduct evaluations and make findings public was another significant challenge. In the words of Sean Phillips, the problem was "a culture of doing things the way they have always been done, as opposed to a culture of continuous improvement and monitoring and reporting for compliance rather than for improvement."

Building demand was addressed through a combination of pull and push factors. The strategic focus was on persuasion and engagement. DPME adopted a participatory approach, working with a mix of incentives, such as carrots (for example, additional funding and awards), sticks (for example, enforcement through Cabinet decisions), and sermons (for example, speeches by the President and ministers, workshops, training, and clinics). Highlighting positive practices in public and addressing resistance in a more internal way helped build demand and reduce resistance.

But there was also realism that persuasion and incentives could go only so far. To kick off the system and expand it, there were also gentle pushes from the top to ensure the system was implemented. They included Cabinet decisions on the use of certain tools (for example, MPAT), the willingness of DPME to be measured by the same yardstick as other departments, and a heavy emphasis on encouraging use of M&E information. As Sean Phillips emphasizes, "Results-based M&E must be coupled with leadership for it to have impact. M&E alone will not result in improved performance—leaders must act on M&E information." For example, the suggestion to have a program evaluated might first come from the technical team. In case of insufficient demand, it might be followed up by a suggestion from a higher level, including the Cabinet, to undertake certain evaluations. The choice of the program to be evaluated might also be part of an informal negotiation process. However, the final decision to conduct an evaluation comes from a cross-government National Evaluation Technical Working Group, and then DPME. Once agreement is reached, the department has to follow the processes established as part of the national evaluation system.

Consensus building was an active part of the engagement strategy with key stakeholders. This was particularly important because DPME did not have the regulatory and financial power of the National Treasury. The President, minister, and DPME management provided strong leadership for the performance M&E system. Cabinet approvals of the system helped raise its profile and enabled the DPME team to work with departments, including some that were not interested in a particular tool, such as evaluation. High-level engagement with ministers, deputy ministers, and directors-general, on a collective or individual basis as needed, helped build support and address concerns at the department level.

National and international workshops, trainings, how-to clinics, and other events helped build interest, enthusiasm, and support for the system and strengthen the technical capacity to demand and use its tools. Moving from a culture of compliance to a culture of continuous learning and improvement helped convey the message that the purpose of the system is not to help DPME collect data on the departments but rather to give the departments tools to continuously enhance their own performance. While DPME is also working with other stakeholders, such as Parliament and the Auditor General's Office to broaden demand and use, continuing to strengthen demand and consensus is likely to be a perennial challenge.

Effective sequencing was another important ingredient in the performance M&E story. The creation of DPME was done using a big-bang approach with the establishment of the work on outcomes. However, once this major change was made, new systems were developed incrementally, introducing new tools in a cautious manner by testing, learning, adjusting, gradually moving to a rollout, and then readjusting and refining. Flexible management arrangements within DPME allowed further evolution of thematic areas, effective collaboration between units, staff mobility between units, and the creation of new units and tools as the need emerged.

The gradual development of other systems was another demonstration of an approach of strategic incrementalism. The management performance assessment tool, for example, was first created at the central level in 2011. It was then rolled out to the provincial and later the municipal level, showing a somewhat linear development. The development of the front-line service delivery system (2011), the evaluation system (2012), the citizen-based monitoring framework (2013), and the ongoing work on medium-term planning (2014) were also developed gradually and expanded in scope over time, based on lessons learned from international experience and testing, as shown in figure 4.1. DPME only brought a

Figure 4.1 Creation and Implementation of South Africa's Performance Monitoring and Evaluation System, 1995–2014

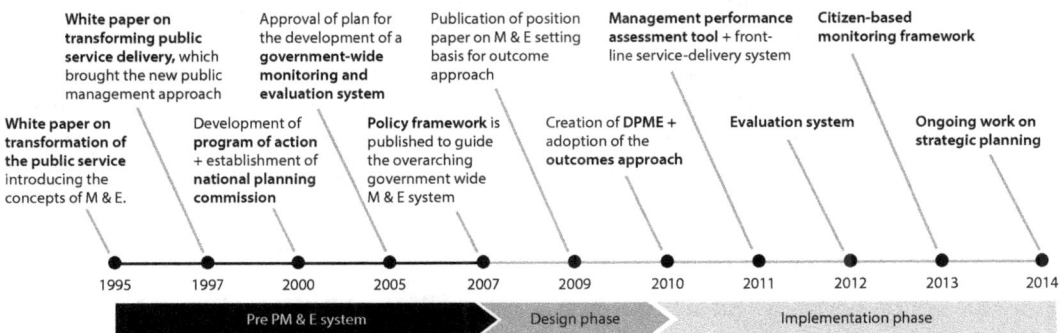

Source: Based on discussions with DPME.
Note: DPME = Department of Performance Monitoring and Evaluation (later renamed Department of Planning, Monitoring and Evaluation); M&E = monitoring and evaluation; PM&E = performance monitoring and evaluation.

new system or tool on the market once it had been tested and reviewed and it was clear that there was demand, response capacity, and interest in rolling it out. This gradual approach also helped build greater buy-in and support. It also made sense politically: the incremental approach helped build buy-in and support over time and did not come at the expense of speed; the system was designed and rolled out within five years, a very fast pace compared with peer countries.

Results Achieved

Given the nature of the system and the time required for changes to take place, it is difficult to quantify its impact—a pending task for DPME. Significant progress has been made in the design of the structure of the system; the development of policies, tools, guidelines, and products; and their early implementation. There is also evidence of important outputs and outcomes that illustrate the initial results achieved.

The outcomes approach has been put into practice across government. It has now been widened from the initial 12 to 14 national outcomes that government is committed to achieving as part of the Medium-Term Strategic Framework (MTSF), now formally linked as the first five years of the National Development Plan. These outcomes cover about 80 percent of government expenditure. All ministers have signed performance agreements that describe the key results the President expects them to achieve for each outcome. For each outcome, delivery agreements have been set up with interdepartmental and intergovernmental plans for key cross-cutting outcomes.[4] These five-year results-based plans outline outcomes, measurable indicators, targets, and key actions; identify required inputs; and clarify roles and responsibilities. The plans have facilitated alignment to strategic and annual performance plans. Implementation fora, based on existing coordination structures, have been set up to help achieve these outcomes.[5] Operation Phakisa, building on Malaysia's Big and Fast Results Initiative, has now started to complement the outcomes approach with an innovative focus on intensive planning, M&E, and problem-solving in selected service delivery sectors, such as the ocean economy and operation of ideal clinics, and is expected to move over time into additional sectors, such as education and mining.

An MPAT has been designed and implemented. It focuses on management performance (for example, human resource management and procurement), building on existing systems. It includes a facilitated self-assessment and subsequent peer monitoring, which strengthen realism and ownership. Established in 2011, following a visit to Canada, and now in its third iteration, it now covers all 155 national and provincial departments. Results are publicly disclosed and discussed by the Cabinet. Since its creation, performance scores have risen across the board. As Ismael Akhalwaya, creator of the MPAT, explains, "Departments are sensitive to naming and shaming." A similar municipal performance assessment tool, the Local Government Management Improvement Model, is being implemented in a phased approach in selected municipalities.

A front-line service delivery monitoring system has been set up. The system was created in response to protests on the ground and to the president's call for more responsive government.[6] Designed to be very practical, it has helped generate visibility on the ground and credibility for DPME. Key features include the following: First, a presidential hotline provides a grievance mechanism for the public. It tracks complaints for resolution by responsible departments and monitors data on sector and geographical trends. By June 2014, it had received more than 190,000 complaints with a resolution rate of more than 95 percent (DPME 2014). Second, unannounced monitoring visits provide a "dipstick" assessment of the quality of front-line services. They focus on facility-specific issues through improvement plans and remonitoring, using a scorecard approach. Third, a citizen-based monitoring framework, which is now being piloted, adds participatory monitoring features to the system. Overall, the front-line service delivery monitoring system focuses not only on receiving feedback but also and more important on improving service delivery standards through improvement plans and other means. As Bernadette Leon, former head of the program, underlines, "Improvement plans facilitate problem-solving, assign responsibilities, and allow tracking of agreed improvements."

A national evaluation system has been developed and evaluations are being rolled out at the national and provincial levels. A national evaluation policy framework and four annual national evaluation plans have been developed and adopted by the Cabinet. Evaluations conducted under the national evaluation system are public, partially financed by DPME and the relevant government department, and undertaken by external service providers, mainly private sector and academia. To facilitate uptake of their findings, they are based on a learning approach, focus on practical matters, and, once completed, include an improvement plan. Fifty evaluations have been or are being conducted, covering about R 75 billion in Medium-Term Expenditure Framework (MTEF) expenditure, at a cost of about R 50 million a year. The official objective is to achieve at least 10 percent in efficiency gains (that is, R 750 million), with the unofficial objective being 50 percent savings and/or improvements in impacts in some cases. Evaluation standards, guidelines, and competences have been developed, an audit of government evaluations was conducted, and an evaluation repository was built. The improvement plans developed by the national and provincial departments as a result of the evaluation are expected to be used for policy making and redesign. Several evaluations, for example, on early childhood development and on the reception year of schooling, have led to encouraging changes in government policies and practices.

The combination of these systems has helped establish a greater focus on key government outcomes, enhancing coordination around these outcomes and strengthening government effectiveness and efficiency. Quarterly reports on the outcomes provide the Cabinet with a strategic agenda, and a quarterly focus on progress with the key priorities of government. "Coordination and government effectiveness have resulted in good progress against key indicators in some sectors (for example, health) and created a whole-of-government

planning linked to key cross-cutting outcomes, clearly linking inputs and activities to outputs and the outcomes. This has also led to a higher level of understanding of how the work of the different departments affects each other
and greater coordination between departments and spheres of government,"
observes DPME Acting Director-General Nolwazi Gasa.

Instruments such as performance agreements and delivery agreements have
helped increase internal accountability in government and, through demand-side
mechanisms, are helping gradually increase external accountability. In terms of
efficiency gains, more systematic M&E through a focus on key outcomes, the
MPAT, and increasingly through the evaluation system is beginning to facilitate a
more efficient use of limited resources, starting to improve focus or generate savings across selected parts of government. DPME's involvement in the budget
process, through joint work with the National Treasury on expenditure reviews,
for example, is also producing efficiency gains. Budget guidelines now require
departments to include linkages with the delivery agreements in their plans, and
DPME checks the strategic plans and annual performance plans to ensure that
the linkages with outcomes are in place.

Equally important is the gradual change from an input- and activity-based
culture with a compliance focus to a results-based culture of continuous learning
and improvement. The emphasis on measuring results is working as a catalyst for
change. Departments are increasingly embracing the approach, putting in place
improvement plans, improving their data, and using the results of M&E findings
for policy making or reviewing policy implementation (for example, from the
evaluation on the reception year of schooling and on nutrition). These changes
have spurred progress against key indicators in some sectors, including health.
These gradual changes have been difficult to quantify, but they have been confirmed in interviews with DPME and other government staff, academics, the
private sector, and other stakeholders.

DPME has also become increasingly transparent and quite candid in its communications on its own performance and that of government at large. By making
information from the performance M&E system public, it has strengthened both
transparency and accountability. In the words of Ian Goldman, "There needs to
be an openness to admitting where things are not working well, so they can be
strengthened."

The magnitude of system design and sophistication is impressive. Comparable
countries, such as Canada, Mexico, and Colombia, have taken one or more
decades to develop their systems. Although each of them had different objectives, focus areas, and tools and some have more advanced systems than South
Africa, the South African system is nevertheless quite comprehensive and has
been developed quite rapidly. First, the combination of the different pillars of
the system, such as the outcomes approach, front-line service delivery monitoring, and the evaluation system shows its far-reaching scope. Second, as opposed
to many countries, the system includes not only the central level of government
but also the provincial and increasingly municipal levels. Third, other initiatives,
such as a national-level citizen-based monitoring framework linking the supply

and demand side, are rare in other countries, where such initiatives are often more local or fragmented. Fourth, the focus on performance as a tool for continuous improvement is promising and helps in starting to institutionalize the system, even though occurring gradually.

The initial impact of the performance M&E system on stakeholders has been rather positive, yet further work is needed. Interviews and surveys with government staff working in national, provincial, and municipal departments show that they have largely welcomed the new system. "It's been a big help," notes one government official. "It has helped us focus our work more, make our programs more effective, helped us make savings, and has taught us quite a bit on being more responsive to citizens' needs." However, stakeholders have expressed concern that the system adds yet another layer of reporting obligations and think that it could be streamlined with other center-of-government initiatives. Some actors also believe that DPME is duplicating the work of the Auditor General, the National Treasury, and other agencies in terms of reporting and compliance monitoring.[7] These concerns need to be addressed in the medium term.

It is still too early to measure the impact on final beneficiaries, but surveys and interviews suggest that it has been overall positive. Feedback on the front-line service delivery tools, the presidential hotline, and the citizens-based monitoring pilots seems to be also largely positive.

Conclusions: Success Factors, Challenges, and Lessons Learned

The development of the South African performance M&E system illustrates a number of success factors and lessons learned. The first is about the strength of the design. DPME was quite strategic and ambitious and focused on building a strong and credible system. To understand best practices, the DPME team reached out to other countries that had national M&E systems in place, to development partners, and to academic experts. It was very careful to adjust these experiences to the local reality, adopting a gradual and government wide approach. It regularly consulted with many stakeholders to obtain feedback on how to further enhance the effectiveness of the system and to build their commitment to the system. The system combined supply-side governance approaches (for example, different monitoring systems) and demand-side governance approaches (for example, engagement with civil society and others through the citizen-based monitoring). This focus on quality was a key ingredient for making the design of the system a regional good practice.

Second, another key lesson is that an effective system can be designed in a narrowing reform space and in a relatively short time period. Critical to this lesson was the importance of technical-driven leadership under political leadership, in a country context of broader governance and service delivery challenges and under a reform space, which 15 years after apartheid had narrowed to the immediate post-apartheid momentum. The system was developed by a technically strong, committed team of individuals. The team managed to build alliances for support, both within DPME, across departments, and more broadly nationally and internationally, and to make progress in targeted, selected areas. The political leadership supported them, enabling the technical team to have a lot of flexibility in the design of the system.

Third, the approach of strategic incrementalism has proved to be most effective. Instead of designing a very comprehensive system at the start, the system was developed over time. The building-block approach allowed officials to learn from the initial parts of the system and build on them in a carefully sequenced way from the outcomes approach, over the MPAT, to the evaluations and citizen-based monitoring. Similarly, within building blocks, the MPAT moved from the national to the provincial and now is moving to the municipal level. A system that was originally more supply-side oriented is being increasingly complemented by demand-side mechanisms, such as training in evidence for directors-general, work with Parliament, and citizen-based monitoring. A pragmatic, flexible, and persuasive approach has helped build demand for the system among various groups of stakeholders. Engagements with departments, for example, through one-on-one high-level meetings, targeted workshops, training, and clinics for departmental staff, helped increase demand for its tools. M&E is increasingly seen not only as a tool for M&E officers but also as a management and learning tool for all levels and types of staff. Offering a menu of tools has helped make the system more attractive, for example, by offering support for evaluations carried out under the national evaluation system or to those conducted directly by departments. A focus on a culture of learning and continuous improvement made departments see the benefits of M&E for their own sectoral objectives. Quick wins, such as pilots, created momentum and showcased early success. As Bernadette Leon emphasizes, "Through our collaboration, creating a community of practice and a focus on quality, we have established a sense of mutual respect between DPME and the departments, which encourages greater demand and ownership in departments of the M&E agenda."

Fourth, there was a lot of focus not only on the design features but also on the implementation arrangements. Whereas some other countries have designed a national development plan/presidential goals/outcomes approach, but sometimes have not paid sufficient attention to implementation, DPME focused on the underlying mechanisms of how to make the system work in practice. This was also important to counter the criticism that government has excellent policies but does not always implement them well. For example, for the outcomes approach, there were clear implementation arrangements, such as the performance agreements, delivery agreements, and implementation fora. There was also a pragmatic decision to continue to let these implementation mechanisms evolve and be adjusted as needed.

Fifth, the availability of funding was another important success factor, helping build capacity, share international experiences, experiment with new ideas, and scale up the system. Through its location in the Presidency, DPME was able to attract sufficient funding to turn the development of the system into a high-level and effective exercise. The President's support helped generate sufficient funding from the National Treasury. But DPME was also very actively engaged in attracting donor funding, through international positioning, engagement with different multi- and bilateral donors, and fundraising tours. Donor funding, for example, from the European Union (EU), the Department for International Development (DFID, United Kingdom), the German Agency for International Cooperation (GIZ), or the World Bank, served two main objectives. First, it helped tap into international experiences and bring them to South Africa, thus strengthening design and capacity. Second, it helped mobilize additional funding for the type of activities that might have been more difficult to fund with national resources, such as international study tours, workshops, and seed money for testing new approaches.

However, as the system evolves, there continue to be important challenges to enhance its design and implementation, such as its linkages with planning and budgeting. First, the integration of the medium-term planning function after the May 2014 elections is therefore a golden opportunity to make this marriage happen. A focus on the design of implementation programs and the design of the medium-term planning framework are first steps in linking planning and M&E. As Ian Goldman, head of evaluation, emphasizes, "We can have the best evaluation system in the world, but if we only focus on this at a late stage in policy, program, and project M&E, our impact will always remain behind. We therefore need to strengthen performance by getting planning right in the first place, as well as performance M&E. Only then can we have a lasting impact on government policies, programs, and projects."

Second, greater integration of M&E with the budget will be crucial. South Africa has an impressive budget performance, recently ranking first or second in the Open Budget Index, and a solid performance-based budgeting system. Whereas in other countries the national M&E system is often based in the Ministry of Finance, facilitating the integration with the budget, there is a need in South Africa to proactively pursue the objective of greater integration while maintaining the benefits of the system's location in the Presidency. This is not only a technical question of how to create the appropriate systems and tools to maximize the impact of the system but also a political question of how to optimize the collaboration between the National Treasury and the Presidency in this regard. In the medium term, what is needed is the greater use of the performance M&E information for budget preparation and execution, to ensure that the budget is aligned with the outcomes approach, and that the M&E findings are actually used for budgetary decision making in all of the stages of the budget process. Further alignment between the National Development Plan, the Medium-Term Strategic Framework,[8] the Outcomes Approach, departmental strategic and annual plans, and the budget will be crucial at the center of government and at the departmental, program, project, and also subnational levels. Harmonizing the use of performance M&E with the use of M&E of public investment to strengthen public investment management efficiency, including in state-owned enterprises, would be another important area where greater integration could be achieved.

Third, other reforms, such as second-generation reforms of performance M&E, will also be needed, such as enhancing data quality. This will include strengthening data, from data availability to the quality of administrative data over single entry of data at field level. It will also require moving toward common data standards across government, including open data standards and the availability and interoperability of the supporting information technology (IT) systems to enhance both the collection and the analysis of data. Ensuring effective coordination and reducing the administrative burden on departments will also be needed to make the system more user friendly. Performance data audits would be useful and help enhance the availability of data, including data to measure DPME's effectiveness.

Fourth, demand by stakeholders needs to be further enhanced to ensure greater use of M&E information for policy making and implementation. Increasing demand is a perennial challenge for all M&E systems, and South Africa is no exception. Limited effective demand is still an obstacle for using M&E tools and M&E findings to change policies. This is partially as a result of the predominance of a compliance culture, the limited culture of accountability, and the lack of a solid incentives framework. Although some encouraging results show the use of M&E findings, such as the briefings to the President, Cabinet, and Parliament and some corrective action following the MPAT, evaluations, and the front-line service delivery monitoring, more needs to be done to enhance use and impact. DPME needs to build stronger alliances with different types of stakeholders, such as with departments, Parliament, the Auditor General's Office, and other oversight institutions, and with the private sector, civil society, the media, and so forth to enhance the demand for the use of M&E tools and findings and promote the use of research for policy making. To do so, an incentives framework of "carrots, sticks, and sermons" with financial and nonfinancial incentives for greater use of M&E tools and M&E findings would be an important next step, ultimately contributing to facilitating greater performance and penalizing poor performance. A systematic review of the performance M&E design and implementation so far, and of its subsystems, such as the upcoming evaluation of the evaluation function, could also help shed light on the necessary structural changes, enhance both supply and demand factors, and help maximize its effectiveness and use.

Fifth, the system needs to include greater built-in locks to increase its sustainability and be protected against policy reversals. Even cases of very successful M&E systems, such as Australia and Chile, show that there can be policy reversals after a change of administration. It would be important to build a solid foundation both on the supply side—for example, by considering a strong legal basis, mandate, and well-established and recognized processes and practices—as well as on the demand side—for example, by setting up a more effective incentives framework for demand and use of the system in government and beyond.[9] Moving toward a more integrated system of performance, with jointly agreed standards, tools, and guidelines from the center of government would also help further institutionalize the system. A solid change and risk management system will be needed to accompany the substantial reforms. Some of the key elements needed to strengthen sustainability are: (i) moving from a directive style to a coordinating style, where DPME is a champion and shows leadership around M&E but builds the involvement and commitment of partners; (ii) enhancing the demand for and use of M&E information, for example, by ministers, directors-general, the Cabinet, and the Parliament, so key decision makers see the value; (iii) building alliances and building fora, that strengthen the M&E voice; (iv) strengthening the perceived value DPME is providing to help departments achieve their objectives to internalize M&E and to use it for improving performance, in the process ensuring that departments take the credit for success; (v) simplifying systems, for example, to reduce duplication in reporting, so increasing the perceived value; and (vi) increasing support by and responsiveness to politicians, so they see M&E as adding value to what they wish to achieve.

Finally, the system needs to mature, in terms of both the development of new tools and the refinement of existing ones. For example, the policy framework for the government wide M&E system needs to be updated. DPME has increased transparency by making a huge volume of information available to the government and the public. Use of this information now needs to come increasingly from other parts of government and external stakeholders, to ensure that government is held accountable.

These lessons learned, success factors, and challenges are widely applicable to other countries, although not all countries might have the significant resources and the political will South Africa has had to invest heavily in the design of the system. Elements that might have triggered the policy challenge, such as the concerns with service delivery challenges, will be similar across countries; and there are lots of lessons to be learned from the success factors and challenges alike. The main message here is that such a system can be designed even in a limited reform space, and even in a relatively short time period. The growing interest in South Africa's experiences by developing and developed countries alike reveals the relevance of its reforms to other countries. South Africa hosted four international workshops in 2014 and 2015 to showcase its system and learn from other regional and global systems. It has hosted several study tours to South Africa to share specific parts of the system, such as the evaluations system and the presidential hotline. More publications on the South African M&E system are emerging. Technical collaboration with other countries (with Canada, for example, on the MPAT); knowledge sharing (through the South Africa Monitoring and Evaluation Association and similar international organizations); and mentoring and coaching are ongoing and expected to be made more systematic. DPME is now working on a framework of national, regional, and global knowledge exchange to make its exchanges, including upcoming study tours to other countries, conferences, and workshops, more systematic and effective. For example, a new regional initiative, "Twende," is being created to support performance M&E in other African countries.

In conclusion, the reform agenda has a solid foundation, and a continued incremental approach can help harvest the benefits of reforms. Given the early years of development of the performance M&E system, there will be a need for greater maturity of the system, in terms of both the development of new tools and the refinement of existing tools. The design is strong, and initial results are encouraging. What the system now needs more than anything is time—time to further develop and fine-tune policies, structures, tools, guidelines, and incentives and to gather further implementation practices. Some reforms will be able to be done in the shorter term, such as the gradual expansion of the evaluations done. Some are in full swing but will take more time, such as a greater integration of strategic planning with performance M&E in the medium term. Others, such as deepening the linkages with the budget, will probably take place only in the long term, when the political timing is adequate. Others, such as use of M&E findings for policy making, the final litmus test of the effectiveness of a performance M&E system, will be an evolving process over time. Finally, in terms of broader government performance, DPME has helped strengthen transparency, making a substantial amount of information on government available to government and the public. Yet the use of the information, not only to ensure transparency but also to create greater accountability, now needs to come increasingly also from other parts of government and external stakeholders, to ensure that government can be held accountable.

Notes

1. DPME's budget for 2014/15 is R 208.3 million, divided into three programs: outcomes monitoring and evaluation (R 78.2 million), institutional performance monitoring and evaluation (R 66.2 million), and administration (R 63.8 million).

2. In 2001 the government of Tony Blair (United Kingdom) created the first prototype of delivery units, the so-called Program Management and Delivery Unit. The creation of delivery units resulted from the need to have a central point in government from which selected service delivery problems could be addressed quickly. The delivery unit was created in the Prime Minister's Office, and its focus was on resolving bottlenecks in major programs or projects and doing so in a pragmatic, practical, quick, and flexible way. It was later dissolved.

3. The management consulting firm Monitor was one of the first private companies to help build strategic support on DPME design of the department and key tools.

4. Delivery agreements are negotiated charters, which reflect the commitment of the key partners involved in the direct delivery process for the achievement of the twelve outcomes.

5. The president and ministers signed 35 performance agreements in April 2010. Between July and November 2010, outcome facilitators at the deputy director-general level were appointed in DPME to support development of the delivery agreements and implementation and monitoring of outcomes. By November 2010, delivery agreements had been concluded and signed by different national departments and provinces. The first quarterly monitoring reports on outcomes were produced in November 2010. This brought about greater focus on performance monitoring and has increasingly made departments and provinces more accountable to the Presidency.

6. In his State of the Nation address on June 3, 2009, President Jacob Zuma stressed the importance of a government that is responsive, interactive, and effective.

7. A research project is underway to examine the extent and nature of the problem.

8. The medium-term national strategic framework is the key instrument to implement the NDP. It identifies the important actions required to implement the aspects of the NDP for which government is responsible over the next five years, from 2014 to 2019 (Presidency, Republic of South Africa 2014).

9. There is a discussion on whether a strong legal basis is needed for the performance M&E system. Proponents argue that it will help raise clarity and enhance sustainability; opponents argue that it will reinforce the compliance element at the cost of the learning element.

References

DPME (Department of Performance Monitoring and Evaluation). 2009. *Improving Government Performance: Our Approach*. Pretoria.

———. 2011. *DPME: National Evaluation Policy Framework*. Pretoria.

———. 2012–14. DPME Presentations and Updates 2012–14. Pretoria.

———. 2014. *Presidential Hotline Update*, June.

———. 2013. *DPME: Improving Capacity to Undertake and Manage Evaluations in South Africa*. Pretoria.

DPSA (Department of Public Service and Administration). 1995. *White Paper on Transformation of the Public Service*.

———. 1997. *White Paper on Transforming Public Service Delivery*.

Engela, Ronette, and Tania Ajam. 2010. "Implementing a Government-Wide Monitoring and Evaluation System in South Africa." Evaluation Capacity Development Working Paper 21, World Bank, Washington, DC.

Goldman, I., R. Engela, S. Phillips, I. Akhalwaya, N. Gasa, B. Leon, H. Mohamed, and T. Mketi. 2014. "Development and Functioning of the National M&E System in South Africa." In *Evaluation Management in South Africa and Africa*, edited by F. Cloete, B. Rabie, and C. De Coning. Stellenbosch, South Africa: African Sun Media.

Phillips, S., I. Goldman, N. Gasa, I. Akhalwaya, and B. Leon. 2014. "A Focus on M&E of Results: An Example from the Presidency, South Africa." *Journal of Development Effectiveness* 6 (4): 392–406.

Presidency, Republic of South Africa. 2007. *M&E Policy Framework*. Pretoria.

———. 2014. Budget Speech by Jeff Radebe, July 21, Pretoria.

World Bank. 2012. "Establishing a National M&E System in South Africa." *PREMNotes* (September).

CHAPTER 5

Creating an Inclusive and Credible Statistical System

Misha V. Belkindas and Phindile Ngwenya

Introduction

Globalization and the revolution in information technology have brought about a fundamental transformation in the way societies conduct their affairs. The transformation of the global economy and its parts has contributed to more transparent and accountable systems of government. The spread of democratic systems of governance has brought about a better-informed citizenry that demands greater transparency and accountability. As a result, people in positions of power are compelled to adopt decision-making processes that are open and grounded in evidence-based approaches.

In such a system, quantitative information plays an important role in policy making, implementation, and monitoring and evaluation (M&E). Official statistics are a vital tool in evidence-based policy making and in enabling citizens to exercise their fundamental rights. Open statistics guide policies and citizen responses to policy implementation. Openness is very important in many governmental processes, including fiscal relations, budgetary process, and M&E.

Under apartheid, South Africa had an opaque, nontransparent, and noninclusive system of government that was accountable to only about 10 percent of the population. Its statistical system was highly distorted in terms of products, data collection methods, geographical location, and staffing. Official statistics were compiled largely on the basis of surveys and administrative records covering only the white minority population. Data on the rest of the (mostly rural and nonwhite) population were based on limited records. As a result, information about the economic and social conditions of South Africa was partial, biased, and

Misha V. Belkindas is Cofounder and Managing Director of Open Data Watch, an international NGO working in the area of openness and national statistical systems. Phindile Ngwenya is a former Research Analyst in the World Bank's Macroeconomics and Fiscal Management Global Practice. This chapter benefited from extensive interviews with current and former government officials as well as from comments by peer reviewer Neil Fantom, Manager in the World Bank Development Data Group.

noninclusive; data released by the authorities lacked credibility; statistics were used as a political tool to sustain a segregated and authoritarian system of government; and policy making and implementation were not evidence based, transparent, or inclusive.

When the democratic government took office in 1994, there was a significant change in the policy focus. Because the statistical system was unable to provide the services for which a statistical system is designed, it required a complete overhaul.

The reform carried out since then has been the fastest and most impressive in statistical reform history. Statistical offices are now located in all nine provinces of South Africa, the staff is demographically representative, methodological weaknesses have largely been addressed, and the products offered by the statistical office—Statistics South Africa (Statistics SA)—have been broadened, in line with the government's policy anchor of reducing poverty and inequality.

This chapter provides a brief overview of the institutional reforms of the statistical system that was in place in 1994. It describes how the national statistics office was transformed into Statistics SA to provide more rigorous and representative statistics. It discusses the key policy challenges of the reforms—including the roles played by stakeholders such as the National Treasury, the Financial and Fiscal Commission, the Reserve Bank, and the academic community—and shows how they were addressed.

The Policy Challenge

The democratic government that took office in 1994 introduced a new priority focus area that was significantly different from that of the previous government. The overarching issue for the government, and indeed the majority of the population, went beyond fiscal and economic management; its focus was on reducing poverty and inequality.

The new government found an institution that was not set up to deal with the country's new priorities. The Central Statistical Services (CSS), as it was known at the time, concentrated on statistics that were linked with issues of economic management, publishing products such as national accounts, price statistics, and income and expenditure surveys. Its work program was tilted toward collecting economic data from the organized sector of the economy, thereby excluding a large segment of the economy. Its products were not credible in light of the new development agenda. The institution's setup had to be realigned in order to be able to produce products that would enable the new government to carry out its mandate of reducing poverty. Major institutional reforms of CSS required organizational, structural, management, physical, and methodological changes.

Under apartheid, the statistical system was racially biased in a variety of ways. Geographically, the CSS served the mainstream economy—composed of the minority white South Africans and urban townships. It paid little attention to the rural areas where most of the African population lived.

CSS services and products were designed to serve white South Africa. Work programs were poorly designed and uncoordinated across the various statistical agencies in the country. These institutions were not equipped to engage in meaningful data collection, and the information that was collected could not be collated to give a holistic picture of the whole economy. Demographically, the staff of the CSS was predominantly white and only English and Afrikaans speaking. The Statistical Council—the entity with oversight responsibilities over the CSS—was similarly structured. At the same time, because of these and other such factors, many members of society did not pay allegiance to, or trust, the state and were therefore not inclined to provide the official statisticians with accurate information about themselves and their environs. Besides this, such accurate data would in many cases invoke charges of illegality in terms of, for instance, sources of income for unlicensed small businesspeople in white South Africa, ethnicity in the context of those located in the "wrong homeland," or filial relations and family size in townships for those not allowed to live in urban areas.

Methodologies were also racially biased. Surveys collected data on the white population and the mainstream white-dominated economy; statistical outputs were similarly structured. Illustrative of the orientation of the system was the manner in which the 1991 Census of Population was conducted. Urban areas, populated largely by the white population, were canvassed through a conventional census; the rest of the country was covered mainly through aerial surveys and data extrapolations. There were also fundamental flaws in the questionnaire design. Most surveys were only in English or Afrikaans; none was produced in the nine African languages spoken by the majority of the population. Moreover, the questionnaire was designed to be self-administered rather than based on interviews conducted by enumerators, even though most Africans could not read English or Afrikaans. All these factors compromised the credibility of the products generated by the CSS.

The Reconstruction and Development Program (RDP) was the policy instrument the new government used to tackle the burning issues of poverty and inequality, complemented by other policy documents over time The new government, and later particularly the newly formed Planning Commission and the Department of Performance Monitoring and Evaluation (DPME) quickly concluded that transforming these policy goals into actionable programs required credible and comprehensive statistical information (see chapter 4). A complete institutional reform of the system was deemed urgent and necessary.

In most countries, reforms to statistical systems are spread over several years. In South Africa the demand for rapid, comprehensive reform of the statistical system was acute. There were no clear examples of reform to statistical systems on the scale or at the speed at which key players wanted to reform. Leaders therefore adopted a learning-by-doing approach with an emphasis on rapid change that brought quick results rather than slow but comprehensive reforms.

Making It Happen • http://dx.doi.org/10.1596/978-1-4648-0768-8

Addressing the Policy Challenge

The transformation of statistical services in South Africa can be attributed to pressure from several fronts. From the bottom, the push for transformation came from statistical practitioners. From the top, the push came from the leadership—politicians who demanded cold hard facts and ministers who fully endorsed and provided financial support for the process. The data generated were criticized by everyone whose goals they did not serve. Users who were not privy to statistical information during apartheid were very critical of any information they perceived to threaten democracy (for example, high unemployment).

The first push came from the formation of a committee of statistical practitioners from the homelands. They recognized that universal statistical coverage was important and that the patchy information collected in various offices without coordination would not bring about an environment in which all people would be treated equally. These practitioners demanded that activities be integrated into the CSS in order to better support the new democratic government in implementing the RDP. Statistical offices needed to be strengthened technically; they needed the relevant autonomy and authority to operate (to carry out their own surveys and statistical programs, for example). Although their efforts met with much resistance from the CSS, their demands gained traction when Mark Orkin, cofounder and formerly deputy director of an anti-apartheid social research agency, Community Action for Social Enquiry, was brought in to head the CSS in 1995. Reform accelerated when Pali Lehohla was brought in from Bophuthatswana to lead the 1996 census.

The other direction of transformation was the leadership, both by politicians and by CSS management. The political leadership acted with remarkable speed and great vision. It took a noninterference approach to the future role of the statistical system. This approach increased the credibility of the organization. Leaders, including all three presidents (Nelson Mandela, Thabo Mbeki, and Jacob Zuma), were very clear in their requests for numbers. They asked for straight, hard facts and informed the statistician general that they did not wish to gloss over anything.

Several figures were instrumental in carrying out the reforms. Much of the credit goes to Jay Naidoo, then minister of RDP, the department in which CSS was located. Initial reforms, including the appointment of Orkin as head of CSS, were undertaken under his leadership. Another important reformer was Trevor Manuel, minister of finance, the minister responsible for statistics. He continued to oversee the statistical function after becoming the minister of the Presidency. "The hallmarks of Manuel's tenure as a minister and one responsible for statistics were trust, rationality, and communication.... My assessment is that he adjudged trust above all else," says Lehohla, who now serves as statistician general.

Manuel accorded the head of the statistical agency the support needed to carry out reforms, in the form of authority, autonomy, and funding. He adopted a tightfisted fiscal stance but had no qualms once a business case was presented to ensure that data needed by policy makers were produced. For example, if there was a methodological dispute in a product, he supported bringing in international consultants to critique the process. Such peer review services ensured that products not only were credible domestically but also met international standards.

Another champion of reform was the first head of statistics in the new democratic government, Mark Orkin, who led CSS and Statistics SA from 1995 to 2000. Orkin was appointed from outside the institution and given the mandate to transform it. Exuding an energetic leadership style that some people found autocratic, Orkin implemented the initial reforms, amalgamating the old and establishing new offices in the newly created provinces. He made the difficult transition rapidly, replacing the apartheid structure of the CSS within 12 months. The major publication of his tenure was the 1996 census. Orkin also ensured the passage of the Statistics Act (described below) shortly before his tenure ended.

A turning point was reached when Pali Lehohla was appointed as his second in command, with the mandate to run the 1996 census. Lehohla had several clashes with the CSS leadership in 1993 under apartheid, when he served on the committee of statistical practitioners in the homelands that had pushed for a more integrated approach to statistics. His previous "difficult" relationship within CSS did not play well with some members of the CSS management.

The 1996 census was a milestone in the transition. Lehohla reports that when Nelson Mandela received the 1996 census, he said, "At last, we have numbers we can work with." Its successful implementation proved that the statistical system could be used to serve all citizens. Statistical practitioners understood that, in the words of Risenga Maluleke, deputy director-general of Statistics SA, "it would serve as a mobilizer of society during peaceful times"—a rare occurrence in South Africa. They understood that the census would go a long way toward making the institution credible in the eyes of society at large. For ordinary citizens, the CSS, which became Statistics SA in 1999, would be a legitimate national statistical office for South Africa. The other function of a census—providing information on society—would play a secondary role.

Building the Legal and Organizational Framework

The new statistical law adopted in 1999 provided a basis for the major reforms. The operations of Statistics SA were to be governed by the Statistics Act (1999), which outlines the activities of the minister, the statistician general, and the Statistics Council. The Statistics Council was reorganized to reflect the diversity of the country. Its members represent the research, academic, business, and government sectors. The Statistics Council provides advice to the minister, the statistician general, and other state organs on statistical matters within Statistics SA as well as on data collected by other government departments, methodology, and prioritization of data needs. The new law took account of international best practices and provided safeguards about statistical integrity and independence from political interventions in areas such as data collection and dissemination.

Making It Happen • http://dx.doi.org/10.1596/978-1-4648-0768-8

Along with the new law, Statistics SA adopted an open and transparent evaluation tool, the South African Statistical Quality Assessment Framework. Under the framework, the statistician general is responsible for ensuring that the entire South African national statistical system produces certifiable standard data that are aligned with international best practice. At the same time, the World Bank extended a grant to develop a comprehensive strategic plan for the statistical system and supported the planning process with technical assistance and advice.

Statistics SA subscribes to the International Monetary Fund's (IMF's) Standard Data Dissemination Standards (SDDS), which set standards for transparency of data and statistical processes. It has also adopted or moved toward adoption of other international standards set by the United Nations (UN) Statistical Commission and other UN agencies. These steps are significant in aligning South Africa's practices with those in many statistically advanced countries.

Although Statistics SA has undergone major reforms and taken on new responsibilities, progress in building up a functioning overall statistical system encompassing statistical units in line departments and agencies has been slow. With the end of apartheid and the dismantling of the homelands, nine new provinces were created. The old statistical offices were incorporated into the main framework of Statistics SA and provided with the resources to carry out their mandate. The number of staff increased from 600 in 1995 to 1,200 in 2005 and 3,500 in 2014; and the agency is more representative of the country's demographic composition. Capacity constraints were addressed by training and retraining staff and implementing an internship program.

Statistics SA has built relationships with universities, such as the ISIbalo Center for Regional and Urban Innovation and Statistical Exploration (CRUISE), based at the University of Stellenbosch. The center immerses officials in technical leadership in urban and regional science and the leading role of statistics. Up to 15 people a year have been enrolled since 2011, when the first intake started, and 34 senior civil servants have earned master's degrees from the center. The program is paying enormous dividends.

Overhauling the Institution

A very important role fell to Pali Lehohla, the statistician general appointed in November 2000. With the success of the 1996 census behind him, he could focus on internal organizational issues, including the reengineering of products and human resource issues through the Organizational development Task Team (OdeTT).

His most immediate objective was to stabilize the institution. This objective was facilitated by his approachable leadership style, which included an open-door policy. Lehohla is also a visionary: over time, he led Statistics SA to become a self-sustaining organization that worked across racial lines and reduced mistrust. He envisaged Statistics SA as producing products that are internationally recognized and play a significant role on the world stage.

Overhauling the statistical system demanded restructuring the institutional framework, adopting a comprehensive work program that was linked to South Africa's overall policy priorities, and adopting international standards and best practices. An overarching goal was the need to develop a sustainable statistical system fully capable of serving the needs of a democratic South Africa. According to Rashad Cassim, the head of the research department at the South Africa Reserve Bank (the central bank) and formerly deputy director-general of economic statistics at Statistics SA, one of Lehohla's key approaches was to retain skilled senior staff from the old regime. By not alienating employees, he retained some institutional memory and critical skills and ensured that reforms did not compromise the quality of the existing products. Upon assuming office, he reiterated that the RDP was the key policy upon which Statistics SA's priorities would be anchored. The other document that would anchor Statistics SA's activities would be the Growth, Employment and Redistribution (GEAR) strategy. One of the outcomes of the transformation of Statistics SA was the emergence of cultural and racial mistrust among staff members. Racial tensions were addressed by the formation of OdeTT, consisting of representatives of trade unions, staff, and management. OdeTT's agenda for change addressed staff development, management and leadership development, systems and processes development, and cultural development. This process helped build trust among diverse constituencies, and it laid the foundations for a technically credible and sustainable organization.

Lehohla engaged in a broad range of techniques to effect his changes. At the start of his tenure, the Public Finance Management Act (PFMA) introduced control instruments. Year-to-year audits of Statistics SA revealed deteriorating results. This weak performance created pressure to focus on a project management system.

Building Institutional Credibility

Democracy ushered in a new breed of data users demanding integrated statistics, but incumbent officials refused to cooperate, resulting in inevitable tensions. Under apartheid, statistics users came mainly from the mainstream—the white-controlled economy, government departments, and academia. Their focus—macroeconomic management—was in line with the government of the day. The new agents demanding statistical services were from the anti-apartheid movement. Like the new government, they were interested in broader socioeconomic transformation and poverty issues.

The tensions were palpable, particularly after the release of the preliminary results of the 1996 census. The results were challenged, and there was a threat of litigation because the premier of the Western Cape believed that the results, which underestimated the province's population, would unfairly deprive it of its equitable share (of subsidies or other benefits provided based on population size). This challenge was overcome by the formation of a technical committee comprising representatives from Statistics SA and the aggrieved premier. Political support from President Mandela and Minister Manuel was instrumental.

Making It Happen • http://dx.doi.org/10.1596/978-1-4648-0768-8

Statistics SA management had to address long-standing issues of the institution's credibility: trade unions, civil society organizations, and the anti-apartheid movement all considered the old statistics unreliable. The new leaders of the CSS wanted to undertake reforms, but parties that supported the old arrangement strongly resisted them.

To gain credibility and support, the leadership of Statistics SA undertook an accessibility policy for statistics users. Journalists were permitted to reach Statistics SA staff at all hours of the day, a step that facilitated the ironing out of any potential data glitches. To improve the perceptions of the organization, Lehohla wrote a weekly column in a national newspaper for 11 years. This commitment showed his desire to connect with the population and increased trust.

Bongani Khumalo, the acting chairperson and chief executive of the Financial and Fiscal Commission (FFC), believes that two events facilitated the successful overhaul of Statistics SA. The first was housing it in the National Treasury, which made it part of the service delivery model. The FFC, which derives its mandate from the Constitution, is responsible for determining the equitable sharing formula of revenues for and transfers to subnational governments, which is done in conjunction with the Intergovernmental Fiscal Review (IGFR) unit at the Department of Finance. This relationship meant that the requirements for broader data collection could take center stage and helped accelerate institutional reforms. FFC's representation by the IGFR meant that it was present at statistical advisory meetings. It also meant that its demands for more credible data and other ways to increase credibility could be addressed.

The second significant step was that the Department of Finance ensured that resources were made available to facilitate the necessary institutional reforms. As the driver of the service delivery model through the IGFR, it also influenced the agenda of Statistics SA. In its yearly submission for the division of revenue, the FFC influenced the kind of data collected by Statistics SA as well as the methodology it used.

Results Achieved

Key results achieved included the following:

First, the coverage of the consumer price index (CPI) was extended to include data from black-owned businesses, small business, and other segments of the country, reducing the metropolitan, white bias. Data collection methods were switched from a system in which questionnaires were mailed to a system in which data are collected by interviewers.

Second, new statistical tools were designed and used. The last population census in a territorially integral South Africa was conducted in 1970. Under apartheid, survey instruments were inadequate, even at the national level. Many urban townships were deemed inaccessible, and mapping was not uniformly available. Aerial photographs were used to estimate the number of dwellings, and the population was estimated using imputation methods based on household densities collected from sample surveys. The 1996 population census remedied some of these problems by collecting information using the same methods all over the country. Labor force surveys were introduced to supplement household activity data collected from censuses. They became important for estimating unemployment. Labor force surveys are now conducted quarterly. The October Household Survey, which evolved into the General Household Survey, was introduced to provide more detailed information on all households' living conditions. It supplements the information collected in censuses. Methodological processes were also streamlined. Missing mapping and demarcation information was collected. Data are now collected in a uniform manner across the country. Surveys are national and use common standards and classifications. With improved sampling frames and mapping, the quality of the data has improved.

Third, a move is underway to strengthen the statistical system by amending the legal stipulation in the Statistics Act that Statistics SA remain the only data collection agency. If the stipulation is passed, Statistics SA would provide oversight of data collection standards and definitions but could accredit other agencies that are carrying out statistical work.

Fourth, Statistics SA was instrumental in supporting implementation of the Reference Regional Strategic Framework for Statistical Capacity Building in Africa, an international effort led by the World Bank to encourage and support reform of statistical systems in Africa. Statistics SA has championed several important initiatives. It created and sponsored the Africa Symposia for Statistical Development, which dealt with population censuses. Partly as a result of these symposia, the 2010 censuses covered many more countries in Africa than the previous round and left out fewer people. The symposia grew into the Africa Program on Accelerated Improvement of Civil Registration and Vital Statistics Systems (APAI-CRVS) movement, which supports the improvement of civil registration and vital statistics systems in Africa. It is supported by the African Union, the *United Nations Economic Commission for Africa (UNECA)*, and the African Development Bank and chaired by the statistician general of Statistics SA.

Fifth, Statistics SA is supporting many international programs. When IMF, the World Bank, and the Department for International Development (DFID, United Kingdom) provided assistance to anglophone countries in Africa that seek to participate in the IMF's General Data Dissemination System, many training workshops were conducted in South Africa and experts from Statistics SA shared their experience with participants abroad. Statistics SA also organized the 57th World Statistical Congress of the International Statistical Institute in 2009, in Durban. The congress clearly demonstrated the maturity of South Africa's statistical system.

Conclusions: Success Factors, Challenges, and Lessons Learned

South Africa has made remarkable progress in restructuring its statistical system to serve the needs of a democratic society. The restructured system has responded to the demands for outputs that are comprehensive, timely, and credible.

It enjoys independence and subscribes to ethical standards in accordance with international norms. These extraordinary achievements were attained in the short space of a decade and a half.

Although not all of South Africa's experience has relevance for other countries engaged in statistical capacity building, some success factors and lessons learned emerge. First, the political leadership was clear in its demand for credible data. The demand was linked to a clearly defined program of economic and social development. Second, the statistical agency was granted autonomy and freed from possible politically motivated interventions. Third, a leading political figure (Trevor Manuel) provided strong and sustained support. Fourth, Statistics SA adopted a comprehensive strategic planning exercise and a work program tailored to the demand from its clientele. The demand-driven work program was accompanied by programs to upgrade staff skills. Linking work programs and skill availability contributed to the development of sustainable capacities Aligning courses offered by academic institutions to the needs of staff played a critical role in equipping staff with the tools they needed to perform their duties.

When undertaking reforms, multiple challenges arise and mistakes are bound to be made. They should not deter policy makers from forging ahead. Mistakes provide platforms to learn and improve. Sometimes very unpopular decisions have to be made, such as introducing new methodology or discontinuing series that have become redundant or irrelevant.

Streamlining processes between Statistics SA and the South African Revenue Service (SARS) has been slow in taking off. Statistical units in line departments and agencies need strengthening. Statistics SA has a role to play in providing leadership and in better integrating its activities into the overall statistical system. Doing so would yield large payoffs and greatly increase the efficiency of data collection.

An area where further investments are needed is the creation of user-friendly databases supported by metadata systems. These investments would greatly enhance the ability of Statistics SA to service its growing clientele in the public and private sectors and civil society at large. Such investment would be consistent with the international trend of establishing open data systems. Further reaching out to users would help overcome any lingering doubts left over from the earlier era concerning the institution's credibility.

Looking ahead, Statistics SA needs to take stock of its strengths and weaknesses. The institution would be well served by using the IMF's Data Quality Assessment Framework (DQAF) to undertake a self-assessment. For such an exercise to have value, relevant stakeholders need to participate.

Another option would be to invite an external agency (for example, Eurostat, the statistical agency of the European Commission) to conduct a global assessment of South Africa's statistical system. It would be extremely useful to understand why the system, which includes Statistics SA and other data collection agencies, is not functioning properly in a country where the national statistics office works well and the statistician general is the head of the whole statistical system.

Such assessment would help in Statistics SA's planning exercises. In the next plan, it will be very important to look into nontraditional areas of labor and economic statistics, the impact of big data on the national statistical system, the steps necessary to make data open, and the preparations needed to prepare the statistical system to report on the post-2015 developments to be able to measure the sustainable development goals.

References

FFC (Financial and Fiscal Commission). 1995. *Recommendations for the Allocation of Financial Resources to the National and Provincial Governments for the 1996/97 Fiscal Year.* Pretoria.

Kahimbaara, J. A. 2001. "South African South-to-South Cooperation." Paper prepared for the PARIS21 Annual Consortium Meeting, Paris, October 4–5.

Lehohla, P. J. 2009. *Statistics South Africa in Transition: Reflections on a Decade of Statistical Practice, 1994–2004.* Cape Town.

———. 2011. "A Decade at the Helm: Critical Reflections." Statistics South Africa. http://www.statssa.gov.za/news_archive/SG_AGM20101206.asp.

Orkin, M. F., P. J. Lehohla, and J. A. Kahimbaara. 1998. "Social Transformation and the Relationship between Users and Producers of Official Statistics: The Case of the 1996 Population Census in South Africa." *Statistical Journal of the United Nations Economic Commission for Europe* 15 (3): 265–79.

Statistics South Africa. 2010. *Strategic Plan 2010/11–2014/15.* Pretoria.

CHAPTER 6

Expanding HIV/AIDS Treatment

Patrick Lumumba Osewe and Yogan Pillay

Introduction

South Africa's history of sustained oppression and two-tier service provision created a deeply unequal society. Although the country has been under democratic rule for two decades and enjoyed solid and consistent economic growth during this period, the gap between rich and poor is widening, and health outcomes are poor in comparison with the level of investment (although they are starting to show some improvement). Challenges are especially acute in remote, rural, and poor urban areas, where unemployment remains high and infrastructure, access to services, and education are inadequate. Apartheid policies spawned high-density urban population clusters in informal settlements that have not improved much, despite a large public housing program.

Although the government spends a larger proportion of gross domestic product (GDP) on health than most other African countries, inequalities mean that outcomes remain far below those of other upper-middle-income countries (table 6.1). About 40 percent of total health expenditure is spent on just 17 percent of the population—people with access to health insurance, largely the formally employed.

These structural, societal, and cultural challenges exacerbate South Africa's high disease burden. The country has a quadruple burden of disease: extremely high prevalence of HIV and tuberculosis (TB), an emerging epidemic of noncommunicable diseases, very high morbidity and mortality from accidents and violence, and high maternal and infant mortality. Of these, HIV and TB (most people with HIV die from TB) are the leading cause of illness and death among working-age South Africans. Both diseases disproportionally affect poor people.

Patrick Lumumba Osewe is the Program Leader for Education, Health and Social Protection for the South Africa Country Management Unit of the World Bank; and Yogan Pillay is the Deputy Director General of the National Department of Health (NDOH), South Africa. This chapter benefited from extensive interviews with current and former government officials as well as from comments by peer reviewer Barry Kistnasamy, Commissioner, Compensation Fund, National Department of Health.

Table 6.1 Health Expenditure and Outcomes in Selected Upper-Middle-Income Countries

Country	Percent of GDP spent on health, 2012	Life expectancy at birth, 2012	Under-five mortality rate per 1,000 live births, 2012	Maternal mortality rate per 100,000 live births, 2013
Algeria	5.2	71	32	89
Brazil	9.3	74	21	69
China	5.4	75	19	32
Ecuador	6.4	76	24	87
Latvia	6.0	74	8	13
Peru	5.1	75	21	89
Russian Federation	6.3	70	12	24
South Africa	8.8	62 (2013 estimates)	41 (2013 estimates)	140
Turkey	6.3	75	20	20
Thailand	3.9	74	13	26

Source: South African statistics for life expectancy and under-five mortality are from the *Rapid Mortality Surveillance Report 2013* (Dorrington and others 2014). All other statistics are from the World Bank.

The priority most keenly felt at the national and provincial levels is the need to cope with the growing demand for antiretroviral therapy (ART). The HIV epidemic in Sub-Saharan Africa reached vastly higher proportions than in any other region in the world. South Africa has the largest number of people infected globally, with an estimated 6.3 million people living with HIV (UNAIDS 2013), and the fourth-highest HIV prevalence. The proportion of people with HIV rose from 10.6 percent in 2008 to 12.2 percent in 2012, although part of the increase may reflect that large numbers of people are on ART and thus living longer (Shisana and others 2014).

South Africa's public policy response to HIV/AIDS dates back to 1992, when the National AIDS Coordinating Committee of South Africa (NACOSA) was formed. In 1994 the first National AIDS Plan (NAP) for South Africa was developed and adopted by the government of national unity led by Nelson Mandela.

The government recognized early on that there was potential for HIV/AIDS to become a major national threat. Affordability of medicines, political differences, and poorly informed policies delayed reform of the health service and the implementation of a robust ART program to cope with the burden, however. Slow development of the HIV program infrastructure, limited political commitment and attention against the backdrop of setting up a new democratic government, and numerous conflicts between stakeholders set the stage for a fractured and ineffective response. As a result, it proved difficult to decrease HIV transmission, and HIV prevalence rose from 4 percent in 1994 to almost 23 percent in 1998 (Simelela and others 2015).

Into the 2000s, the formal positions of the second democratic government on the link between HIV and AIDS were undercut by reluctance on the part of government to acknowledge such causality. This, and the prices of antiretroviral medicines delayed funding for appropriate medical treatments. After more than a decade of denial, controversies, and weak responses, South Africa emerged as one of the countries most affected by HIV/AIDS.

International and domestic pressures from a growing civil society movement, heavy criticism of the then health minister's stance that nutritional choices could benefit people with HIV more than ART, and a rapidly expanding HIV/AIDS epidemic eventually led the government to resolve the debates and focus on ART as one of the central elements of the national HIV response.

Since 2009 South Africa has mobilized massively to address the challenge. ART has been expanded to millions of people. A countrywide HIV prevention program launched in 2010 has counseled and tested more than 15 million people, and the country is currently implementing the largest ART program in the world (WHO, UNAIDS, and UNICEF 2013). Domestic funding for the HIV response was estimated at $1.9 billion in 2011 alone, with strategic assistance and additional funding provided by the U.S. President's Emergency Plan for AIDS Relief (PEPFAR) and the Global Fund to Fight AIDS, Tuberculosis and Malaria (the Global Fund). These efforts have led to impressive results, including a sharp decline in new HIV infection among children, an estimated eight-year gain in average life expectancy at birth (from 54 to 62 years), and the provision of HIV treatment to some 2.2 million people in 2012 (WHO, UNAIDS, and UNICEF 2013; Dorrington and others 2014; Shisana and others 2014).

How did South Africa achieve these results? How did it improve the availability and quality of HIV treatment? This chapter examines the key institutional reforms that catalyzed the rapid turnaround in the national ART program.

The Policy Challenge

For well over a decade, the HIV/AIDS policy-making and policy-implementation process in South Africa was widely criticized. A highly fragmented post-apartheid health system combined with political and ideological conflict between various HIV/AIDS stakeholders—including AIDS activists, civil society, political leaders, and the scientific and medical communities—led to a very slow start in addressing the country's need for a universal ART program (Schneider and Stein 2001; Wouters, van Rensburg, and Meulemans 2010). The establishment of the national ART program in 2003 and its massive scale-up from 2009 onward thus represented a huge shift in the country's HIV/AIDS policy.

In 1992 the government created NACOSA. Shortly thereafter, the government crafted the NAP, which the new government of national unity led by Nelson Mandela adopted in 1994 (Schneider and Stein 2001; Wouters, van Rensburg, and Meulemans 2010).

Under the new government, AIDS was prioritized as a "presidential lead project," which meant that it received preferential funding. A National AIDS Program was quickly established, with its program director situated within the Department of Health. Placing the program director within the Department of Health was viewed as problematic because it designated HIV/AIDS as a health issue rather than as a multisectoral issue, which international best practices have long recommended. It also meant that implementation of the NAP would be overseen by provincial AIDS coordinators who were recruited from old structures, rather than the new network of AIDS activities, and who had limited authority and limited connections with civil society (Schneider and Stein 2001; Wouters, van Rensburg, and Meulemans 2010). This dynamic, coupled with limited political commitment and attention against the backdrop of setting up a new democratic government, contributed to the slow development of the HIV/AIDS program infrastructure. Early implementation of the NAP was embedded within the wider framework of democratic transformation, evolving decentralization, and weak health system capacity—all of which limited the government's ability to implement its policy.

In 1999, approximately 4.2 million South Africans were living with HIV (Wouters, van Rensburg, and Meulemans 2010). In 2000 the South Africa National AIDS Council (SANAC) was established to build consensus across government, civil society, and other stakeholders in the response to HIV; and the government launched its first five-year Strategic Plan for HIV, AIDS, and Sexually Transmitted Infections (STIs) (2000–05) (Willian 2004; Wouters, van Rensburg, and Meulemans 2010). The prevailing view at the highest level in government at the time, however, was that ART was not effective, not affordable, and not an appropriate policy response to HIV/AIDS (Nattrass 2008; Wouters, van Rensburg, and Meulemans 2010); the government rejected the widely acknowledged scientific evidence that HIV caused AIDS. While the position of the technical staff in government was in line with the widely acknowledged scientific evidence that HIV caused AIDS, the questioning of this at the highest level created confusion and undermined focus on the key actions required.

A weakened healthcare infrastructure was another key institutional constraint in the early 2000s. Human resources capacity gaps in the health sector posed a risk to the scale-up of a national ART program (Butler 2005; Dickinson and Buse 2008; Wouters, van Rensburg, and Meulemans 2010). Compared with other diseases and health issues, HIV/AIDS was neglected; where available, ART drugs were distributed mainly by nongovernmental organizations (NGOs). According to Johnson (2004, 123), the "centralized and closed leadership style ... rendered the bureaucracy largely unable and unwilling to mobilize and coordinate around a common vision a range of actors inside and outside of government, and across social and sectoral divides."

Civil society formally challenged the government's position and authority in the Constitutional Court. In 2002 the Treatment Action Campaign (TAC)—a leading advocate of HIV/AIDS treatment and health care—along with the AIDS Law Project (now called Section 27) challenged the government's policy on HIV treatment in court, arguing for universal provision of ART to HIV-positive mothers through the public health system (Butler 2005; Venter 2013). Invoking the constitutional right to health for all South Africans case, the TAC won a landmark victory that influenced the future course of government HIV/AIDS policy (Jones 2005; Vandormael 2007). "Government policy, and, more accurately, by implication, key figures within it, had been openly questioned in public and ordered by the court to be changed," writes Jones (2005, 441). Also during this period, two provinces (Gauteng and KwaZulu-Natal) asserted their provincial autonomy and announced their decisions to expand their pilot programs to provide ART to HIV-positive mothers, defying national government policy (Dickinson and Buse 2008; Simelela and Venter 2014). In the face of mounting international and domestic public pressure, including a civil disobedience campaign, formal litigation through the Constitutional Court, and the strategic use of mass media led by the TAC and other civil society actors, the government reviewed its approach to HIV/AIDS policy.

Two competing policy models were advanced: a social mobilization/biomedical paradigm, supported largely by AIDS activists, and a nationalist/ameliorative paradigm, supported largely by the government (Butler 2005). Proponents of the biomedical model advocated for clear political leadership to lead the national response, increased mobilization of resources to address the epidemic, the use of ART to prevent mother-to-child transmission of HIV, and a significantly expanded national ART program. Advocacy for HIV treatment was viewed within a rights-based framework and as a class-based struggle to secure access to treatment for the poor (Dickinson and Buse 2008).

Civil society, AIDS activists, scientists, and health professionals pushed for widespread provision of ART. Initially, they were unsuccessful because of the government's arguments about the prices and toxicity of the drugs and exploitation by pharmaceutical companies, and the refusal to recognize the need for reform (Nattrass 2008).

The second model questioned the scientific evidence that HIV causes AIDS. It supported mass communication campaigns and life skills education emphasizing prevention and behavioral change, the use of nutrition and traditional medicine in HIV treatment, and antipoverty programming to address the social determinants of the disease (Butler 2005).

Several theories have been posited to explain why elements within government questioned the scientific evidence that HIV caused AIDS. Some have claimed that this reflected anticolonial, Africanist ideology and a desire not to see Africa blamed for a sexually driven epidemic (see Nattrass 2008 and Butler 2005). The government's position was challenged by scientists, activists, and health professionals.

The cost of the government's position was enormous. According to one estimate, 330,000 premature deaths (or 2.2 million person-years) could have been prevented if ART had been provided and widely administered between 2000 and 2005 (Chigwedere and others 2008).

Addressing the Policy Challenge

Before 2004 ART was available through the private sector and a small number of NGOs. Systematic reforms to South Africa's HIV policy addressed the rapidly escalating need for treatment in the public sector and equal access to health care, especially for marginalized groups.

Making It Happen • http://dx.doi.org/10.1596/978-1-4648-0768-8

Policy Making

The combination of international and domestic criticism and the Constitutional Court decision eventually led to consensus over HIV policy (Fassin and Schneider 2003). In April 2002, the Cabinet decided to implement a number of measures to reinforce ART. These efforts included strengthening civil society partnerships and developing a plan to roll out ART nationwide. In July 2002, the government established a joint task team with the Department of Health and the Treasury to investigate the financing of an enhanced response to HIV/AIDS and examine treatment options that would enable the public health sector to provide comprehensive care. During this process, clinical experts developed treatment protocols that included ART for adults and children. Support from international donors—such as the Clinton Foundation and PEPFAR—accelerated progress (Simelela and others 2015).

In August 2003, the government announced a significant shift in its commitment to making HIV treatment available throughout the public sector. Tensions within the Cabinet were cited as having had a significant effect on the government's decision to roll out ART. Senior party officials such as the ANC's head of elections, Manne Dipico; the former director-general of health, Olive Shisana; and the party's chief strategist and government communications head, Joel Netshitenzhe, were believed to have been instrumental in driving the change (Nattrass 2008).

At its August 2003 meeting, the Cabinet received the task team's report, which included options for scaling up access to ART (Willian 2004). The Department of Health was instructed to develop a detailed operational plan by the end of September 2003, including development of provincial implementation plans, a schedule for rollout across district hospitals and health centers, and a forecast of staffing requirements. The Cabinet announced the first Operational Plan for Comprehensive HIV and AIDS Care, Management and Treatment for South Africa, in November 2003; and the Mbeki government initiated the ART program in December 2003, through the national Department of Health, with the goal of having 54,000 people in treatment by March 2004.

By March 2005, all of the country's 53 districts had at least one service point for AIDS-related care and treatment (Simelela and others 2015), but scale-up remained slow because of long public debates about the toxicity and economics of the drugs. During this time, external funding—from donors such as the Global Fund and PEPFAR—continued to play a significant role in supporting the country's HIV care and treatment services.

As a result of these efforts, in 2006 SANAC developed the National Strategic Plan for HIV, AIDS, and STIs 2007–11. The process—considered "laborious, politically charged, but widely consultative" (Simelela and Venter 2014, 250)—involved an expert team of clinicians, scientists, economists, and activists. The plan outlined an ambitious target of providing ART to 80 percent of eligible people by 2011. In September 2005, only 85,000 people were enrolled in ART.

By December 2007 an estimated 424,000 people were receiving ART in the public health sector (Simelela and Venter 2014).

Policy Implementation

South Africa's HIV/AIDS response evolved rapidly after 2009; the program is now the largest in the world. The national election in 2009 resulted in a change of leadership and a heightened political commitment to HIV testing, treatment, and care. The new president, Jacob Zuma, and his minister of health, Aaron Motsoaledi, quickly launched a comprehensive government response to tackle the AIDS epidemic, including outspoken public acknowledgment of the urgency required to address the challenges, a countrywide prevention and testing campaign that greatly increased the testing rate, and treatment for all HIV-positive babies under the age of one. The open and consultative leadership style exhibited by the new government on this issue helped facilitate the rapid scale-up of South Africa's ART program.

In 2010, the first year of Zuma's administration, a wide-scale national initiative was launched aimed at counseling and testing 15 million people by June 2011 as a precursor to boosting ART program enrollment. The president himself was publicly tested for HIV during this campaign, in an effort to promote openness and expand knowledge and understanding of the epidemic. In his 2011 health budget policy speech, Health Minister Motsoaledi announced that 11.9 million (of 50 million) people had been tested for HIV that year. The Department of Health's role was particularly instrumental in building the capacity of the National Health Laboratory Service to test large numbers of people. By June 2012, 20 million people had been counseled and tested, according to the government.

In addition to testing and counseling, the government strategically leveraged the nationwide campaign to promote behavior change and regular condom use, voluntary medical male circumcision, and prevention of mother-to-child transmission. Minister Motsoaledi has been noted for his strong leadership, especially his efforts to engage civil society and key political leaders, mobilize public support for the nationwide testing and counseling campaign, and revitalize the public health sector (Joachim and Sinclair 2013). Renewed political will coupled with political backing to implement a more robust HIV response helped increase public buy-in and support, paving a path forward.

Under Motsoaledi's political leadership, HIV treatment services expanded by 75 percent between 2009 and 2011 (UNAIDS 2012). In 2010 South Africa released new guidelines on prevention of mother-to-child transmission that were in line with recommendations by the World Health Organization. Since its first plan, it has elaborated two additional strategic plans, the most recent one published in early 2012. The National Strategic Plan on HIV, STIs, and TB 2012–16 has articulated ambitious HIV treatment goals, including enrolling at least 80 percent of eligible people in ART programs by 2016 and reducing the mortality rate five years after initiation to 30 percent.

In 2010 the government also introduced task shifting as a key strategy to increase access to ART, provide more points of care, and improve adherence to and management of ART. Before this shift, ART services were primarily doctor initiated and hospital based. Under the new model, nurses were trained to administer ART, community health workers (or lay counselors) were trained to perform HIV tests, and pharmacy assistants were trained to dispense ART (Wet, Wouters, and Engelbrecht 2012). Task shifting was key in addressing the chronic shortage of health care workers, reducing bottlenecks in the health care system, and supporting government treatment targets. Expansion of the ART program led to an increase in ART facilities countrywide, estimated at 2,552 in 2011 (SANAC 2011).

As the program has been scaled up, quality—as defined by the number of patients receiving a viral load—has decreased.[1] In addition, poor infrastructure, drug stock-outs, lack of training in the treatment and care of children, and worker burnout have led to dissatisfaction among health care workers and negative patient perceptions about the quality of care they receive. These issues threaten the successful expansion of the ART program and need to be adequately addressed.

When Motsoaledi was appointed minister of health, he presented the country's HIV statistics to President Zuma, who asked him to present them to the Cabinet. Given the scale of the problem and the devastation the epidemic had caused, the Cabinet decided that additional domestic funding would have to be found in the national health budget to accelerate the response.

The government's commitment has been financed primarily through the national health budget. The Comprehensive HIV/AIDS Conditional Grant (ring-fenced transfers from the national department to provinces) remains the main funding mechanism for HIV/AIDS in the health sector. South Africa significantly increased public expenditure to meet its targets for initiating ART (estimates indicate that public sector AIDS spending in South Africa increased fivefold between 2006 and 2011), with an estimated $1.9 billion from public resources spent in 2011 alone (WHO, UNAIDS, and UNICEF 2013). The initial cost of the ART program was estimated by a model put together in 2000 by the Actuarial Society of South Africa. This estimate was used by the Joint Health and Treasury Task Team to calculate the likely budget for a comprehensive care and treatment package. Flexibility was built into the initial budget in order to cover escalating implementation costs.

A National AIDS Spending Assessment was completed in 2011. It examined the money spent on different aspects of the HIV program and assessed whether it produced value for money. The AIDS 2031 consortium examined various policy scenarios to estimate the future costs associated with each. According to an August 2013 report, the estimated cost of maintaining the country's 2.3 million patients on ART in 2012/13 ranged from R 6.8 billion to R 11.6 billion, depending on the costing model used (see table 6.2).

The government's decision to invest in new technologies, particularly GenExpert for rapid diagnosis of TB, and its commitment to develop

Table 6.2 Annual Expenditure on Antiretroviral Therapy in South Africa, 2007–12

Year	Total expenditure (millions of rand)	Percent of public health expenditures	Percent of total public expenditures	Percent of GDP
2007	2,006.2	14.8	0.4	0.097
2008	2,885.4	17.6	0.5	0.125
2009	4,376.1	22.8	0.6	0.179
2010	6,051.8	26.2	0.7	0.227
2011	7,493.0	29.1	0.8	0.257
2012	8,824.6	32.0	0.9	0.276

Source: SANAC 2013.
Note: $1 = R 8.3. Figures for 2011 and 2012 are estimates.

state-owned pharmaceutical manufacturing capacity, which should significantly reduce the future costs of ART, have also strengthened implementation of the HIV treatment policy.

Overcoming Obstacles

From 1999 to 2008, political resistance to the scale-up of ART, particularly from the Mbeki administration, was a primary obstacle to changing the country's HIV policy. Mbeki himself was the primary skeptic. Along with his minister of health and a few allies, he was very isolated in his denial.[2] From 1999 to 2008, reticence to the scale-up of ART, particularly from the Mbeki administration, was a primary obstacle to the effectiveness of the country's HIV program.

Civil society strategically used social mobilization and advocacy to apply political pressure on the government. The civil disobedience campaign launched by the TAC, coupled with its direct engagement with formal institutional channels through litigation, leveraged action. Although the ruling by the court did not precipitate a direct change in the general HIV/AIDS policy at the time, it is widely considered to have paved the way for universal access to ART (London and Schneider 2012; Joachim and Sinclair 2013). Strategic alliances with other civil society organizations, including the Southern African HIV Clinicians Society and Médecins Sans Frontières, facilitated a broader social response and a united front against the government's intractability (Venter 2013). The change of guard during the 2008 election (more precisely Mbeki's resignation) provided the catalytic shift in overcoming political resistance to ART.

Poor relations between government and civil society threatened the scale-up of HIV treatment. Renewed political leadership and commitment by the Zuma administration played a critical role in gaining the trust of civil society and reenergizing the public health sector to take on the task of improving HIV policy and service delivery. In sharp contrast to the previous administration, in 2009 Minister of Health Motsoaledi acknowledged that South Africa had "spent the last 10 years pedaling backwards" (Simelela and others 2015, 4–5).

On World AIDS Day in December 2009, President Zuma announced significant changes to the national AIDS prevention and treatment policies, signaling a break with the previous administration's position and ushering in a new era in South Africa's HIV/AIDS policy making. Both the health minister and President Zuma considered the swift reversal of the HIV policy a political priority. They were vocal and highly visible in their efforts to support rapid change and build consensus among key stakeholders, publicly campaigning for and championing HIV prevention and treatment.

Once the ART policy was approved, initial access to drugs for public sector patients was limited, in large part by the doctor-centric, hospital-based approach of the health system at the time. The 2003 operational plan indicated that the Department of Health planned to inspect all facilities that were preparing to offer ART treatment, with the aim of awarding one-off accreditation. The procedure was based on the reasoning that assessment was necessary to ensure that facilities had staff with sufficient skills to deal with the complexity of the program and to administer drugs safely and effectively. No arrangement was made for periodic reaccreditation or regular inspections.

Because of the large numbers of patients and the challenges brought by the bureaucratic process of accreditation, the plan was abandoned. In 2009 the accreditation system was revised in favor of a broad training and facilitation scheme for all institutions, devolution of responsibility for treatment (task shifting) from clinicians to nurse practitioners, and the setting of targets. This strategy ensured that all public health facilities were equipped with the capacity to provide ART.

Sequencing Reforms

The development and rollout of South Africa's HIV treatment policy has been a long and complex process. It has included both watershed moments and incremental approaches.

Three politically related phases framed the key policy challenges around South Africa's ART program, each testing assumptions and leading to certain changes in the policy process. Years of international and domestic pressure led to a dramatic shift in the government's HIV treatment policy in 2003/04. The shift was profoundly influenced by the TAC's court victory against the government in 2002, which tested assumptions about civil society's role in effecting policy reform and the degree to which the courts could intervene in executive decision making on social policy (Fassin and Schneider 2003). From 2004 to 2008, although the government made a significant shift in its commitment to making HIV treatment available throughout the public sector, lack of political will and obstruction from senior political figures stalled effective implementation, and change was slow. After 2008 a new political dispensation steered by President Zuma and the more open and inclusive leadership of Minister of Health Aaron Motsoaledi helped facilitate the massive and rapid scale-up of the program (Venter 2013). In this period, as a consequence both of pressure on pharmaceutical companies with the support of international organizations such as the Clinton Foundation and of economies of scale, the prices of antiretroviral (ARV) drugs had significantly declined.

Making It Happen • http://dx.doi.org/10.1596/978-1-4648-0768-8

Results Achieved

South Africa's ART program was widely and rapidly implemented, and positive results are starting to be reported. These achievements were attained against a background of "multiple system failure across a range of programs, including maternal and child health, HIV/AIDS, TB and others, with a devastating combined impact," according to Vision 2030, the government's National Development Plan (NPC 2011). HIV had a huge, rapid, and transformative impact on the country's disease burden and health system demands, leaving policy makers floundering to address the constantly changing epidemiological profile.

In the past decade, South Africa extended treatment to almost 35 percent of infected people (2.2 million of 6.3 million), including almost 80 percent of people classified as needing treatment under previous technical guidelines (before changes to the qualifying CD4 [a glycoprotein] count). Average life expectancy at birth increased from 54 in 2006 to 62 in 2011, and new infections among children declined by 63 percent (WHO, UNAIDS, and UNICEF 2013; Dorrington and others 2014).

The ART program also spurred the transition to primary health care in a series of nationwide health reforms. It catalyzed significant investments to strengthen the national health care system. The government is strongly pushing management of HIV down to the lowest levels of the chain, creating the incentives necessary for upgrading and extending the primary health care network. The government's success with ART was the motivating force for completing the wider health system reform embarked upon in the immediate post-apartheid era. That reform is intended to address fundamental problems in access, quality, and poor return on health investments.

What strategy will be successful in achieving universal health care coverage remains unclear, however. With plans to move forward with a national health insurance scheme, the central government is attempting a major reform to create universal coverage. It is hoped that this reform will leverage some of the gains that have resulted from the ART program in access to services and strengthening of the primary health care system.

Conclusions: Success Factors, Challenges, and Lessons Learned

Despite more than a decade of denial and the fact that a robust five-year plan for ART was elaborated only in 2003, expansion of services and coverage has expanded rapidly and broadly throughout all provinces of South Africa since 2009. Improvements are evident, with the number of people accessing ART and life expectancy rising and new infections among children falling.

Several key success factors and lessons learned led to the rapid turnaround in South Africa's HIV treatment program. The first was renewed political leadership and commitment. Motsoaledi's appointment as minister of health in 2009 marked a reversal in the country's controversial HIV treatment policy and response. Motsoaledi quickly prioritized HIV prevention and treatment;

advocated for better integration between the HIV, TB, and antenatal programs, and supported task shifting to lower cadres of staff; his style was more open and democratic. He reasserted the government's commitment to stemming the tide of the epidemic as he embarked on a highly publicized crusade to expand prevention and treatment efforts (Joachim and Sinclair 2013).

The second factor was a well-articulated national policy and the alignment of the architecture of the ART program with the National Strategic Plan 2012–2016. In 2011 SANAC revised and released the National Strategic Plan on HIV, STIs, and TB 2012–2016. The National Strategic Plan 2012–2016 sets out the target of enrolling 80 percent of the estimated 2.5 million people in need of treatment by 2016. The government has pledged to increase its budget allocation for ART treatment to meet the 80 percent goal by 2016. Changes, however, are occurring in the context of a huge nationwide health reform aimed at refocusing the health system on primary health care and raising the quality of health services in preparation for the launch of a national health insurance scheme. Piloting of this reform, which is envisaged to take 14 years, began in 2012. The plan demonstrated a renewed government commitment to reset it targets, aim higher, and provide universal access to life-long ART. The policy clearly integrated HIV/AIDS and TB, which was particularly important given high coinfection rates, and identified the most at-risk populations (including mobile and migrant populations, sex workers, drug users, and men who have sex with men) and transmission "hot spots." Partly because of these robust policy changes, the ART program expanded widely, leading to reductions in deaths from HIV. The changes in the health service that are already underway—related to changing over to mainly primary health care and full integration with the other public health programs, such as TB and maternal and child health, and screening and early diagnosis—are in line with the goals of the National Strategic Plan. The strengthening of prevention of new infections in children, adolescents, and adults is also in line with those goals.

Third, programs need to be well designed and implemented to allow them to address inequalities and establish an effective health system. South Africa's hospital-based ART program provided services initially because it bypassed the most severe constraints of service access to target populations as patients had to go to specialist hospital facilities. As the number of patients diagnosed increased, the economic toll and workloads became too great for the country and its hospitals. Although South Africa had started to show good progress in health outcomes, even without strong political backing domestically, other much-needed health system reforms were hindered. With widespread and diverse system constraints, the only plausible way to tackle HIV was to institute a program that provided effective services within the normal health delivery system but that had its own supply chain, staff, and clinic space. Decentralization of the ART program facilitated this process. As a result, the ART program has been an effective vehicle for accelerating primary health care reform.

In particular, task shifting became crucial. A key obstacle to the expansion of ART was the shortage of doctors trained in initiating treatment. By adopting nurse-led ART and additional task shifting to lower-level staff, South Africa reduced the cost of treatment, improved access to services, and reduced the burden on clinics providing ART. In line with international best practices, in 2009 the minister of health requested that every facility in the country have at least one nurse trained to provide ART. In 2010 South Africa introduced nurse-initiated ART and allowed community health workers to perform finger-prick HIV testing (Wet, Wouters, and Engelbrecht 2012). As a result of this process, ART treatment was devolved to lower-level facilities, increasing access to a much larger number of patients. This decentralized model demonstrated in inner-city sites and elsewhere that primary health care clinics have the capacity to effectively initiate and monitor ART, according to Venter (2013).

Fourth, a participatory approach, engaging patients and other stakeholders, is key. For example, the inclusion of patient advocates can improve policy implementation. Studies indicate that the inclusion of lay people as patient advocates and the idea of an "informed patient" in the ART program have been extremely important in increasing retention of patients, including children (Grimwood and others 2012). High adherence levels and problem-solving ability have been observed in patients taught how to manage their illness (Venter 2013). As a result of patient engagement and inclusion, particularly in communities with high treatment literacy interventions, patients have staged protests over drug stock-outs or perceived poor service delivery. They have improved dialogue between patients, communities, and health care providers and facilitated resolution of emerging issues (Venter 2013).

Strategic collaboration with other stakeholders, particularly civil society, is also critical to the success of HIV/AIDS response efforts. Community leadership by members of social advocacy groups and other grassroots organizations has been essential worldwide in driving the response to the epidemic (Trapence and others 2012). In South Africa, collaborative and constructive partnerships with civil society were critical to the success of the institutional reform objectives. The growth of a strong, vigorous civil society movement rooted among people living with HIV/AIDS was a defining feature of the country's response and the growing inclusiveness of government policy debates. Civil society proved more successful than the government in educating people in the community, including young people in schools. These groups not only advocate for equitable access to relevant health care but are also involved in wider approaches, such as research and advocacy of human rights.

Finally, the use of international benchmark prices can reduce the cost of ART. Reforming its tender process to increase competition among suppliers and improve transparency saved the South African government millions of dollars. Key factors in the success of this process were the careful review of tender language, the inclusion of preference points for local manufacturing, and the implementation of mechanisms to strengthen a fair and transparent evaluation process. These and other reform strategies allowed the government to reduce ART costs by 53 percent between 2011 and 2012 (UNAIDS 2013). These lessons have been shared largely through UNAIDS and articles on South Africa's HIV program.

Despite the progress made, several challenges need to be addressed. First, monitoring and evaluation are inadequate. The initial reporting procedure adopted in 2004, based on World Health Organization recommendations, proved too burdensome. As a result, most sites abandoned it. Local registers were created, but reporting on key indicators was inconsistent and sometimes inaccurate. Because of costs and limited staff capacity and training, outcome reporting has been supported primarily by research-driven, donor-supported sites that have the resources to invest in more sophisticated monitoring and evaluation systems. The Department of Health has introduced a new three-tier strategy for monitoring ART provision that seeks to address these weaknesses (Venter 2013).

Second, the sustainability of the ART program needs to be addressed in the context of other health reforms. In 2010 the government revised its guidelines on who should be immediately enrolled into the ART program and who should be referred to a wellness program. It continually updates these guidelines to take into account new scientific evidence and international recommendations (from the World Health Organization, for example). Estimated unit costs from 2007 to 2010 show that delivery efficiency is increasing but that drivers of expenditure vary across provinces. Comparison of provincial spending with the estimated numbers of people in need of treatment indicates that allocations and spending seem to be determined based on capacity to deliver rather than need. In the Northern Cape and Western Cape provinces, for example, spending was far higher than necessary given the HIV prevalence, whereas in KwaZulu-Natal and Gauteng, expenditure fell far short of need. As spending on ART has dramatically increased, sustainability at the national level is a concern (Simelela and others 2012). Robust models of care need to be developed and implemented to increase access and lower costs (Cleary 2010). The social grant system is also in the process of being overhauled; it is at the consultation stage. This reform aims to tackle the key questions of access, beneficiary identification and verification, and grant distribution.

Finally, although users largely welcomed the reformed health policies (Harrison 2009), nurses felt overwhelmed. A countrywide strike was called as a protest against the lack of increase in salary in relation to the heavier workload. Looking forward, the ART program should capitalize on nurse-driven health care to counteract the shortage of doctors.

Notes

1. Personal communication from Yogan Pillay, National Department of Health (NDOH), February 11, 2015.

2. Personal communication from Nicolli Nattrass, University of Cape Town, February 10, 2015.

References

Butler, A. 2005. "South Africa's AIDS Policy: 1994–2004: How Can It Be Explained?" *African Affairs* 104 (417): 591–614.

Chigwedere, P., G. R. Seage, III, S. Gruskin, T. H. Lee, and M. Essex. 2008. "Estimating the Lost Benefits of Antiretroviral Drug Use in South Africa." *Journal of Acquired Immune Deficiency Syndrome* 49 (4): 410–15.

Cleary, S. 2010. "Equity and Efficiency in Scaling Up Access to HIV-Related Interventions in Resource-Limited Settings." *Current Opinion in HIV AIDS* 5: 210–14.

Dickinson, C., and K. Buse. 2008. "Understanding the Politics of National HIV Policies: The Roles of Institutions, Interests and Ideas." Technical Approach Paper, HLSP Institute, London.

Dorrington R. E., D. Bradshaw, R. Laubscher, and N. Nannan. 2014. *Rapid Mortality Surveillance Report 2013*. Cape Town: South African Medical Research Council. http://www.mrc.ac.za/bod/RapidMortalitySurveillanceReport2013.pdf.

Fassin, D., and H. Schneider. 2003. "The Politics of AIDS in South Africa: Beyond the Controversies." *British Medical Journal* 326: 495–97.

Grimwood A., G. Fatti, E. Mothibi, M. Malahlela, J. Shea, and B. Eley. 2012. "Community Adherence Support Improves Programme Retention in Children on Antiretroviral Treatment: A Multicentre Cohort Study in South Africa." *Journal of the International AIDS Society* 15: 173–81.

Harrison, D. 2009. "An Overview of Health and Health Care in South Africa 1994–2010: Priorities, Progress and Prospects for New Gains." Department of Health, Pretoria.

Joachim, M., and M. Sinclair. 2013. "Reflections on Ministerial Leadership: HIV/AIDS Policy Reform in South Africa." *Harvard School of Public Health*. http://www.ministerialleadershipinhealth.org/wp-content/uploads/sites/19/2013/07/HIV-AIDS-Policy-Reform-in-South-Africa-The-Transformation-after-2009.pdf.

Johnson, K. 2004. "The Politics of AIDS Policy Development and Implementation in Post-apartheid South Africa." *Africa Today* 51 (2): 107–28.

Jones, P. S. 2005. "A Test of Governance: Rights-Based Struggles and the Politics of HIV/AIDS Policy in South Africa." *Political Geography* 24 (4): 419–47.

London, L., and H. Schneider. 2012. "Globalisation and Health Inequalities: Can a Human Rights Paradigm Create Space for Civil Society Action?" *Social Science and Medicine* 74: 6–13.

NPC (National Planning Commission). 2011. *The National Development Plan: Vision 2030*. Pretoria.

Nattrass, N. 2008. "AIDS and the Scientific Governance of Medicine in Post-Apartheid South Africa." *African Affairs* 107 (427): 157–76.

Schneider, H. 2002. "On the Fault-Line: The Politics of AIDS Policy in Contemporary South Africa." *African Studies* 61 (1): 145–67.

Schneider, H., and J. Stein. 2001. "Implementing AIDS Policy in Post-Apartheid South Africa." *Social Science and Medicine* 52: 723–31.

Shisana, O., T. Rehle, L. C. Simbayi, K. Zuma, S. Jooste N., Zungu, D. Labadarios, D. Onoya, and others. 2014. *South African National HIV Prevalence, Incidence and Behaviour Survey, 2012*. Cape Town: HSRC Press.

Simelela, N., S. Senabe, C. Sozi, H. Damisoni, and T. Guthrie. 2012. "Spending on ART by Provinces in South Africa: Trends, Cost Drivers, (In)Efficiencies and Sustainability." Paper presented at the 19th International AIDS Conference, Washington, DC, July 22–27.

Simelela, N., and W. D. F. Venter. 2014. "A Brief History of South Africa's Response to HIV." *South Africa Medical Journal* 104 (3): 249–51.

Simelela, N., W. D. F. Venter, Y. Pillay, and P. Barron. 2015. "A Political and Social History of HIV in South Africa." *Current HIV/AIDS Reports* 12 (2): 256–61.

SANAC (South African National AIDS Council). 2011. *National Strategic Plan, 2012–2016*. Pretoria.

———. 2013. *August 2013 Report on Costing Provincial Implementation Plans for HIV/AIDS, STIs, and TB*. Pretoria.

Trapence, G., C. Collins, S. Avrett, and others. 2012. "From Personal Survival to Public Health: Community Leadership by Men Who Have Sex with Men in the Response to HIV." *Lancet* 380: 400–10.

UNAIDS (Joint United Nations Programme on HIV/AIDS). 2012. *UNAIDS World AIDS Day Report 2012*. Geneva: UNAIDS.

———. 2013. *Efficient and Sustainable HIV responses: Case Studies on Country Progress*. Geneva: UNAIDS.

Vandormael, A. 2007. "The TAC's 'Intellectual Campaign' (2000–2004): Social Movements and Epistemic Communities." *Politikon: South African Journal of Political Studies* 34 (2): 217–33.

Venter, F. 2013. "HIV Treatment in South Africa: The Challenges of an Increasingly Successful Antiretroviral Programme." In *South African Health Review 2012/13*, ed by A. Padarath and R. English. Durban: Health Systems Trust.

Wet, K., E. Wouters, and M. Engelbrecht. 2012. "Health System Barriers to Implementation of Collaborative TB and HIV Activities Including Prevention of Mother to Child Transmission in South Africa." *Tropical Medicine and International Health* 17 (5): 658–65.

WHO (World Health Organization), UNAIDS, and UNICEF (United Nations Children's Fund). 2013. *Global Update on HIV Treatment 2013*. Geneva: WHO.

Willian, S. 2004. "Briefing: Recent Changes in the South African Government's HIV/AIDS Policy and Its Implementation." *African Affairs* 103: 109–17.

World Development Indicators. http://data.worldbank.org/data-catalog/world-development-indicators. World Bank, Washington, DC.

Wouters, E., H. C. J. van Rensburg, and H. Meulemans. 2010. "The National Strategic Plan of South Africa: What Are the Prospects of Success after the Repeated Failure of Previous AIDS Policy?" *Health Policy and Planning* 25: 171–85.

CHAPTER 7

Reforming the Social Assistance System

Lucilla Maria Bruni

Introduction

In 1994 South Africa's social assistance system had fewer than 3 million beneficiaries, and the system was characterized by low coverage, strong imbalances, and discrimination. Today it covers nearly 16 million people, through a set of transfers that are considerably more progressive and pro-poor than those of other middle-income countries, with 69 percent of all cash transfers going to the bottom 40 percent of the income distribution (World Bank 2014). Government resources devoted to social assistance rose from R 14 billion in 1994 to R 111 billion in 2014. The 2014 figure represents 3.4 percent of gross domestic product (GDP), a larger share than the average for Sub-Saharan Africa (2.8 percent) and many Asian, Latin American, and European countries.[1] Empirical research suggests that the grant system helped reduce poverty, stabilize the annual growth of real earnings, and increase employment and labor force participation among women (Eyal and Woolard 2011; Bhorat and Cassim 2014).

Reforming social assistance in South Africa has been a long and complex process that began in the mid-1980s and is still ongoing. The apartheid government had slowly started opening the social assistance system to the African population; by 1994 benefit programs for old age and disability had been extended to all groups (van der Berg 1997; Woolard and Leibbrandt 2011).

As of 1993, however, little was being spent on children, and coverage was limited and highly unequal by race: only 0.2 percent of African children were receiving maintenance grants, compared with 1.4 percent of white children, 4.0 percent of Indian children, and 5.0 percent of Coloured children (van der Berg 1997; Woolard and Leibbrandt 2010).

The author is an Economist in the Social Protection and Labor Global Practice at the World Bank. This chapter benefited from extensive interviews with current and former government officials as well as from comments by peer reviewers Alan Gelb, Frances Lund, and John Kruger.

The new government started addressing these challenges through both policy and administrative reform. The main policy step was the introduction of the child support grant in 1999. The grant was designed to follow the child rather than the biological caregiver. Assigned on the basis of poverty status, the grant phased out the old state maintenance grant, a benefit paid mostly to Coloured and Indian single mothers that was eliminated in 2001. The government has since significantly expanded coverage of the child support grant by raising the age of eligibility: the child support grant expanded from 150,000 beneficiaries at its inception in 1998 to about 11.2 million in 2013. The government also pursued a strong administrative reform agenda, by overhauling the management of grants, harmonizing procedures across regions, and greatly improving the administrative process. A remarkable step in this area was the creation of a specialized agency, the South African Social Security Agency (SASSA), responsible for all aspects of administering grants, including application, verification of eligibility, payments, case management, and upkeep of the beneficiary roster.

SASSA started operating social grants in 2006. Since then, an estimated R 2 billion a year has been saved by eliminating ghost beneficiaries and reducing turnaround time. Significant efforts have been devoted to standardizing business processes and improving service. State-of-the-art biometric identification and electronic payments were introduced; they now represent the sole mode of delivery of payments. In 2013/14, 90 percent of all new applications were processed within 21 days across all provinces, and the average cost per transaction fell to R 16 a month, about 5.4 percent of the value of the benefits delivered (SASSA 2014).

Such successful expansion and improvement of the social grant system is unique in Africa and remarkable worldwide. This case study analyzes how South Africa managed such reform. It shows that a combination of commitment, leadership, backing from the constitution, focus on technical soundness, broad countrywide dialogue, and engagement with civil society contributed to this success.

The Policy Challenge

One of the most pressing challenges for the new South African government in 1994 was how to address the high levels of structural poverty and inequality inherited from the apartheid era. More than half the population lived in relative poverty (Leibbrandt and others 2010); this situation was acutely visible because of poverty's correlation with ethnicity and coexistence with great affluence (Seekings 2007). A number of policy instruments were examined to address these challenges, including housing, social services, nutritional support, early childhood development programs, social funds, and traditional welfare programs (Lund 2008).

The government identified social grants as a central instrument, partly because South Africa's Constitution mandates the right to social assistance when individuals cannot provide for themselves or their families and partly because of mounting evidence of the positive impacts that existing social grants (the old-age pension and the disability grant) had on poverty reduction (Case and Deaton 1998). Some observers also viewed social grants as a necessary means to compensate the population for the sometimes tough economic reforms the new government undertook under the Growth, Employment and Redistribution strategy (GEAR), introduced in 1996.

The outcome of the negotiations that led to the democratic government meant that the apartheid-era social assistance system remained largely intact after the elections. Although this system needed deep policy and administrative reform, it provided an existing platform to build such reforms on. The apartheid government had started opening the social assistance system to the black population long before 1994. The old-age pension—the largest program until the child support grant—was extended to the black population in 1944. In 1978 blacks made up 70 percent of pensioners but received 43 percent of the total pension value; by 1990 that proportion had increased to 67 percent (van der Berg 1997). In 1994 social assistance reached less than 3 million people (about 7 percent of the population at the time) (van der Berg 1997), and there were great disparities in the efficiency and reliability of social assistance administration across provinces and regions. The Self-Governing Territory Constitution Act 21 of 1971 established the creation of four independent states (bantustans) and six self-governing territories, "with state and administrative apparatuses as if they were fully functioning countries with their own education, health and welfare services" (Lund 2008, 11). The system led to administrative fragmentation, with 13 national and 4 provincial offices, plus 3 coordinating departments, a costly system aimed strictly at separating the provision of welfare across the races (Lund 2008). Thus, the legacy of apartheid meant that in 1995 the Department of Social Welfare operated with vastly different standards (Patel 2011). Access to public offices was difficult for the majority of poor people, and limited administrative capacity created barriers for basic documentation and registration services.

The state maintenance grant was highly differentiated along racial lines. It was paid mainly to Coloured, Indian, and a small number of white single, widowed, or separated women. Although all South Africans in the former Republic of South Africa were formally eligible for it, in practice African women were largely excluded from access because of the fragmentation in administration described above (Skweyiya 2011).

To address the problem, the government embarked on the long and ambitious reform path to design the right instruments, expand coverage, strengthen the developmental impact, and improve the administration of the social grants system. Harmonization of segmented welfare departments, which had begun during the previous regime, was a key objective of the new government.

The constitutional underpinnings of the right to social assistance gave a great deal of momentum to the harmonization process, through a famous constitutional court case, *Mashavha v. the President of the Republic of South Africa* (box 7.1), in which, for the first time, the Constitutional Court upheld the constitutional right to social assistance. It ruled that delivery of social assistance

Box 7.1 *Mashavha v. the President of the Republic of South Africa*

In 1992 Mr. Mashavha, a manual laborer, was injured in a collision that left him with a permanent disability. In October 2000, he applied for a disability grant in Limpopo and was referred for a medical examination. He was advised that he could not work again and told to come back for the grant three months later. By November 2001, he had not received any transfer. His attorney wrote to the local pension office. He started receiving his grant on January 25, 2002, but he received less than what he was owed in arrears.

With the support of a nongovernmental organization, Mr. Mashava took his case to the Constitutional Court, challenging the delegation of administration of social assistance to provincial governments. The court ruled that "social assistance is indeed a matter that cannot be regulated effectively by provincial legislation, or that to be performed effectively, it requires to be regulated or coordinated by uniform norms and standards."

Source: Mashava v. President of the Republic of South Africa, 12 BCLR 1243 (CC 2004).

at the provincial level meant that some citizens got better access to their constitutional right than others and called on the government to promptly reform the system in a manner compliant with the constitution.

Addressing the Policy Challenge

The formal objective of the reform was to establish a social assistance system that addressed socioeconomic challenges in a manner compatible with the Constitution. The informal objective was to respond to the demands of a poor black electorate that had experienced one of the worst forms of segregation in recent history. Social grants were seen as one of the key instruments of compensation and redistribution that had been proved effective by rigorous research and a means to strengthen the social compact between the people and the new government. The specific objectives evolved as the reform progressed, starting from big-picture policy objectives such as reducing poverty and inequality to the more specific goals of addressing challenges in administration and the delivery of social grants.

Policy Making

Discussions on the role of social assistance in addressing poverty and inequality took place within the African National Congress (ANC) even before the 1994 elections. "The right to education, welfare and health care consistent with the needs of the people and the resources of the state" was included in the ANC's proposal for a democratic South Africa of 1991 (ANC 1991). Section 27 of the Bill of Rights of South Africa's Constitution includes the right to "social security, including if they are unable to support themselves and their dependents, appropriate social assistance." These rights are to be realized progressively, to the best of the state's ability, contingent on available resources.

In 1996 the government asked a group of experts, the Lund Committee on Child and Family Support, to review the state of child and family support systems in South Africa and recommend options for addressing the pressing social challenges families with children faced. The committee recommended the introduction of a flat-rate child support benefit (the child support grant) and the corresponding phase-out of the state maintenance grant. The child grant was the first means-tested child support benefit in South Africa to be paid to a primary caregiver, whether or not he or she was the biological parent. It expanded the number of beneficiaries from 150,000 at its inception in 1998 to about 11.2 million in 2013. The ceiling for eligibility increased progressively from 7 years in 1999 to 18 currently.

Support from leadership—particularly two successive pairs of ministers and directors-general of the Department of Social Development—was key to the success of the reform, according to the head of the committee, Professor Frances Lund. The committee started its work under the first minister of welfare of the democratic government, Abe Williams, but it operated mostly under Geraldine Fraser-Moleketi, who replaced Williams in 1999. Being new to welfare, Minister Fraser-Moleketi "worked hard and read widely" to learn about the sector; she was "willing to listen and rapidly recognized that the reform had political clout" (Lund 2008). She quickly became a champion of reform, providing the necessary political endorsement within the Cabinet. Leila Patel, acting director-general (later confirmed), enabled the work of the committee under Minister Williams and provided the necessary continuity when Minister Fraser-Moleketi took over. As one of the few senior staffers with theoretical understanding of the redistributive role of social assistance and its contribution to poverty alleviation, she was instrumental (Lund 2008).

Under Fraser-Moleketi's political guidance, and with the intellectual leadership of Leila Patel, the Department of Social Welfare adopted the White Paper for Social Welfare. The White Paper "marked the transformation of the welfare sector from a narrow, strictly welfare focus to a broad context-relevant developmental social welfare perspective" (Skweyiya 2011). As an emblem of the shift from welfare to development, the Department of Social Welfare was renamed the Department of Social Development. The White Paper, along with all the groundwork done by Fraser-Moleketi and Patel, set the vision for the reform process to follow.

Zola Skweyiya, who followed Fraser-Moleketi as minister in 1999, remained in office until 2009. He carried the reform forward with great impetus. "Considered one of post-apartheid South Africa's most successful ministers, he has turned around an often unsympathetic and dysfunctional department that now ensures that almost 13 million South Africans access social grants," wrote the *Mail & Guardian* in 2009 (Tolsi 2009). Vusi Madonsela, director-general of the Department of Social Development under his leadership, credits Skweyiya with having "led a social policy revolution in South Africa" (Madonsela 2013). Passionate about the socioeconomic challenges the country faced, Skweyiya set his key strategy as building engagement with people and bringing the pressing poverty challenges to public attention.

Skweyiya surrounded himself with capable staff. Director-general Vusi Madonsela was an effective leader and one of the key intellectual forces in the department. Professor Vivienne Taylor, who was appointed advisor to the minister in 1999, recalls how Skweyiya and his staff would travel to the provinces and organize dialogues with local communities in an effort to bring the Parliament closer to the communities. "He was trying to change the way politicians engaged with people, and thus built up a type of legitimacy that others did not have. He became known by people," she recalls.

Minister Skweyiya put great emphasis on training personnel. "For the Department of Social Development to discharge its mandate of being the lead department in addressing poverty in post-apartheid South Africa, we needed to build sound expertise in social policy and evidence-based policy making," he wrote (Skweyiya 2011). He created the Strengthening Analytical Capacity in Evidence-Based Decision Making Program, funded by the U.K. Department for International Development (DfID). Since 2005 this program has trained more than 300 senior South African policy makers, with strong support from the Department of Social Policy at Oxford University (Skweyiya 2011).

In 1999 Minister Skweyiya appointed a second policy committee, the Taylor Committee of Inquiry into Comprehensive Social Security, led by Professor Taylor. Its role was to elaborate options for a new social security system based on the concept of developmental welfare, explore their viability, and formulate recommendations. The committee presented its recommendations in 2002. They centered on the idea that a comprehensive social protection system should be put in place to ensure all citizens a minimum acceptable standard of living and strengthen the state's contract with the people. "In placing social grants as a key pillar of a broader social protection strategy, South Africa is moving away from a piecemeal residual and reactive approach to poverty to an approach that is socially and economically empowering for individuals" (Taylor 2010).

Throughout the reform the main discussion of policy alternatives centered on whether grants should be universal (given to all South Africans); categorical (given to all individuals within a vulnerable group, such as children or the elderly); or means tested (given only to the poor, whether or not they belong to a specific group).

Discussions around the idea of a basic income grant that would provide a guaranteed minimum income to all South Africans started around this time. The prevailing assumption was that a basic income grant would not be sustainable. To find out if the assumption was valid, the Cabinet tasked the Taylor Committee with examining its fiscal sustainability. The Committee found that the grant was indeed fiscally feasible, under various scenarios, and proposed its (progressive) introduction. Despite its recommendation, in 2002 the decision was made not to introduce a basic income grant, although the matter is subject to discussion to this day.

As for means testing, both the Lund Committee and the Taylor Committee recommended that the child support grant not be means tested. However, the government strongly endorsed the idea of (self-declared and unverified) means testing. "It was too soon into the post-apartheid era to gain acceptance of a new benefit that would include white people," writes Lund (2008, 86).

There has been some speculation that having a more ambitious alternative (the basic income grant) might have facilitated the passage of (relatively) more modest measures (Lund 2008): a child-related grant appears to be more sustainable and less controversial than a universal transfer. Similarly, an expansion of the existing state maintenance grant would have been unsustainable because the benefit paid was very high; thus, the alternative of a lower yet meaningful benefit like the child grant appeared more appealing.

On the administrative side, a key reform introduced during Skweyiya's tenure was the creation of SASSA. The agency has the mandate to "act, eventually, as the sole agent that will ensure the efficient and effective management, administration and payment of social assistance; serve as an agent for the prospective administration and payment of social security; and render services relating to such payments," according to the Social Assistance Act of 2004, which established it. With the introduction of SASSA, the policy and administrative functions of social assistance were separated, with the Department of Social Development responsible for policy and SASSA for administration.

The decision to separate the two and create SASSA was made to provide uniform norms and standards of service across the country, as set out in the Social Assistance Act of 2004 and mandated following *Mashava v. the President of South Africa* case (see box 7.1). According to some SASSA officials, it was also made as a way to separate the delivery of social assistance and social welfare services (noncash support services), which had historically been neglected. Dividing administrative responsibility between SASSA and the Department of Social Development would allow resources to be devoted to welfare services, according to key people involved at the time. It was also hoped that establishing SASSA would allow the government to fight corruption in grants administration more effectively, according to Professor Lund—although because most SASSA staff came from the Department of Social Development, it is unclear the move would have that effect (and indeed allegations of corruption remained after SASSA was established).

During the reform the government made extensive use of both technical expertise and international best practice examples. In the early stages of the reform, policy makers paid great attention to the technical soundness of policy and implementation design, as embodied by the establishment of the two high-profile policy committees (Lund and Taylor), which comprised academics, practitioners, and civil society leaders. Their purpose was indeed to provide technical recommendations and build consensus around their recommendations, thereby helping reconcile technical aspects with stakeholder interests.

The two committees made use of local as well as international expertise. In May 1996, Professor Lund organized a retreat (called the Itala Think Tank) for the members of the Lund Committee and other experts in order to brainstorm and make key decisions. The location of the retreat was remote; participants had to commit to stay for the whole period and to take part in the deliberations on policy recommendations made at the end (Lund 2008). A number of international experts took part. They were asked not to speak the first day, "in order for them to learn about the local context and discourse" before contributing to the discussion, according to Professor Lund.

International experience also played an important role in the administrative reform. SASSA was modeled after Centrelink, the Australian social grants payment agency. Study tours were organized to various countries, including Australia and the Netherlands, though emphasis was always put on adapting what was learned to the unique South African context, according to SASSA officials. Some officials believed that even more exposure to international experiences on the nuts and bolts of setting up an agency would have been useful during implementation.

Implementation

The Department of Social Development faced three key implementation challenges: managing the progressive phase-out of the state maintenance grant, expanding the child support grant from all children under 7 in 1998 to all children under 18 in 2012, and overhauling the way social grants were administered, by centralizing all social assistance functions across the country through the establishment of SASSA.

Early and consistent evidence on the success of social grants in combatting poverty was the basis for gathering resources for the expansion of coverage. The constitutional right to social assistance also provided a strong underpinning, as it required the government to provide resources for the progressive realization of this right (see the next section on consensus building). Funding for the establishment of SASSA was mobilized under the promise that both the centralization and the new agency would address fraud and leakage in the system, thereby saving resources in the longer term.

In 1997 an implementation task team began phasing out the state maintenance grant and phasing in the child support grant. An innovative public-private partnership (PPP) called the Program Management Service facility financed the changes. It allowed civil servants to purchase skills from the private sector, learn from them, and eventually take over the outsourced functions. Civil servants headed the task team's operations, but the work was carried out largely by consultants. This model was effective at overcoming hurdles and completing the phasing in and phasing out work that had begun in 1998 (Lund 2008).

Use of information technologies (IT), especially the adoption in the early 2000s of a management information system, led by some of the provincial Departments of Social Development (Eastern Cape first, followed by the Free State and Gauteng), played a big role in managing the expansion in the number of grants. A SASSA official said, "The provincial Department of Social Development had adopted a Management Information System that improved service delivery to a great extent. This system was brought over from the province and is still in operation today. Besides improving control and turn-around time (improved from about 106 days on April 1, 2006, to 3 days currently with regard to the applications), it also took the place of many of the manual registers. Better performance with application taking meant a reduction in time wasted to deal with enquiries and complaints—a byproduct of increased efficiency."

With the support of a consulting firm, the Department of Social Development separated the functions it handled from those taken over by SASSA. In 2002 Minister Skweyiya created a Project Implementation Unit (PIU) within the Department of Social Welfare to handle establishing SASSA and managing the transfer of functions. Deloitte, a management consulting firm, supported the PIU throughout the process. The PIU dealt with many aspects of the implementation of the reform, including legal issues and staffing. Development of the legislative acts involved extensive consultations and appearances before Parliament. Most staff who carried out front office functions within the Department of Social Welfare were moved over to SASSA, but staff for support functions such as human resource, finance, legal, and IT had to be recruited.

According to members of the PIU, the ability to plan dynamically was a key factor of success: continuously restaging processes and systems according to the challenges faced allowed the team to address issues effectively. The governance structure within the central administration (the PIU, the Department of Social Development, Treasury, and the Department of Public Service and Administration) allowed for very good dialogue and flow of information. Reportedly, the governance structure and resulting flow of information between the central administration and the regions were not as good, creating some resistance to reform in the provinces (see section on consensus building).

Strong leadership within SASSA was not present at the beginning. "The leadership issue was not the primary focus at [the initial] stage, as the emphasis was on integrating previously disparate provinces into a functional whole (…) [A dynamic] leader has now come into the organization and the results are clearly visible," reports one SASSA official, referring to Virginia Petersen, the chief executive officer (CEO) of SASSA appointed by Minister Bathabile Dlamini in 2011. She has driven key activities, including the reregistration of beneficiaries and the introduction of the electronic payment and identification card. She also introduced a "corporate brand," by improving, standardizing, and curating the image of SASSA offices, officials, and materials.

A key obstacle that SASSA had to overcome was fraud and corruption in the system. In April 2005, Minister Skweyiya set up a special investigating unit to review people who had permanent positions in the public service but deliberately misrepresented their positions in order to obtain social grants (*Mail & Guardian* 2008). Thanks to this special unit, nearly 2,600 government employees were removed from the social grants roster. Disciplinary action ranged from warnings to dismissals. The investigation reportedly yielded significant savings (*Mail & Guardian* 2008).

Fraud and corruption persisted despite these improvements. The Social Assistance Act established an Inspectorate for Social Security to operate as watchdog over SASSA, conduct investigations to ensure the integrity of the social assistance system and management, and fight against the abuse of social assistance. The Inspectorate was never established, however.

In 2012 Minister Dlamini and CEO Petersen adopted a new strategy, requiring all social grant beneficiaries to reregister with SASSA. Upon registration, beneficiaries' data were (and still are for new beneficiaries) collected and stored on a biometric ID card. Once a month, all beneficiaries need to present their proof of life by scanning their fingers or speaking into a voice recognition machine. The ID also works as a debit card, linked to the account into which benefits are paid.

Reregistration led to the removal from the system of more than 640,000 ineligible beneficiaries (South Africa, National Treasury 2014) and to savings of roughly R 2 billion a year (interviews with SASSA officials and Ensor 2014). According to media reports, the cost of the reregistration exercise was R 275 million, or roughly 10 percent of the annual savings (Yahoo Finance 2014). The reregistration process faced great opposition by people who lost benefits because of fraudulent claims. Top personnel at SASSA are reported to have received death threats (eNews Channel Africa 2014).

The SASSA ID is one of the most advanced social security identification systems in the world. Its introduction has not been without problems, however. In April 2014, a court declared the tender for the distribution of payments (which includes the biometric ID system) invalid and ordered SASSA to reopen it for a period of five years. SASSA is scheduled to take over the payment mechanism by 2017.

Consensus Building

According to Minister Skweyiya, there was broad agreement within the Cabinet that social assistance was needed as a key instrument of compensation and redistribution and a means to strengthen the social compact between the people and the new government. "Many members of the Cabinet came from poverty; they thus fundamentally understood the role social assistance can play in improving the livelihoods of the poor. People were promised a better life and equal treatment with the new government, and such a promise was recognized as an agreed basis for working together," he said.

There were differences and disagreements over the scale, effect, and sustainability of the social grant system within the Cabinet, however. Minister Skweyiya and Professor Taylor recall many intense discussions with Finance Minister Trevor Manuel on the fiscal sustainability and economic effects of various aspects of the expansion of the social grants system, particularly the appropriateness and feasibility of the basic income grant.

Forming a coalition outside government was very important in building consensus within government, according to Skweyiya. Garnering support from faith-based organizations and nongovernmental organizations (NGOs) that were vibrant supporters of the role of social grants in poverty reduction was fundamental. The two technical committees also played a role in building consensus. Their broad membership implied strong ideological differences among their members but also broad support once recommendations were made. The committees had to engage in a consultation processes with all stakeholders as part of their terms of reference, although Professor Lund recalls being given insufficient time for consultations and pushing for more. A group of NGOs reports that the Taylor Committee's work was generally perceived as "competent, collegial and open to public comment" (South African Council of Churches 2002).

During implementation, criticism from inside and outside the Department of Social Development was a key challenge. When SASSA was being established, the governance structure at the central level allowed for a good flow of information internally. Less attention was given to the flow of information at the decentralized level, according to SASSA officials. Provinces were reportedly consulted in the process, but there was constant jostling for position and interests because representatives from the provinces were not formally included in the process, making it difficult for them to provide input. According to one SASSA official, "the Minister and the CEO played a crucial role in negotiating with the Provinces about the transition. Their message was that the change was not negotiable, but how it occurred and the processes were negotiable. In this manner, they did manage to garner support from the Provincial government."

Outside the Department of Social Development, various NGOs vocally opposed the creation of SASSA and the transition from provincial government to SASSA. Their views were reportedly not taken into account. Some SASSA officials believe that more attention should have been paid to those critics, as doing so would have allowed for a better process and better outcome. Other officials believe that "external stakeholders like the Black Sash and the Legal Resources Centre were also instrumental in the change, as they were responsible for the legal challenge in the Mashavha case. They thus further gave legitimacy to the process."

Minister Skweyiya believes the media also played an important role in increasing consensus around the reform process. By disseminating information on the prevalence and depth of poverty and sharing information on the reform plans and its progress, the media helped increase the reform's transparency and legitimacy.

Sequencing

Discontinuing the state maintenance grant was challenging on both political and ethical grounds because it meant that nonblack single mothers would lose support. Human rights groups threatened to legally challenge the withdrawal of the grant for existing beneficiaries on the basis that it violated the Constitution, according to Professor Lund, although they never carried through with such action.

The Lund Committee conducted solid statistics-based background work to estimate the effects of the policy change; it sought advice to evaluate the likelihood of encountering legal issues; and it was transparent and open about the implications of reform and explained the rationale of the choices it made (Lund 2008). On the basis of this work, the committee recommended the gradual phasing out of the state maintenance grant over five years, as children reached the end of their eligibility. The phasing out would coincide with the five-year phase-in of the child support grant.

Despite Minister Fraser-Moleketi's staunch advocacy, this approach did not find support at the political level. "Too many wanted the state maintenance grant to disappear right away," recalls Professor Lund. A compromise solution of three years, later extended to four, was reached. By 2001 the state maintenance grant had ceased to exist.

Introduction of the child support grant required two sequencing decisions. The first was whether to immediately extend coverage to all eligible children or to limit coverage to newborns. The second was whether to progressively increase the age threshold. Both were political decisions: the Cabinet decided to immediately extend coverage to all age-eligible children (children under the age of seven at the time) on the basis of the right of all children to receive assistance, and to raise the eligibility age in order to mimic the age eligibility of the state maintenance grant (Lund 2008). Pilot projects were not launched, as there was a perception among the various stakeholder groups that they "would not be constitutional or fair" (Lund 2008).

The sequencing approach of the establishment of SASSA combined the sequential and the big bang approach. Implementation took place in three phases:

1. In the *stabilization* phase, SASSA took over all functions previously performed at the provincial level and ensured continuity.
2. In the *standardization* phase, all provinces were brought up to the same level of performance.
3. In the *optimization* phrase, overall performance was enhanced, through the use of technology.

The big bang approach came in the stabilization phase: on a single day (April 1, 2006), SASSA took over all provincial functions across South Africa. "There were too many reasons why an incremental approach [for a take over of functions] was not going to work. First, the staff had to be transferred as a going concern—the date of transfer was the same for all staff. Second, the court order had to have everything under a national umbrella by a certain date. Third, the legislation had to be implemented on the same date in all provinces," recalls one SASSA official.

All provincial social assistance workers were automatically moved over to SASSA, and on April 1, 2006, everyone continued to perform their jobs the way they had the previous day. New posts were quickly filled by identifying and prioritizing pressure points at the local office level. Core local office staff were also appointed from staff shifted from the provinces. "Astute planning contributed to very little disruption of services," according to one SASSA official. "The situation was managed, although long hours were sometimes put in to achieve goals."

Results Achieved

The number of social assistance beneficiaries quintupled, from fewer than 3 million in 1994 to 16 million in 2014. The cash grant system as a whole is strongly progressive and pro-poor, raising the market incomes of people in the bottom decile of the income distribution by a factor of 10, according to analysis by the World Bank. This impact is far greater than in other middle-income countries, including Brazil, which is celebrated worldwide for the success of its antipoverty cash transfer system (World Bank 2014). Overall, 76 percent of total expenditure on grants is allocated to the poorest 40 percent of the population (Bhorat and Cassim 2014). Most grant recipients are children under 18 (70 percent of grant allocation), old people (17 percent), and disabled individuals (7 percent) (Bhorat and Cassim 2014).

There is strong evidence that increased access to safety nets has reduced poverty rates and inequality (Bhorat and Cassim 2014) and had positive development impacts on health, schooling, and labor supply (Duflo 2000; Department of Social Development, SASSA, and UNICEF 2012). There is no support in the literature for the claim that social grants discourage work or incentivize teenage pregnancy (Leibbrandt and others 2013).

At the institutional level, the key achievement of the reform is the establishment of an agency (SASSA) accountable to citizens for the quality, reliability, and transparency of payments it provides. Rules of eligibility for benefits are clear, applications are processed much more rapidly than they used to be, and people receive what they are entitled to in a reliable and convenient way. The average cost of transaction decreased from R 30 to R 16 per transaction per month, and an estimated R 2 billion a year has been saved by eliminating ghost beneficiaries and reducing turnaround time. Furthermore, centralization of the administration of grants simplified financing processes and reduced scope for misuse for political patronage: budgeting used to be a complex bargaining process between provincial and national levels and was subject to misuse for political patronage by provincial governments. Centralization allowed for more straightforward and transparent budgeting.

A notable by-product of the expansion of grants is the spectacular rise in birth registration during the first year of life, which rose from 24 percent in 1991 to 95 percent in 2012 (UNICEF 2013). The requirement that a birth certificate be presented in order to obtain social grants—especially the child support grant—has worked as a major incentive to early registration. In order to allow for accessible birth registration, the government has established fixed service centers as well as hospital registration points, mobile units, and multipurpose community centers (UNICEF 2013).

Conclusions: Success Factors, Challenges, and Lessons Learned

The end of apartheid and the beginning of a new era based on freedom and democracy gave singular momentum to reform in South Africa. Although these circumstances were unique, many aspects of reform can nevertheless be replicated in other countries.

Several factors were key to success. First, credible leadership was exerted throughout the process at different levels. Second, building on the existing system inherited from the previous government, even if this is in need of deep reform, can provide a substantial starting point; scrapping the system and starting from zero would have proven much harder. Third, the constitutional underpinning of the right to social assistance gave the reform both legitimacy and momentum. Fourth, the inclusiveness of the reform process, especially at the design stage, meant that reform was known, discussed, and accepted. Adequate resources could therefore be devoted to it. Fifth, the embrace of technology helped address capacity and human resources constraints. Sixth, a relatively well-functioning system for birth and ID registration of both children and caregivers (partly the consequence of the requirement to obtain ID books in order to vote in the 1994 elections) facilitated administration of the expansion in coverage.

These achievements are impressive, but reform is not complete: the fact that South Africa remains one of the most unequal countries in the world—with a poverty rate that is twice as high as the average upper-middle-income country, according to the World Development Indicators—suggests that much work remains to be done. Application and case management systems are not yet fully computerized, procedures are often onerous for beneficiaries, payment administration is still outsourced to a private company, allegations of fraud persist, and the cost and fiscal sustainability of the system has been questioned in the context of pressure on public budgets. In addition, the social grant system is not fully integrated with health, education, and other social services, hindering synergies and efficiency. A more holistic approach to social grants might yield better human capital development and increase efficiency. Attempts to move in this direction were unsuccessful, because challenges within each sector made harmonization a low priority.

Five key lessons can be learned from South Africa's experience in reforming social assistance. First, establishing a legal (possibly constitutional) foundation for social protection set a solid ground for building the consensus, momentum, and financing needed to establish an extensive cash transfer system.

Second, dialogue and consensus building are key at all stages of reform, from design to implementation. Allowing for some compromise between achieving technical soundness and efficiency and building a wider consensus can help a reform to succeed.

Third, attention to the technical soundness of policy, through the use of committees of experts to formulate policy proposals, increased the effectiveness and sustainability of programs.

Fourth, if well managed, ambitiousness can create momentum and a real sense of positive change, as evidenced by the plans for expanding the child support grant, the overhauling of delivery through the centralization of social assistance functions from one day to the other, the herculean reregistration effort undertaken in 2013, and the introduction of cutting-edge technology in the delivery system (biometric ID and smart payment cards).

Fifth, communicating results may garner support for the reformed programs. The perception that social grants induce dependency or encourage teenage pregnancy remains widespread among some groups. More could be done to counter such perceptions by publicizing the actual estimated impacts of social grants.

Note

1. Social assistance expenditure is 0.4 percent of GDP in China, 1.4 percent in Brazil, and 1.8 percent in Croatia (Weigand and Grosh 2008).

References

ANC (African National Congress). 1991. *Constitutional Principles for a Democratic South Africa*. Pretoria.

Bhorat, H., and A. Cassim. 2014. *South Africa's Welfare Success Story I* and *South Africa's Welfare Success Story II*. Washington, DC: Brookings Institution.

Case, A., and A. Deaton. 1998. "Large Cash Transfers to the Elderly in South Africa." *Economic Journal* 108 (September): 1330–61.

Department of Social Development, SASSA (South African Social Security Agency), and UNICEF (United Nations Children's Fund). 2012. *The South African Child Support Grant Impact Assessment: Evidence from a Survey of Children, Adolescents and Their Households*. Pretoria: UNICEF South Africa.

Duflo, E. 2000. "Child Health and Household Resources in South Africa: Evidence from the Old Age Pension." *American Economic Review* 90 (2): 393–98.

eNews Channel Africa. 2014. "Top Sassa Officials Receive Death Threats." April 20, 2014. http://www.enca.com/south-africa/top-sassa-officials-receive-death-threat.

Ensor, L. 2014. "Re-registration of Social Grant Recipients Saves R2bn." *Business Day BDLive*, February 5. http://www.bdlive.co.za/national/2014/02/05/re-registration-of -social-grant-recipients-saves-r2bn.

Eyal, K., and I. Woolard. 2011. "Female Labour Force Participation and South Africa's Child Support Grant." Paper prepared for CSAE 25th Anniversary Conference 2011: Economic Development in Africa, March 8.

Leibbrandt, M., K. Lilenstein, C. Shenker, and I. Woolard. 2013. "The Influence of Social Transfers on Labour Supply: A South African and International Review." SALDRU Working Paper 112, South Africa Labour & Development Research Unit, University of Cape Town, Rondebosch, South Africa.

Leibbrandt, M., I. Woolard, A. Finn, and J. Argent. 2010. "Trends in South African Income Distribution and Poverty since the Fall of Apartheid." OECD Social, Employment and Migration Working Paper 101, OECD Publishing, Paris. http://dx.doi.org/10.1787 /5kmms0t7p1ms-en.

Lund, F. 2008. *Changing Social Policy: The Child Support Grant in South Africa*. Pretoria: HSRC Press.

Madonsela, V. 2013. "Current Issues in South African Social Policy and the Role of Local Government." Lecture presented at the University of Oxford, October 23.

Mail & Guardian. 2008. "More Than 5,000 Public Servants Convicted for Fraud." January 29. http://mg.co.za/article/2008-01-29-more-than-5-000-public-servants-convicted-for-fraud.

Makiwane, M., and E. Udjo. 2006. *Is the Child Support Grant Associated with an Increase in Teenage Fertility in South Africa? Evidence from National Surveys and Administrative Data.* Pretoria: HRSC Press.

Patel, L. 2011. "Child Support Grants in South Africa." In *Sharing Innovative Experiences: Successful Social Floor Experiences*, 361–84. New York: International Labour Organization/United Nations Development Programme.

SASSA (South African Social Security Agency). 2014. *Annual Performance Plan 2014/2015.* Pretoria.

Seekings, J. 2007. "Poverty and Inequality after Apartheid." Paper prepared for the second "After Apartheid Conference, Yale University, April 27–28.

Skweyiya, Z. 2011. "Building on Inclusive, Comprehensive and Nondiscriminatory Social Welfare System in Post-apartheid South Africa: A Reflection on Achievements and Continuing Challenges." Lecture delivered at the Oxford Institute of Social Policy, Oxford, May 17. https://www.spi.ox.ac.uk/fileadmin/documents/PDF/ZS_final _version_oxford_lecture_as_delivered_on_17_May_2011_1700.pdf.

South Africa, National Treasury. 2014. *Full Budget Review.* Pretoria.

South Africa News. 2012. "New Biometric Card to Boot Out Social Grant Fraud," June 8. http://www.sanews.gov.za/south-africa/new-biometric-card-boot-out-social-grant -fraud/.

South African Council of Churches. 2002. "Coalition Endorses Revolutionary Report's Big Anti-poverty Plan." May 16. http://www.sacc-ct.org.za/taylor.html.

Taylor, V. 2010. "Foreword." In *Social Assistance: A Reference Guide for Paralegals.* Cape Town: Black Sash.

Tolsi, N. 2009. "Conscience from Beyond." *Mail & Guardian*, May 9. http://mg.co.za /article/2009-05-09-conscience-from-beyond.

UNICEF (United Nations Children's Fund). 2013. *Every Child's Birth Right. Inequities and Trends in Birth Registration.* Paris.

van der Berg, S. 1997. "South African Social Security under Apartheid and Beyond." *Development Southern Africa* 14 (4): 481–504.

Weigand, C., and M. Grosh. 2008. *Levels and Patterns of Safety Net Spending in Developing and Transition Countries.* Social Protection Discussion Papers 44857. Washington, DC: World Bank.

Woolard, I., and M. Leibbrandt. 2011. "The Evolution and Impact of Unconditional Cash Transfers in South Africa." In *Annual World Bank Conference on Development Economics 2011* edited by Claudia Sepúlveda, Ann Harrison, and Justin Yifu Lin, 363–84. Washington, DC: World Bank.

World Bank. 2014. *South Africa Economic Update #6. Special Focus: Fiscal Policy and Redistribution in an Unequal Society.* Washington, DC: World Bank.

World Development Indicators (database). World Bank, Washington, DC. http://data .worldbank.org/data-catalog/world-development-indicators.

Yahoo Finance. 2014. "Net1 Finalizes Recovery of Additional SASSA Implementation Costs." June 6. http://finance.yahoo.com/news/net1-finalizes-recovery-additional -sassa-143000056.html.

CHAPTER 8

Improving the Delivery of Identification Documents to Facilitate Access to Services

John Carneson and Zandile Ratshitanga

Introduction

In 1994, the "rainbow people" of South Africa underwent a momentous change to forge a new common national identity, marking the end of apartheid. This was embodied by the issuance of the same compulsory identity document (ID) to all citizens irrespective of race. Without an ID a citizen cannot register for school, vote, get married, draw social grants, be buried, open a bank account, or obtain any kind of official license.

The identity value chain starts with the registration of a new citizen at birth on the National Population Register (NPR). When citizens turn 16, they are issued their first ID. Both IDs and passports are issued against the record in the NPR, which is secured through early birth registration and updated when there are changes in status, such as marriage or death.

The new democratic government inherited a fragmented civil registration system[1] that was used to systematically deny citizenship to the majority of the people on the basis of race and ethnicity. Under apartheid, only the 4.5 million people classified as white could access an acceptable level of civic services because only whites were accorded full citizen status.

The first policy focus of the new government was to build a single nonracial population register of citizens to restore citizenship and dignity to the majority who were denied these rights. The register was also the basis of the

John Carneson is the Chief Director, Policy and Strategic Management, at the Department of Home Affairs, South Africa; Zandile Ratshitanga is a Senior Communications Officer at the World Bank. This chapter benefited from extensive interviews with current and former government officials as well as from comments by peer reviewer Steven Friedman (director of the Centre for the Study of Democracy at Rhodes University and the University of Johannesburg).

voter roll, which enabled the holding of the first democratic election. The main policy driver over the following decade was to expand these civic services to all 40 million citizens, with priority given to rural areas and marginalized communities.

The Department of Home Affairs (DHA) has a sole mandate to issue birth certificates, IDs, passports, marriage certificates, and death certificates and to verify civic status and identity. By 2006 the quality of the delivery of these services had reached crisis proportions. The department was characterized by uncaring staff, chronic delays, and high levels of corruption, which put the integrity of the national identity system at risk. The media dubbed the department "the Department of Horror Affairs" and reported daily on lives destroyed because citizens struggled to get these enabling documents that gave them access to basic rights and services.

In response to the crisis, the government shifted its policy focus after 2007 to transforming the department into a modern, efficient organization that is responsive to the service-delivery and security needs of South African citizens, residents, and visitors. Implementation of this policy was successful thanks largely to the strategy of using internal reforms to effect visible improvements in services that in turn built the confidence necessary to mobilize support for deeper reforms. Key stakeholders in this process were the political leadership, including the president, the Cabinet, the parliamentary portfolio committee and DHA ministers, DHA staff, the National Treasury, national and provincial government departments, local government, communities, and the private sector.

The department implemented this strategy in relation to the three documents that have the most direct impact on the everyday lives of citizens: birth certificates, IDs, and passports. It drastically improved its ability to deliver services, with the average turnaround times for issuing IDs reduced from more than 140 days in 2006 to 40–45 days by 2009–14. Even more important was the increase in reliability, which surveys showed was valued by citizens above speed of service.

The modernization program initiated in 2013 reduced turnaround times for the delivery of IDs, in the form of the new "smart card," by another 5–10 days. The average turnaround time for passports was reduced from 12 weeks in 1994 to 2 weeks from 2009 for applications that are captured digitally. Between 2010 and 2015 steps were taken that increased the number of births registered within 30 days from 46 percent in 2010/11 to 64 percent in 2014/15.

The policy to turn around the DHA is remarkable because it happened despite very limited recognition of the scope and strategic importance of the department's civic and immigration mandates. Between 1994 and 2014, the DHA expanded its civic services footprint to cover every municipality in the country. In 2000 there were 200 local and regional offices. A fleet of 112 mobile units with satellite connectivity was added, and by 2014 the footprint had expanded to 405 offices at which the public could access DHA services. In real terms, however, the growth of the budget and staff complement did not match this expansion. Despite increased demand for services, budgets have not allowed for significant investment in infrastructure, systems development, training, or security.

Table 8.1 shows the growth in the production of selected documents, the staff size, and the budget of the DHA during critical phases of the transformation of the department. The budget covers the civic functions of the DHA (the focus of this chapter) and immigration functions.

Historically, the DHA was considered a department that provided routine administrative services of relatively low value. Its classification by the National Treasury as a "general public service" department means that it is not regarded as either a mainstream service delivery or a security department. The much smaller Department of International Relations and Cooperation (DIRCO), which is similarly classified, had a budget of about $670 million in 2013/14, about 50 percent more than $440 million allocated to DHA.

The international, border, and domestic functions of the South African Revenue Service (SARS) are more comparable to the DHA; it received $1.1 billion. Both SARS and DIRCO have staff with higher-level and more specialized skills than the DHA, and their core and support systems are more integrated, up to date, and secure. Yet the DHA delivers a wider range of services to a larger client base and plays a critical role in national security. It is also a key enabler of service delivery in both the public and the private sectors. There is growing pressure for a new policy shift: the repositioning of DHA so that it can deliver its full mandate as a key element of an effective, citizens-oriented state.

Table 8.1 Performance by the Department of Home Affairs, 1994–2013

Year	# Birth certificates	# IDs issued	# Passports issued	# Staff	Budget (thousands of rand)
First phase: Expansion of services					
1994/95	574,980	4,636,995	454,498	6,941	356,928
1995/96	966,696	2,830,940	502,489	7,549	424,454
1996/97	1,064,662	2,222,441	510,245	7,619	471,820
1997/98	1,775,662	2,498,970	889,340	7,907	587,785
Second phase: Turnaround program					
2006/07	1,068,934	2,759,949	1,006,060	8,341	2,800,405
2007/08	1,279,828	2,054,272	1,081,771	8,560	2,906,230
2008/09	163,151	2,499,419	1,115,711	12,186	3,606,271
2009/10	1,726,766	2,567,414	9,023,80	10,494	3,807,884
Third phase: Modernization					
2010/11	2,183,110	2,216,652	946,512	9,259	4,186,331
2011/12	1,979,299	2,275,461	748,477	9,091	4,816,566
2012/13	1,259,491	1,936,475	580,215	9,198	4,376,678
2013/14	650,682	1,789,671	614,008	9,664	5,198,858

Source: DHA 2001–2014.

The Policy Challenge

By 2006 a dysfunctional DHA was becoming recognized as a material risk at home and abroad because of its failure to adequately deliver services and security. In its election manifesto, the government committed to building a capable modern state that could lead development. Such a state needs efficient and secure identity and immigration systems and the confidence of its citizens and the global community. At a symbolic and political level, the new identity system was essential to achieving social justice through the restoration of basic rights that had been denied to the majority of South Africans under apartheid.

Profoundly concerned about this state of affairs, Minister of Home Affairs Nosiviwe Mapisa-Nqakula saw that it was necessary to go beyond the department to find the solution to the problem. "Only a forensic view of Home Affairs thorough, unsentimental, professional, without fear or favor would give us the detailed understanding of what has to be fixed," said Mapisa-Nqakula to Parliament (Budget Vote speech, National Assembly, June 7, 2007).

The path adopted was to involve relevant state actors with the support of the Cabinet. She drew a Support Intervention Team from the Public Service Commission, the National Treasury, and the Department of Public Service and Administration. This team's summary report, presented to Parliament in early 2007, called for the department to take drastic action to address deep-seated problems of leadership, management, systems, technology, organization, and corruption. Minister Nkosazana Dlamini-Zuma, who succeeded Mapisa-Nqakula, said she had in the later years undertaken unannounced and disguised ministerial visits to service delivery points to experience the quality of service firsthand.

The policy option of initiating a large-scale turnaround program was presented to the Cabinet and approved. The National Treasury agreed to an initial grant of approximately $20 million. The decision to comprehensively overhaul the department to achieve a dramatic improvement in service delivery was the best policy option given political and social pressures and the need to holistically address the institutional issues of leadership, governance, operations, and culture.

From 2010, building on the momentum generated by the turnaround, very substantial progress was made. There was no way in which deeply rooted problems could have been resolved in three years or in some areas even five. The decision to focus attention and energies on ensuring the successful transformation of the ID and passport processes was correct in that it acted as a catalyst for larger changes in the medium and longer terms.

Addressing the Policy Challenge

Institutional Reform Objectives

The primary stated objective of the turnaround program was to drastically improve service delivery, starting with the issuance of enabling documents. This was done through addressing the serious institutional challenges the Support Intervention Team had identified. Stating this as a government priority, President Thabo Mbeki mentioned in his 2007 State of the Nation Address that "we will bring the operations of the Department of Home Affairs to full capacity" (National Assembly, February 9, 2007). Specific areas to be addressed were service delivery and facilities, people and organizational structure, corruption, security and risk, and information technology (IT).[2]

The turnaround program was formally launched in June 2007. "We want to ensure that we deliver services efficiently and in predictable time frames," said Minister Mapisa-Nqakula at a press briefing (statement issued by the DHA, November 14, 2007).

At the strategy level, the minister and director-general, supported by lead consultants, agreed that the success of the turnaround hinged on making a quick and visible impact on the lives of citizens and that the most important service in this regard was the issuance of ID books. This strategy was highly successful, but it narrowed the objectives of the turnaround. Less attention was paid to other critical areas, such as immigration and the coherent development and security of the entire national identity system. Apart from funding constraints, the capacity of the DHA was not sufficient to manage more than one large-scale project at a time, such as addressing the complex challenges presented by the broader national identification system and birth registration.

An immediate informal objective was to deal decisively with weak leadership and management, an aspect that received intense media and political attention. The appointment of a new director general of DHA, Mavuso Msimang (dubbed "Mr. Fix-It" by the media) was an important step. He had a track record of improving public institutions. He gave the turnaround a public face and served as a spokesperson who could articulate the policy internally and externally and provide progress on what was being done to address the service delivery challenge. This interface with the public showed that the department was responsive to the needs of citizens and went a long way toward changing public perceptions.

The second policy objective was to achieve a profound cultural change in the way managers viewed and executed the mandate of the DHA. It was critical that officials begin to put service to the public first and to take control of the business processes for which they are responsible. These concepts were alien in the DHA. Most staff came to work not understanding or caring about the value they could add to the lives of citizens or their own careers. This is despite the adoption of government-wide legislations in 1995 of "Batho Pele" principles,[3] meaning putting people first in order to transform public service delivery (South Africa, DPSA 1997).

A third policy objective was to ensure political and public support and funding for the program. The strategy was to establish an effective partnership between the minister and the director-general, supported by a well-funded and competent communications team. Such a partnership provided leadership that could point to progress, manage risks, and maximize gains. Most important, channels were created to allow the minister to communicate directly with staff and the public. "I am new and want to work with you to improve Home Affairs. Good or bad, let me know—we will fix it together," said Minister Nkosazana

Dlamini-Zuma when she joined the department in 2009. This kind of direct interaction encouraged the staff to own the process as valued participants and assured the public that something was done to address their problems.

Policy Making

Essential to success was selecting which "quick wins" to focus resources on. The decision was critical, because failure to deliver might have had a fatal impact on the program.

The obvious choice was the issuance of IDs, because they have an immediate impact on the lives of citizens. Typically a grandmother sharing a small pension with many dependents in a rural area may have to forgo several meals to pay for transport to a DHA office in order to acquire an ID, which is needed to access the child support grant.

The consultant conducted an in-depth study of the ID production process, which indicated that there were gross inefficiencies that if corrected would result in a dramatic improvement in service delivery. The ID process in 2007 included too many manual handovers, redundant and duplicated areas, little use of metrics for efficient management, and a lack of basic monitoring and controls. The systematic implementation of operational management principles was key to the transformation of all business processes involving production.

Because of funding constraints, the complexity of the reform challenge, and organizational capacity, birth registration was initially not prioritized, despite its fundamental importance for the security of the population register. Passports were also not prioritized, because they were issued mostly to people who could afford to travel rather than to the mass of impoverished people who needed DHA services most.

In 2009, under Minister Dlamini-Zuma, a clear strategy to deal with birth registration and the issuance of birth certificates began to emerge. The main policy objective of the DHA was securing the NPR rather than speeding up service delivery. The logic was that, as custodians of identity and citizenship, the DHA must make security of the NPR and related processes its primary concern. Without a secure NPR, the value of DHA services and the security of the state and individual citizens would be at serious risk. It was taken forward under the leadership of a new director-general, Mkuseli Apleni, and a skilled management team that had the confidence to take the transformation of the department to the next level without reliance on consultants.

Under apartheid there was no systematic registration of the births of Africans; and, since 1994, in a democratic South Africa, various campaigns were run to persuade parents to register children after birth to secure their citizenship and identity. The Births and Deaths Registration Act as amended in 2005 requires birth registration within 30 days. About 1.1 million new citizens are born each year in South Africa, and in the financial year ending in March 2011 a total of 946,031 births were registered—representing 86 percent of total births. However, only 46 percent of births were registered within the required 30 days. By March 2015 the number of births registered within 30 days had increased by about 5 percent a year to

64 percent (DHA Annual Reports). Although important, this gain in early birth registration falls short of what is required to secure the population register.

Further amendments to the Births and Deaths Registration Act (2010) were to make it easier for caregivers to register the birth of their wards and for orphans to be registered. This was in response to the reality that many babies are brought up by relatives.

Implementation

The first vehicle used to implement the reforms and achieve the policy objectives was the turnaround program. A service provider with a track record in business process and institutional transformation was contracted to partner with the department.

Among the many projects initiated were the radical transformation of the ID process, the establishment of a modern passport production facility, the training of staff on the new systems, the launch of a 24-hour client service center, the upgrading of frontline offices, and the implementation of a major change management subprogram. Direct expenditure on turnaround projects from the special grants and baseline budget exceeded R 1 billion ($84 million).

As with any large-scale reform, it was important to learn from people who had been through similar processes. Senior managers began to develop the understanding necessary to appreciate lessons learned elsewhere and adjust them to DHA. Benchmarking was used as a standard tool in projects, and senior consultants shared their experiences of reform management in other projects in South Africa and abroad. Lessons learned from the turnaround of SARS were particularly important. Two meetings were held to exchange experiences between DHA top management and managers driving several large projects in countries such as the United Kingdom.

The policy objectives were largely achieved because the governance and administration of this complex program were sound and an appropriate project methodology was adopted and implemented. For Director-General Mavuso Msimang, the immediate challenge was to build—from a very low base—a leadership team that could mobilize the department in support of the turnaround program. Senior managers were sent for competency assessments, and a number were replaced. New structures, including steering committees and a program management office, were established, with the minister herself chairing the highest-level committee. Metrics and dashboards—data visualization tools that display the current status of metrics and key performance indicators of the project—were developed and used to make quick and effective decisions at each management level using operations management principles. As a result, funds were enabled and capacity could be used strategically.

One of the most successful innovations was a standard project methodology. The approach was to derive maximum benefit from the involvement of consultants, ensure that the DHA was in charge, and create an environment for the effective transfer of skills and knowledge. "You cannot improve service delivery by relying on consultants. The public and officials must own the change process," said Minister Nkosazana, emphasizing the critical role stake-holders had to play. This strategy also created opportunities for identifying and building effective managers and leaders such as Vusumuzi Mkhize, who went on to lead the civil service unit responsible for the production of IDs as the new deputy director-general. "We identified knowledgeable, capable staff from Provinces and Head Office as champions of change and created incentives for staff," said Mkhize.

At the level of projects, the key to success was to form mixed teams of staff and consultants led by a DHA project leader who worked closely with a consultant counterpart. Reporting lines were clear. Poor performance was identified and dealt with while good performance was celebrated.

Addressing the problem of late registration of birth could not be done only through reforming DHA business processes but required action at the level of communities and institutions such as schools and hospitals. Minister Nkosazana Dlamini Zuma actively promoted early registration of birth through community-based and national campaigns, hospitals were connected to DHA systems to facilitate registration, and laws were amended to address gaps and increase penalties for fraud. There was also a program in collaboration with the Department of Education to ensure that 16-year-olds received their ID by capturing their biometrics and issuing them with an ID.

In March 2010 President Jacob Zuma launched the NPR Campaign. A robust and creative communication campaign used every available channel, from radio to meetings to football matches and appearances by the minister in a drama series and commercials for diapers. For maximum reach, partnership with the Departments of Health, Education, Police, and Social Development was essential, as was the support of provincial and local governments. By 2014 a total of 389 hospitals and clinics were connected to DHA systems in order to facilitate the registration of birth within 30 days after birth (DHA *Annual Report 2013/14*).

Overcoming Obstacles

An essential part of the strategic management of the program was identifying major risks and threats up front. It was imperative that the unions and the officials in general co-own the process because the program involved changes that would have a direct impact on the working conditions of a highly unionized staff. The transformation of the ID and passport processes was particularly vulnerable to union action. Apart from general resistance to change, there was also a serious threat of sabotage by the minority of staff who had exploited deficiencies in the old system to conduct fraudulent activities.

What was effective was adopting the mitigating strategy to convince staff that there would be no redundancies, that they would acquire skills and opportunities, and that their working environment would improve, according to Msimang. An agreement with the unions was signed to ensure their support for the turn-around, and a "transformation forum" was established in which staff representatives were kept informed and could raise issues with management. The minister and director-general engaged directly with staff members, through Short Message

Service (SMS) and creating a temporary internal TV channel. All of this effort was a powerful motivation for staff to promote and defend the turnaround.

For the public, publicizing manager's names, pictures, e-mail addresses, and phone numbers in every DHA office and on the department's website ensured that citizens had recourse, said Minister Dlamini Zuma.

Operations management methodology is a tested way to optimize and monitor workflows and remove obstacles. "We adopted a totally new approach in government called 'Operations Management' with all its tools and dashboards as well as holding without fail morning productivity meetings with performance feedback," said Deputy Director-General Mkhize. Every day a three-person team met for 20 minutes to effect changes in frontline offices, once a week a meeting chaired by the director-general was held, and every month the steering committee chaired by the minister met. Issues that could not be resolved at one level were escalated to the next level. Governance structures relied on reports from project teams, with dashboards reviewed to ensure that no issues were hidden. Problems and solutions could be identified because the metrics produced for the dashboards were designed to monitor key points in a workflow, such as the number of ID applications; the average time of delivery to Head Office; the time taken to scan, compile, and print documents; and the time taken to deliver the ID to the office of application.

Consensus Building

The need to involve all his staff in the change process was stressed by Deputy Director-General Vusi Mkhize: "We had a strong change management program that included round tables, quality circles, and engagements at every level to ensure involvement of all staff. We focused on the rationale and benefits to themselves; and we created a statement about the value of change and the turnaround project for the nation."

To sustain a positive relationship with staff and citizens, the communications unit produced good-quality content for internal and external stakeholders using a variety of media. "We gave feedback to staff and acknowledged the good work that was being done and accounted to the public through regular media briefings on the progress made," Msimang explained. Appearing on radio talk shows, the director-general actively encouraged members of the public to comment about the improved experiences they were having with the department and to make known service delivery problems and instances of corruption.

As the DHA modernized its technology and systems, it built support for its programs by signing formal agreements with the banking sector and other departments that allowed them to verify the identity of their clients online. This step provided solid support for national efforts to combat fraud and corruption. The breakthrough was the development of an online fingerprint verification system, which was part of the project to transform the ID process.

Less formal but more important in the short to medium term was the need to keep key government and political role players, such as the Director-General's Forum, the National Treasury, and relevant Parliamentary committees, informed and involved. It was also important to manage relations and acceptable service levels with departments on which the DHA depends, such as the Department of Public Works and the State Technology Agency. As the DHA has moved away from paper-based to digital systems, dependency on unreliable networks with limited bandwidth has become the largest single constraint to making further improvements to service delivery.

On securing the NPR, the underlying policy thrust was for citizens to take coresponsibility for securing their identity and citizenship through individual actions and through participation in the Stakeholder Forums that were established in 90 percent of local municipalities. The nonpartisan fora identify local needs in terms of DHA services, have oversight over local offices, and support campaigns. Local government plays a leading role in the fora, and national and provincial departments participate.

Sequencing

The department adopted an incremental approach to turnaround. In the first six months (Phase 1), it developed a five-year strategy for improving key management functions and processes and responding to customer needs. Major targets included stabilizing and improving key support systems such as finance and communications, management structures, risk management, and the management of contracts. Management of contracts produced more than $9 million of savings, which was used to support projects that required new contracts, such as the customer call center.

The largest project with an organizational focus was "vision and design," which addressed structural challenges and included a comparative study of departments that carried out DHA functions in a range of countries. At the same time, baseline studies of the ID and other systems were conducted and resources put in place to enable the transformation of the production of IDs.

In the following 12 months (Phase 2), the highest priority was given to ensuring the success of the project to transform the ID process. This a large-scale national project aimed at progressively reducing the average turnaround times for issuing an ID to 40–45 days from more than 130 days. The introduction of scanners in 250 offices to track applications and IDs and the retraining of staff was a massive undertaking, as was the reduction of the number of production stages from 85 to 35. What took most time and effort, however, was the training of officials from individuals who carried out routines without understanding or measuring their efforts to civil servants who enthusiastically embraced operations management. This transformation was partially achieved throughout the process; where it was fully achieved, as in the document scanning unit, productivity rose by a factor of at least three, and morale was maintained at a high level.

The introduction of digital online verification of fingerprints enhanced security and meant that temporary IDs could be issued immediately. Citizens could use the temporary IDs for most transactions, including voter registration and voting.

By 2009 the average turnaround time had fallen to 45–55 days, down from 147 in 2006/07. Even more important was the increase in reliability, which surveys showed citizens valued above speed of service, and the significant reduction in error rates.

During this phase of operations, the most decisive success factor was the supportive environment created by Vusumuzi Mkhize. Without his leadership the use of consultants would not have been effective and skills would not have been transferred at the necessary rate and level.

In the last 18 months of the turnaround project, the priority was to replace the outdated passport and national identity system with a secure, modern, digital printing system. This process leveraged the experience gained in transforming the ID process. Time frames were much tighter, and the project was far more technically challenging, however.

A large part of the passport process was digitized and automated, starting with the "live capture" of biometrics (fingerprints, signatures, and photographs). Doing so represented a quantum leap in technology use, in part because the output had to be a digitally printed passport that met the highest international standards.

This process also involved coordination of external players, such as the Government Printing Works, and international service providers. Gaps in capacity, such as the lack of IT specialists and suitable trainers, created risks; and the DHA was overly dependent on private providers and consultants. Once the technical problems were overcome, improvement in service delivery was dramatic. In regional offices, which were reconfigured to enable the full digital capture of biometrics and other details of citizens, average turnaround times were reduced from 12 weeks to 2; and the process became far more reliable and secure. These results were crucial proof of concept in terms of the DHA moving to a paperless, integrated digital environment.

An important component of the integrated digital platform and national identity system is a smart ID card (a card with a programmable chip), which will eventually replace the old ID book. In partnership with other departments and agencies, the DHA has designed and tested an award-winning smart ID card. The Government Printing Works has acquired the capacity to print the cards overnight and deliver them for collection within 5–10 days. More than 70 frontline offices have been converted to run fully digital systems. By March 2014, 1.6 million smart ID cards had been issued to the first target groups, 16-year-olds and pensioners.

Results Achieved

The possession of an identity document is critical in the life of all who are eligible for a South Africa ID because it is needed to access both public and private services. They want to apply for and receive an ID at a nearby Home Affairs office without having to wait in long queues and within an acceptable and consistent period. They also want to be able to enquire easily about the progress of their applications and they expect to be protected against errors and identity theft or fraud. The overall result achieved by the implementation of the policy reform is therefore the improvements in the speed and consistency in the delivery of this

Making It Happen • http://dx.doi.org/10.1596/978-1-4648-0768-8

enabling document: 92 percent of first-issue IDs were delivered within 54 days in 2013/14, as compared with 61 percent in 2010/11. The reliability of delivery of ID reissues has improved even more each year, from 50 percent within 47 days in 2010/11 to 98 percent in 2013/14. Since 2009, with digital verification of fingerprints, temporary IDs can be issued on the spot, and the new smart ID is produced within 24 hours and reaches the citizen within 5–7 days.

The production of passports was the first process to be digitized, and since 2009 the great majority of citizens applying at the forty largest offices have received their passports within two weeks. In 2013/14 a total of 96 percent of passports applied for at these offices were received within 13 days. A state-of-the-art printing system incorporates advanced security features.

The birth registration process itself has been reformed. From 2013 a full birth certificate is now being printed on the spot with the details of both parents rather than the much less secure abridged birth certificate. The mass registration campaign launched in 2010 had three objectives. One was to register about a million South Africans who had never been registered and who now have their identity and citizenship secured. The second was to establish the importance of birth registration firmly in the popular consciousness. The third was to lay the basis for introducing, from December 2015, a far more stringent system for late birth registration plus the envisaged introduction of escalating administrative fines. Access to birth registration services has been largely assured through connecting all the larger health care facilities (398) to DHA systems.

Another most significant result of policy and institutional reforms of the DHA has been the emergence of a much more advanced understanding of the department's mandate in line with African and global developments. As a key enabler of development and security, it has begun putting in place the elements of a single integrated digital platform at the heart of which is a new National Identity System. This will be fully comprehensive and will contain the status, identity, and biometrics of everyone who has resided in South Africa or who has visited the country.

In terms of the magnitude and scope of the reform, the banks and other departments such as Social Development have established interfaces with the DHA that allow them to verify identity online to prevent and detect fraud. The Master of the High Court, another client, using this system, detected fraud against a fund held for widows and orphans, leading to the prosecution of officials involved. Enabled by the new digital systems, the first online applications, payments, and appointments system for IDs and passports is planned. This will greatly reduce the time needed when visiting offices. After signing agreements with major banks, clients will be able to access DHA officials stationed in their largest branches.

The department has been able to develop a cadre of professional officials armed with appropriate values and skills needed to manage and protect identity and immigration systems of the DHA. The number of senior and middle managers has grown from 660 middle and senior managers in March 2011 to 932 in March 2014. Apart from improving the management of back office systems, the public benefits directly by having higher-level managers who are able to make decisions in frontline offices.

Another result of the effective institutional reforms is the establishment of a DHA Learning Academy that delivers courses leading to a dedicated and recognized higher education qualification. Under the category "Humanities," the DHA was ranked in 2015 as among the top 10 institutions to work for (private and public) in a Universum survey of 65,000 students and professionals (Universum Global 2015).

The reform has had a major impact on a critical stakeholder, members of the public who require the enabling documents delivered by the DHA; as shown by research commissioned by the DHA in 2013, a strong relationship has formed between the DHA and citizens, particularly among the poor, those in rural areas, and those serviced by small offices. Changes such as extended opening hours were appreciated, but the main reason given was dealing with a knowledgeable, caring staff. Citizens agreed that, between 80 and 89 percent of staff were polite and honest, provided sound advice, and addressed complaints. In urban areas, and among higher income groups, expectations were higher and citizens were generally more critical. This is the segment of the population that going forward will benefit the most from new channels, such as online applications.

In 2014 a survey on government's service trends rated DHA service delivery as among the best within government, with only the SARS rated higher (Public Service Commission, September 2007).

Conclusions: Success Factors, Challenges, and Lessons Learned

The chapter has shown how a more efficient and reliable service delivery of birth certificates, IDs, and passports to citizens was achieved. The following are the salient success factors and lessons learned from the reform process. First, leadership was given at the political (executive) and departmental (executing) levels by ministers who worked in close partnership with directors-general of the department. This leadership was sustained in spite of the appointment of four ministers between 2007 and 2014. The current minister, Malusi Gigaba, is driving the modernization process launched by Minister Naledi Pandor.[4] The factor of continuity has saved time and ensured that results were visible faster, according to Minister Nkosazana Zuma.

Second, the transformation process became a national issue and a de facto national project around which public support and a wide range of institutional and political stakeholders could be built and mobilized at national, provincial, and local levels. There was a clearly defined public information strategy that required quick wins that would visibly impact the lives of citizens, particularly the poor and marginalized, and in so doing advance the national agenda. This aligned the reforms with the actual and symbolic transformation of South African society. There was also international recognition. For example, in 2009 the DHA was awarded the prestigious public service delivery to citizens award by the United Nations Commission for Africa, in Ethiopia.

A third factor was to focus attention and resources on internal change management to transform the organizational culture toward a greater service delivery orientation. The most sophisticated systems and advanced forms of organization are completely dependent on the people charged with their management and operation. In this regard, the paradigm shift that had to happen was to move from a traditional inward-looking approach to an outward-looking, client-centric approach. It also meant that officials who were initially supported by management consultants had to take charge. This required a strategic decision to use consultants only when necessary rather than using them as substitutes for government officials. Adapting management methods that work effectively in the private sector, such as operations and project management, helped facilitate this change. The transfer of skills such as operations and project management, together with a paradigm shift to a client-centric approach, were perhaps the most important internal achievements of the reform. This was reinforced by an understanding that technology, if deployed appropriately, helps solve problems that would otherwise seem impossible to tackle. Finally, it meant leveraging reforms on the work done by other government institutions to learn from others and save time and costs.

Fourth, openness to learn from others also played an important role in the turnaround. By looking at international experiences and by comparing management strategies, organizational changes, and change management as applied in other institutions in the country (for example, SARS), DHA was able to extract important experiences and lessons learned. By working with external consultants who brought precious private sector management consulting experiences, additional valuable expertise was brought in. Peer-to-peer learning across government, and inspiration from other institutions that managed to achieve important changes, thus became an important motivating and knowledge-contributing factor of institutional reforms.

Last, it was the implementation of a highly visible communications strategy that helped win staff over and changed public perception as the department gave regular progress reports in the media and demonstrated with specific cases how it was improving the lives of people. This ultimately improved the image from the "Department of Horror Affairs" to one that puts the people first.

The reforms, however, also encountered challenges. First, capable, motivated managers who could provide leadership, rapidly acquire skills, and create an appropriate organizational environment were scarce. This problem was characteristic of support functions, which remained largely undeveloped because of a lack of specialists and leadership.

Second, most IT systems and production processes were outdated and partly paper based, making it difficult to extract accurate statistics and develop dashboards, perform efficiently, and maintain security.

Third, the multitude of projects overstretched resources and created change overload. The program became too complex and it should have focused on fewer objectives. The governance structure and management were too weak to resist pressure to create projects to deal with short-term problems.

Fourth, the poor positioning of DHA within the state created chronic underfunding. The DHA has been widely perceived as a routine administrative department producing low-value products. Most of the budget is allocated to expanding, improving, and maintaining civic services, leaving too few resources for security and immigration.

Fifth, the reforms thus remain works in progress, and sustained efforts are needed to further respond to the needs of citizens. The next reform challenge will be to move from the traditional current NPR toward a full-fledged integrated digital National Identity System, which is currently being designed.

Notes

1. The civil registration system provides the basic legal document that helps the individual in proving his or her identity, nationally and claiming his or her individual rights and privileges.

2. Presentations to the Portfolio Committee in 2008.

3. Batho Pele principles are drawn directly from the Constitution on dealing with public service.

4. Minister Gigaba had been deputy minister of home affairs from 2004 to 2010 during the turnaround project.

References

Ask Afrika. 2014. "Ask Africa Orange Index." 2014. Ask Afrika, Pretoria. http://www.askafrika.co.za/orange_index.

Hausman, David. 2013. *Reforming without Hiring and Firing: Identity Document Production, South Africa 2007–2009.* Innovations for Successful Societies Case Studies, Princeton University, Princeton, NJ. http://www.fevertreeconsulting.com/assets/princeton-report-id-project-turnaround.pdf.

South Africa, DHA (Department of Home Affairs). Various years. Annual Reports. Pretoria. http://www.home-affairs.gov.za/index.php/about-us/annual-reports.

———. 2007a. Internal report (November 2007). Pretoria.

———. 2007b. Press statement by Minister of Home Affairs, Nosiviwe Mapisa-Nqukula, July.

———. 2007c. "N Mapisa-Nqakula: Home Affairs Budget Vote 2007/08." Speech by Home Affairs Minister Nosiviwe Mapisa-Nqakula for Budget Vote 2007, National Assembly, June 7. http://www.gov.za/n-mapisa-nqakula-home-affairs-dept-budget-vote-200708.

South Africa, DIRCO (Department of International Relations and Cooperation). 2007. State of the Nation Address of the President of South Africa, Thabo Mbeki: Joint Sitting of Parliament, February 9. http://www.dfa.gov.za/docs/speeches/2007/mbek0209.htm.

South Africa, DPSA (Department of Public Service and Administration). 1997. "White Paper on Transforming Public Service Delivery." September 18. http://www.dpsa.gov.za/dpsa2g/documents/acts&regulations/frameworks/white-papers/transform.pdf.

———. 2007. "Citizen Satisfaction Survey 2006/2007." Public Service Comission Pretoria. http://www.psc.gov.za/documents/2007/PSC%20CSS%202007%20%28Screen%29 .pdf.

Statistics South Africa. 2005. *Achieving a Better Life for All: Progress between Census '96 and Census 2001*. Pretoria. http://www.statssa.gov.za/publications/Report-03-02-16 /Report-03-02-16.pdf [23 May 2015].

Universum Global. 2015. "The World's Most Attractive Employers 2015." Stockholm, Sweden. http://universumglobal.com/worlds-most-attractive-employers-2015/.

CHAPTER 9

Protecting Biodiversity, Rehabilitating Ecosystems, and Promoting Conservation for Development

Christopher J. Warner, Claudia Sobrevila, and George C. Ledec

Introduction

As part of its development agenda, South Africa has made significant progress since 1994 in rehabilitating and conserving its biodiversity and ecosystem assets at the landscape level.[1] Biodiversity is defined as the diversity of plants and animals. An ecosystem is a community of plants and animals in conjunction with the nonliving parts of the environment, especially land and water. Ecosystems provide the foundation for all life and deliver important goods and services to the economy and community. Along with all natural capital, they form a part of a nation's wealth (World Bank 2006).

These issues are particularly important for South Africa, for several reasons. First, ecosystem services may be equivalent in value to 7 percent of South Africa's gross domestic product (GDP) (Department of Environmental Affairs and SANBI 2010). Second, South Africa is a water-scarce country. One way to increase water availability is by removing alien invasive plant species, which consume up to 7 percent of South Africa's freshwater resources, according to the Working for Water program (World Bank 2002).[2] Third, conserving and rehabilitating landscapes is a critical element in strengthening adaptation to climate change and fostering resilience, as South Africa's National Development Plan 2030 recognizes. The vegetation of the Cape Floristic Region, for example, has evolved under conditions of drought, fire, hot summers, and cool winters.

Christopher J. Warner is a Senior Technical Specialist, Claudia Sobrevila is a Senior Environment Specialist, and George C. Ledec is a Lead Ecologist—all in the World Bank's Environment and Natural Resources Global Practice. This chapter benefited from extensive interviews with current and former government officials as well as from comments by peer reviewer Saliem Fakir (head of the Living Planet Unit, World Wildlife Fund [WWF], South Africa).

Its vegetation cover is therefore the most suitable and cost-effective for coping with the key impacts of climate change (increased drought and fire). Allowing alien invasive plants to destroy that land cover increases fire risks and reduces water runoff, both of which would be extremely costly to address. Fourth, South Africa has a global responsibility to conserve its biodiversity because of its richness. The Cape Floristic region is the world's smallest and most threatened bioregion, containing more than 9,600 plant species, 69 percent of which are found nowhere else on the planet (SANBI 2006). South Africa contains four other biodiversity hotspots and is home to 95,000 plant and animal species. Fifth, South Africa's biodiversity treasure trove, landscape beauty, and abundance of wildlife form the foundation of the tourism sector, which has consistently outperformed the rest of the economy. Tourism grew at an average annual rate of more than 7.3 percent for 20 years, employing 4.6 percent of the workforce. In 2012 it directly contributed $10 billion to GDP, according to the minister of tourism.

This chapter analyzes how South Africa has mainstreamed biodiversity and ecosystems management into development. It identifies the institutional reforms, challenges, and lessons learned.

The Policy Challenge

Recognizing the importance of creating a framework for promoting sustainable development, South Africa decided to include an environment right in its new Constitution. It reads as follows:

> Everyone has the right to an environment that is not harmful to their health or well-being and to have the environment protected, for the benefit of present and future generations, through reasonable legislative and other measures that prevent pollution and ecological degradation; promote conservation; and secure ecologically sustainable development and use of natural resources while promoting justifiable economic and social development. (Constitution of the Republic of South Africa 1996)

Chapter 4 of the Constitution makes the environment and nature conservation concurrent national and provincial functions (exceptions are national parks and national botanic gardens).

In 1994 national parks covered only 4 percent of South Africa's land area, and many of the country's important biodiversity assets and key ecosystems lay outside protected areas. Although the protected area network was small, qualified scientists and other professionals supported the country's environment and conservation institutions. However, as Brian Huntley, the former chief executive officer (CEO) of the South African National Biodiversity Institute (SANBI) notes, before this change,

> while scientists enhanced their understanding of how South Africa's ecosystems functioned, a void existed between science and the socioeconomic aspect. The issue at the time—early 1990s—was that we had good biophysical scientists, and some

good human science research outside of the Human Sciences Research Council, but the link between these two streams in both research and policy was not made. Success had been made in linking the two in some of the Cooperative Scientific Programs—Fynbos, Karoo programs—but it was the motivation for me working with Clem Sunter to point out the challenges in our book—*South African Environments into the 21st Century*—which preceded and underpinned the bioregional approach that I introduced in NBI/SANBI with the appointment of Khungeka Njobe and Kristal Maze in the late 1990s.

"The apartheid government could clearly not provide a link between environment and development. Conservation was seen as being antidevelopment and antipeople because of the history of displacement of African people from their land to make way for conservation. This was a major source of friction and in the post-apartheid era great effort had to be made to rectify this," says Saliem Fakir, a manager at the World Wildlife Fund (WWF) South Africa.

South Africa faced three broad policy options: (i) to prioritize job creation and poverty eradication over biodiversity and ecosystem considerations (under this scenario South Africa would have witnessed accelerated biodiversity losses and environment and conservation institutions would have been allowed to wither); (ii) to largely continue business as usual while addressing land claims and deracializing environment institutions; and (iii) to give full effect to the constitutional environment right, through both policy and institutional transformation. It selected the third option.

Addressing the Policy Challenge

One of the first objectives of the Department of Environmental Affairs (South Africa's lead national government environment institution) was to bring South Africa in line with international environment conventions, create new updated environment legislation, and develop new institutions around the revised legal and policy objectives. According to Mike Knight, the head of Planning and Development at South African National Parks (SANParks), South Africa's national-level park authority, SANParks pursued three objectives: (i) to secure conservation assets, which meant creating an ecologically representative system of national parks able to adapt to climate change; (ii) to promote tourism and the sensitive commercialization of parks, recognizing that they are key to South Africa's tourism product; and (iii) to develop parks that contribute to the local economy and provide value to local communities.

At the provincial level, the reform agenda was less ambitious. It focused on creating new park and conservation agencies from existing ones, including former homeland structures; deracializing the agencies; and putting them on more of a commercial footing. David Daitz, the CEO of the Western Cape Nature Conservation Board, recalls,

I inherited an organization in which 65 percent of the budget was being spent on staff salaries, leaving little room for any other expenditure. One of my first tasks was to broker a deal with the unions and staff to create severance packages in order to free up capital for park development Although we asked staff whether they would elect to go voluntarily on the basis of declared severance conditions, we made it clear from the outset that the retrenchments would be management driven. However, we committed to doing our best to take people's declared preference to leave the organization into account. In the end, only 12 out of 208 were involuntary severances, but all of the others had put up their hands. These were not voluntary severance packages in the normally accepted definition of the term. Indeed, had they not been management determined, the benefits available to the retrenches from the Government Employees Pension Fund would have been much less attractive.

In 1998 the Botanical Research Institute and the National Botanical Gardens were amalgamated to form the National Botanical Institute (NBI). With the promulgation of the Biodiversity Act of 2004, the NBI became SANBI, South Africa's lead biodiversity agency. As SANBI began to demonstrate its research, project management, and biodiversity capabilities, it emerged as a logical home to take on the higher-level planning and monitoring functions for national biodiversity and ecosystem conservation. As part of meeting its legal requirements, it is committed to ensuring that its research and mainstreaming work is useful to decision makers and that its botanical gardens and programs have relevance to the community. It places considerable emphasis on generating income from botanical gardens in order to reduce reliance on the government for its operating budget.

Policy Making

In keeping with the Constitution, which required cooperative governance between the national and provincial spheres of government, in 1994 South Africa created coordinating structures for all key concurrent national and provincial functions. These structures are known as Minister and Executive Council Meetings (MINMECs). To advise the MINMECs, a similar structure was created at the technical/official level involving the provincial heads of departments for the environment and nature conservation. These structures are called Technical Committees to MINMEC (MINTECHs). The intention was that MINMEC and MINTECH would help coordinate policy development, including by bringing various provincial-level constituencies on board.

With South Africa's reemergence in the international area, accessing finance from the Global Environment Facility (GEF) became possible.[3] The way in which the first program came about and was implemented reveals the characteristics of the institutional setting and shows how reformers drove innovation and change.

In 1998 the World Bank approved the GEF-financed Cape Peninsula Biodiversity Conservation Project. The program included three components, two implemented by WWF South Africa and one by the National Parks Board.[4] In the words of David Daitz, then manager of Table Mountain National Park, "the program was an astonishing success and pioneered the toolbox and landscape management approach for South Africa. It facilitated voluntary cooperation between

15 and 16 organizations aimed at finding cooperative solutions to issues." To a large extent, the program demonstrated that landscape-level programs could be successfully led through cooperative governance structures other than government—a feature of the design and implementation of landscape programs in South Africa.

Implementation

SANBI organized itself around seven program areas—conducting research, performing monitoring and assessment, managing biodiversity information, strengthening South Africa's biodiversity assets and ecological infrastructure, providing science-based policy advice, unlocking the benefits of its botanical gardens, and developing skills and promoting community awareness—according to Tanya Abrahamse, CEO of SANBI. Program areas were carefully selected to align with South Africa's socioeconomic priorities in order to ensure continued demand for services and funding. Programs are well managed through an annual target-setting exercise and the monitoring of performance.

SANBI's botanical gardens represent South Africa's rich plant biodiversity and demonstrate the links between biodiversity and development. SANBI is able to attract funding for its own use as well as for managing programs because it has received several years of clean unqualified audit reports and demonstrated its project management expertise. It raises its core budget (of about $30 million a year) domestically, generating about $4.3 million from gate fees from its 1.3 million visitors, rentals, and other sources of income (SANBI 2013).

A major thrust of SANBI's work has been developing an array of mechanisms to encourage landowners to voluntarily bring land into the conservation estate (box 9.1). These programs have been highly successful because they enable landowners to switch to more profitable conservation land use; undertake their activities in a more sustainable manner; market their products as

---

Box 9.1 Finding Win-Win Cooperative Solutions to Sustainable Potato Growing in the Western Cape

Potato farmers in the Western Cape were rapidly plowing up the last remnants of the endangered Sandveld vegetation and depleting the groundwater for irrigation purposes. To address the problem, CapeNature, the Western Cape biodiversity conservation agency, organized a series of stakeholder meetings that included owners of 65–70 percent of the potato-growing land area (Potatoes South Africa 2012).

These meetings culminated in the development of a scheme to encourage sustainable potato farming. The scheme provides information to farmers on how to practice biodiversity-friendly potato farming by leaving natural vegetation corridors along rivers, cutting back fertilizer and pesticide use, removing alien invasive plant species, reducing grazing pressure on

box continues next page

Box 9.1 Finding Win-Win Cooperative Solutions to Sustainable Potato Growing in the Western Cape *(continued)*

remaining natural vegetation, adopting proper fire management procedures, and setting aside a portion of their land for natural vegetation.

Each year farmers assess their own performance against a scorecard that is jointly audited by Potatoes South Africa and CapeNature, the provincial conservation authority. Points are awarded for various categories, including setting aside land for conservation use. Upon each successful audit, the farmer is issued a producer member certificate.

Audit results demonstrated improvement in 14 of 18 farmers (Department of Environmental Affairs and SANBI 2010). The program demonstrated to the community that win-win solutions are possible when parties engage one another around the table. Similar initiatives have been brokered elsewhere, and policy implementation has evolved through these types of engagement.

Source: Department of Environmental Affairs and SANBI 2010.

more sustainable; address threats to biodiversity, such as fire and alien invasive vegetation; and access national and local tax breaks.

The financial health of SANParks improved significantly as a result of its commercialization program. In 2012/13 revenues from gate fees, accommodations, support services, and game sales amounted to about $100 million, about 85 percent of its operating income. In a bid to further improve its financial strength, SANParks embarked on a public-private partnership strategy in 2002. It has netted $55 million from the relationship since then (SANParks 2013).

Another important area the conservation authorities had to address is land claims by previous black landowners who had been evicted from land to make way for national parks. For land claims within parks, the government faced two broad choices: allowing land to be "de-proclaimed" from national parks and given back to communities or keeping the land within parks but entering into comanagement or stewardship agreements. The first option was found to be impractical, and it risked undermining conservation objectives. Comanagement agreements with the community emerged as the preferred option.

A good example is provided by SANParks, which helped establish the Mayibuye Ndlovu Development Trust (MNDT) in 2004 to support communities around the Addo Elephant National Park (AENP) develop economic activities compatible with the park's values. In response to the threats posed by invasive alien vegetation on the Sundays River system around AENP and the productive soil in the valley, MNDT and the Sundays River Citrus Company (Pty) Ltd., one of the largest packers and marketers of citrus fruit in southern Africa, launched a joint commercial initiative, the Mayibuye Ndlovu Compost Project. This project sought not only to address the problem of invasive plant species but also to support sustainable agriculture and promote sustainable employment for people from surrounding communities. The MNDT supported the creation of two local small or medium-size microenterprises. The self-sustaining microenterprises harvest alien vegetation and process the raw material for compost manufacturing. This material is then distributed to citrus growers and other commercial buyers in the region. The Mayibuye Ndlovu Compost Project has helped revitalize the local environment and economy by providing an opportunity for local communities to benefit financially from the removal of invasive alien vegetation. It serves as a benchmark for future community development projects.

Andrew Zaloumis, CEO of the iSimangaliso (St. Lucia) World Heritage Authority, recounted how "the Reconstruction and Development Program, the then key program of government, identified a series of spatial development initiatives across South Africa with the objective of largely promoting major new development. One of them was the Lubombo Spatial Development Initiative, which identified the iSimangaliso/St. Lucia Wetlands World Heritage Site as a key conservation and ecotourism asset as part of the initiative." The project is a good example of how government sought to actively promote sustainable development.

Another good example of how emerging policy was linked to jobs is the Working for Water program, highlighted in box 9.2.

Box 9.2 Protecting Biodiversity, Increasing Water Flows, and Creating Jobs

In the early days of the transition, it was extremely important for the government to demonstrate quick wins in the sector—to provide tangible examples of how it intended to address poverty and conservation issues. In 1995 Kader Asmal, minister of water affairs and forestry, listened to a presentation by scientists on how alien vegetation was reducing the country's water supplies and how, through labor-intensive techniques, it could be removed. Asmal realized that such an approach could provide multiple benefits, including job creation, restoration of the health of ecosystems, and reduction of fire threats, thereby supporting the conservation of South Africa's biodiversity, especially the threatened Cape Floristic region. Convinced of the benefits, he set aside $3.2 million for the Working for Water program.

This highly successful program has grown each year and spawned similar initiatives, including the Working on Wetlands and Working on Fire programs. Between 1995 and 2009, the program spent $519 million, created 15,500 jobs among previously unemployed youth and women in poor communities, and increased annual water flows by an estimated 48–65 million cubic meters a year—equivalent to the water capacity of a large water storage dam (Department of Environmental Affairs and SANBI 2010). The benefits of the program are visible across swathes of the landscape. The effort spawned other industries, including charcoal, light furniture, and timber manufacturing. Its quick start and high visibility soon after the establishment of democracy gave credibility to the policy change that emphasized linking conservation to job creation and poverty reduction.

Source: Department of Environmental Affairs and SANBI 2010.

How Were Obstacles Overcome?

The first obstacle to overcome was the notion that job creation was more important than environmental protection and that South Africa could not afford to invest in biodiversity and ecosystem services. Enshrining an environmental right along with all other rights set forth in Chapter 2 of the Constitution silenced this debate. It challenged the sector to find creative and innovative ways to demonstrate the value of this right.

A second obstacle was the old way of doing business. Under apartheid, regulation was used to enforce environmental decisions. Recognizing that environmental issues needed to be resolved in an interdisciplinary way, the sector demonstrated through the Cape Action Plan for the Environment (C.A.P.E.) program that partnerships involving relevant stakeholders provide a better way of resolving issues.[5] If programs are well coordinated, they draw on the collective capabilities of the various stakeholders, reducing the need for large organizations and budgets.

A third obstacle was underfunding. Well-managed agencies delivering results managed to increase funding by demonstrating their value added. In addition, switching from land acquisition to land stewardship models reduced future capital budget requirements for bringing land under conservation management.

Consensus Building

Consensus building has been one of the most critical success factors in the sector. It is best demonstrated in the C.A.P.E. program, which laid a foundation for how landscape-level programs would evolve in the sector. The enlightened leadership within the Department of Environmental Affairs, SANParks, and SANBI, coupled with programs such as Working for Water, disarmed skeptics about the need to consider biodiversity and ecosystem services in development.

One of the areas where consensus was not initially reached was the applicability of South Africa's environmental impact assessment regulations to the mining sector. A decision was made that the regulations would not apply because the mining sector already followed a form of environment assessment. Several years later, however, mining and biodiversity guidelines were developed and approved by the two ministers concerned (box 9.3).

Box 9.3 Getting Sectors to Embrace Environmental Considerations

South Africa's economy was built on mining. Government policy has therefore been promining, which has often had negative consequences for the environment, including biodiversity. The environment sector struggled to find a mechanism to encourage mines to include biodiversity considerations in their planning and development.

The biodiversity sector began to engage with the organized mining sector in 1999. "After several years of negotiation, in 2013, the Minister of Water and Environmental Affairs and the

box continues next page

Box 9.3 Getting Sectors to Embrace Environmental Considerations *(continued)*

Minister of Mineral Affairs jointly published mining and biodiversity guidelines in 2013," explains Kristal Maze, chief director at SANBI. "It took long and hard work, but we got the job done" (Maze, Driver, and Brownlie 2004).

In another example, asking key players to subscribe to the conservation and development vision—not assuming a no answer to a request for support—was critical, according to Andrew Zaloumis. He explained that the former South African National Defense Force was one of the largest landholders in South Africa, including in areas of high biodiversity importance, such as around the St. Lucia wetlands and the missile testing ranges in the Cape. In the case of St. Lucia, he was able to request the defense force to transfer the St. Lucia land, which they were no longer using, to the World Heritage Authority. On another occasion, he heard SAFCOL (the South African Forestry Company Limited) was also going to dispose of some of its key forestry land on the Western and Eastern Shores of St. Lucia. He acted swiftly to demonstrate, using soil maps, that a portion of that land formed part of the St. Lucia wetland system. He was able to get it transferred to the World Heritage Authority while the rest of the land was sold off by SAFCOL.

Source: Department of Environmental Affairs and SANBI 2010.

Sequencing

The sector has seen three broad stages of development. The first stage involved establishing the powers and duties of national and provincial governments and enacting new overarching legislation. An overlapping stage involved demonstrating the program and policy concept through early programs, such as C.A.P.E. During this stage, the lower-than-expected capacities of provincial and of local government structures became apparent. The third stage involved granting SANParks and SANBI new mandates and empowering them to fulfill them. They have done so with confidence, delivering strong results.

Results Achieved

The institutional model for conserving and rehabilitating South Africa's biodiversity and ecosystem assets shifted from a largely public sector activity to a model in which the private sector participates. At a more local level, the focus has shifted from conservation of park assets to development of the biodiversity economy and the creation of benefits for local communities.

In order to create a system of national parks that was more representative of South Africa's diverse ecosystems, South Africa expanded its area under some form of protected area management from 6.0 percent in 2008 to 7.8 percent in 2013 (SANBI 2012[6]) against a target of 8 percent by 2010 set by the Department of Environmental Affairs in 2005. "SANParks has expanded its area under conservation by 600,000 hectares to 4.2 million hectares and established four new national parks, as well as corridors linking parks. In addition, four or five parks cover their operating costs, and approximately half are about to break even," notes Mike Knight. With more than 85 percent of its operating costs covered, SANParks may have achieved the highest level of self-financing of any park service in the world. In addition, it has established several marine protected areas adjacent to national parks. Conservation on private land has taken off. For example, 140,000 hectares of land is being conserved under the Wine and Biodiversity Initiative, and Kwa-Zulu Natal Wildlife Service has 170,000 hectares under stewardship (KZN Wildlife 2013). Twenty-one marine protected areas cover 20 percent of the coastline, a key step in restoring inshore fish stocks and protecting fish breeding grounds.

The success of the Working for Water program was discussed earlier. It pays unemployed members of the community to systematically remove alien invasive plants in priority areas.

The science behind ecosystem planning has been strengthened within SANBI, and SANParks is routinely recognized by the professional community as being world class. South Africa has developed a strong legal framework for the sector and reformed the key national institutions steering the sector—SANBI, SANParks, and the Department of Environmental Affairs.

A series of highly innovative models was developed for advancing the landscape management approach and mainstreaming biodiversity and ecosystem considerations into land use. At the forefront are models that support and enable landowners and communities to contract portions of their land into conservation use.

South Africa has achieved very significant reforms, which appear to be sustainable. The Department of Environmental Affairs receives a modest but sustainable portion of the government's annual budget, and both SANParks and SANBI have increased their operating income. Policy makers are mindful of the fact that tourism is the most rapidly growing sector of the economy and is largely nature based. With poverty levels still high, public works programs such as Working for Water receive an increased share of the national budget, thanks to their demonstrated results, visibility, and popularity.

Reforms engaged key national ministries, provincial and local governments, and special purpose bodies, such as SANParks and SANBI. A hallmark of the sector has been the extent to which it has engaged private and communal landowners through cooperative models to contract land into the conservation estate. Landowners have bought into several initiatives to strengthen biodiversity management in working landscapes. Nonprofit organizations—including key international environment organizations, bilateral and multilateral development agencies, including United Nations (UN) agencies, the World Bank, and the GEF—have lined up to support South Africa's biodiversity agenda. South Africa's stakeholder engagement model has proven sustainable because it leverages the strengths of agencies, involves cooperative governance, and takes into account all views.

An important part of developing the new environment institutions has been promoting good governance and combatting corruption, as illustrated in box 9.4.

Box 9.4 Combatting Corruption

South Africa has adopted a number of innovative measures to support good governance, promote transparency, and combat corruption. The Department of Environmental Affairs set up a 24-hour environment crimes and incidents hotline. SANParks established a crime and ethics reporting email address and contact number, managed independently by KPMG. SANBI also established a whistleblower hotline, administered by the South Africa Corporate Fraud Management Institute (SACFMI). All procurement documents carry a whistleblower telephone number to report fraud or corruption. From time to time, SANParks also posts reports on its website of the outcome of high-profile investigations involving allegations of fraud or corruption against staff.

The Department of Environmental Affairs created a high-profile National Environment Management Inspectorate, known as the "green scorpions," which operates as a network of government agencies from the national to the local level. It made 1,818 arrests in 2012/13, up from 1,080 in 2011/12. The boards of SANParks and SANBI play oversight roles, as does Parliament. The public protector also investigates complaints in the sector, including against government ministers.

Sources: SANBI, SANParks, and Department of Environmental Affairs Annual Reports from 2012 to 2014.

Conclusions: Success Factors, Challenges, and Lessons Learned

The South African experience in shifting from poor conservation practices, which were largely established for white South Africans, to being inclusive for all South Africans and in strengthening biodiversity management yields several success factors and lessons learned.

First, the Constitution elevated the importance of appropriate biodiversity management coupled with the need to address poverty as well as land rights. This created an important space for ensuring that people would never again be unfairly evicted from land to make way for conservation and that people needed to be placed at the forefront of conservation efforts. It also recognized that development could not take place at the expense of the environment. This approach was included in the Reconstruction and Development Program (RDP).

Second, significant organizational change and the development of major new programs require visionary leadership. A strong constitution alone does not drive the process. Only after inspiring leaders took over did the Department of Environmental Affairs begin to demonstrate results and win the confidence of other national departments, the provinces, and the private sector. Inspiring leadership led to the Department being viewed in a more senior light. Creating the NBI at arm's length from government worked: SANBI is able to act nimbly, with some independence from the regular government bureaucracy. These experiences show that reforming existing institutions can be preferable to creating new ones. In this case, institutions with dedicated professionals, middle management, and procurement and financial management capabilities were willing to take on new and wider policy mandates. Investing in good staff is crucial, and staff at all levels should be properly compensated and barred from running their own parallel businesses or taking on external assignments.

Third, sequencing is key. A program is most successful when the concept is first accepted among a few willing stakeholders before the program is scaled up. A good example is the land stewardship program, which was developed over time. To help gather greater support, good news stories have also been essential for getting the attention and support of the public and decision makers.

Fourth, investment is needed in the sector by the government, the private sector, and landowners, which requires the development of partnerships. Investing in biodiversity and ecosystem assets pays returns, in the form of increased tourism, private enterprise development, and poverty alleviation. Whenever possible, biodiversity organizations should develop their own income streams and as far as possible begin to cover their own operating costs. Turning to the international community for assistance on incremental program financing and design played a key role in developing the subsector. It allowed for a "learning-by-doing" early start model, which was later replicated. The learning-by-doing approach enabled the sector to test and implement models and activities that work (such as the highly successful landscape-level planning models, stewardship programs, and commercialization of parks).

Fifth, successful donor-supported biodiversity programs established small project management units. To the extent possible, program activities were farmed out to other implementing partners. At the same time, South Africa's strong domestic funding and professional capabilities enabled the country to implement programs with little external technical support. Bold program designs that delivered results on time created demand by new stakeholders to enroll in activities.

Many challenges remain. The *Fifth Biodiversity Assessment Report* (SANBI 2012) does not confirm that the decline in the overall health of South Africa's ecosystems and biodiversity assets is being reversed. Nevertheless, the results section of the report indicates impressive gains that would not have taken place without the reforms. First, mainstreaming biodiversity and ecosystem assets into development will require continuous innovation in response to new and emerging threats, including climate change. Part of the challenge will be to develop models that better value ecosystem services while protecting ecosystem assets that do not demonstrate economic value. This will also require a further strengthening of programs at the provincial and local government levels, where most conservation authorities remain weak.

Second, rhino poaching, as an example, has reached epic proportions in South Africa because of the illegal international demand for rhino horn. Existing or future programs to address this crisis will need to demonstrate greater success to keep South Africa's populations of both black and white rhinos from declining further toward extinction.

Third, investment is needed to build a constituency of black professionals in the sector. "With hindsight we should have invested more heavily in addressing this issue," notes Abrahamse. The national Jobs Fund allocated $30 million over three years to the Groen Sebenza program (which supports youth in biodiversity jobs) and placed 818 unemployed students in 43 different conservation-related institutions to get working experience.

Fourth, progress in marine conservation has been slower than expected. Although SANParks has established a number of inshore protected areas, South Africa's offshore marine ecosystems remain poorly protected.[7] The poaching of marine resources is a serious problem for some key species. Another challenge is the settling of all land claims, which has still not been completed in a number of conservation areas.

Reforms in the sector are largely complete. The focus is now on expanding programs and responding to emerging challenges. The institutional setting has settled down, and the key national institutions are in good health. The marine environment is perhaps the one area in which reform is needed. In particular, offshore protected areas need to be established, and measures to rebuild inshore fish stocks and reduce the poaching of high-value species, such as abalone and crayfish, must be strengthened. Other issues the sector is addressing include bringing more black professionals into the sector; making use of new technologies to make information more readily available to decision makers and the public; reviewing how best to unlock the value of natural assets, including potentially through payment for ecosystem services, something SANParks is interested in; and ensuring that local communities benefit from parks.

Notes

1. "Landscape" refers to large areas (often hundreds of square kilometers) that share certain common biodiversity features.

2. The Working for Water program pays unemployed members of the community to systematically remove alien invasive plants in priority areas.

3. The GEF provides grant financing to developing countries primarily to implement various international environment conventions.

4. Now South African National Parks (SANParks).

5. The C.A.P.E. program is a major landscape-level program to conserve the Cape Floristic Kingdom, the world's smallest and most threatened plant kingdom. It includes flora found only in the southernmost part of South Africa.

6. According to SANBI this includes some privately owned nature reserves that were not included in a previous 2011 figure and that still need to be verified.

7. South African Government. http://www.gov.za/about-sa/environment.

References

Department of Environmental Affairs. 2005. *National Biodiversity Strategy and Action Plan.* Pretoria: Department of Environmental Affairs.

———. 2015. *State of the Environment.* Pretoria. http://soer.deat.gov.za/1218.html.

Department of Environmental Affairs and SANBI (South African National Biodiversity Institute). 2010. *Biodiversity for Development: South Africa's Landscape Approach to Conserving Biodiversity and Promoting Ecosystems Resilience.* Silverton, South Africa.

Jobs Fund. "Welcome to the Jobs Fund." http://www.jobsfund.org.za/.

KZN Wildlife. 2013. *Annual Report.* South Africa: KZN Wildlife.

Maze, Kristal, Amanda Driver, and Susie Brownlie. 2004. "Mining and Biodiversity in South Africa: A Discussion Paper." Forest Trends Association, Washington, DC. http://forest-trends.org/documents/files/doc_602.pdf.

Potatoes South Africa. 2012. "Potato Fact Sheet." http://biodiversityadvisor.sanbi.org/wp-content/uploads/2012/11/Potatoes-fact-sheet.pdf.

Republic of South Africa. 2012. *South Africa's 5th National Report to the Convention on Biodiversity.* Silverton, South Africa. https://www.cbd.int/doc/world/za/za-nr-05-en.pdf.

SANBI (South African National Biodiversity Institute). 2006. *Fynbos, Fynmense, People Making Biodiversity Work.* Silverton, South Africa: SANBI. http://www.sanbi.org/sites/default/files/documents/documents/biodiversityseries4.pdf.

———. 2012. *Fifth Biodiversity Assessment Report.* Pretoria: SANBI.

———. 2013. *Annual Report.* Pretoria: SANBI.

———. 2015. *South African Mining and Biodiversity Forum (SAMBF).* Pretoria: SANBI. http://biodiversityadvisor.sanbi.org/industry-and-conservation/conservation-and-mining/connect-2/south-african-mining-and-biodiversity-forum-sambf/.

SANParks (South African National Parks). 2006. *Annual Review 2006/07.* Pretoria: SANParks. http://www.sanbi.org/sites/default/files/documents/documents/annualreport 2006-2007.pdf.

———. 2013. *Annual Report 2013/14.* Pretoria: SANParks. http://www.sanparks.org/assets/docs/general/annual-report-2013.pdf.

———. 2015. "The South African National Parks Ethics Line." SANParks, Pretoria. http://www.sanparks.org/about/crime/default2.php.

World Bank. 2002. *Mainstreaming Biodiversity in Development: Case Studies from South Africa.* Washington, DC: World Bank.

———. 2006. *Where Is the Wealth of Nations? Measuring Capital for the 21st Century.* Washington, DC: World Bank. http://siteresources.worldbank.org/INTEEI/214578-1110886258964/20748034/All.pdf.

CHAPTER 10

Improving the Management of the National Road Network

Ben Gericke

Introduction

In 1994 the South African government recognized that a change in policy direction was required to address the transportation legacy, which reflected the discriminatory practices of the previous regime. One priority area was the management of the national road network of about 7,200 kilometers, the backbone of the South African road network of about 747,000 kilometers. Under earlier governments, management of the national road network had been the responsibility of the Department of Transport (DOT), which was responsible for the planning, design, construction, and operation of the network; maintenance responsibility had been delegated to the provinces. The national road network had been developed to support the industrial and economic centers, with little regard to the transportation needs of workers. People living in remote townships and homelands had poor access to growth centers and cities. In addition, there was a substantial decline in road construction and maintenance, in line with overall public investment trends during the 1980s.

The post-apartheid government sought to realign public expenditure and finance public services to redress these imbalances and deficit in public investment, but it was unable to efficiently respond to the lack of road services. Road traffic was continuing to grow, and the commute from rural areas to economic centers remained long and difficult. "The time cost of commuting for working families was destroying family life," said the first minister of transport in the democratic government, Mac Maharaj, who served in 1994–99. Road services were not delivering on people's needs because funds to expand or improve the network were not available. The democratic government had to first attend to the social infrastructure neglected by the previous regime and reprioritize its expenditure accordingly.

The author is a Program Leader and Lead Transport Specialist in the Africa Region of the World Bank. This chapter benefited from extensive interviews with current and former government officials. The author thanks Peter Freeman for excellent peer reviewing of this chapter.

This chapter describes the transformation of the management of the national road network and explains how—through the establishment of the South African National Road Agency, Limited (SANRAL), in 1998—the government created a more efficient delivery mechanism for responding to the demands of a growing South Africa.

The Policy Challenge

Before 1994, management of the national road network was the responsibility of the DOT. This centralized delivery model had serious disadvantages. The key challenge for the incoming government was to find a delivery model that would respond to and implement the post-1994 policies. "There was an urgent need to develop an integrated and rapid transportation system that increased the access to the economy for large segments of the country's population," recalls Maharaj.

The incoming government faced several unique issues. The road network had not been developed to take the transport needs of the whole population into account, leading to long commute times and poor access to the economic centers of South Africa for a large part of the population. Earlier governments under-funded road construction and maintenance, especially in rural areas, even though constant traffic growth required network and capacity expansion.

Road maintenance was poorly supervised, with provinces not always able to show the DOT where and on which roads maintenance funds had been spent (Bennet 2011). The DOT did not have the network and management systems in place to provide management information to justify rehabilitation and mainte-nance requirements on a network-wide basis.

The functions of the South African National Roads Board, established in the 1930s, had largely been absorbed into the DOT, with the director-general of the DOT serving as chairperson. There was thus little opportunity for independent review of development needs and accountability.

Addressing the Policy Challenge

Minister Maharaj felt strongly that transport had a significant role to play in social and economic development. "Improvements in transportation are vital to provide equal opportunities to participate in the economic growth of South Africa," he said (Bennet 2011). He ordered the development of a white paper on national transport policy, to be published in 1996. It would review the challenges, recommend improvements, and provide the necessary policy guidance to imple-ment them.

Maharaj identified the need for a new growth and financing model. He wanted to look critically at the role of government in transport. Together with Ketso Gordhan, who was first appointed as adviser to the minister and later appointed director-general of the DOT; Harold Harvey, then deputy director-general of the DOT; and Nazir Alli, chief director of roads, he led a process of reviewing the existing national transport policy. Consultations were held with more than 300 organizations and people from the transportation industry and business, government, and the academic community. The outcome of the consultations led to the preparation of a green paper on transport in March 1996. It was refined after further comments and presentations by stakeholders and finalized as the *White Paper on National Transport Policy* in August 1996 (South Africa, DOT 1996).

The white paper recommended that government adopt a more commercial approach to road management through the establishment of an arm's-length institution that would undertake "certain elements of government's current activities in service provision and operations more efficiently and cost-effectively, giving higher levels of service to consumers which would be paid for by direct or indirect user charges. This could be done through professionally managed arm's length agencies functioning according to commercial principles, with government retaining the responsibility of ensuring that minimum standards are maintained, and that essential services are provided" (South Africa, DOT 1996).

As part of the transport policy review, in 1995 delegations from the DOT traveled to other countries to learn from their experiences. Gordhan and Alli visited Malaysia, New Zealand, and the Philippines. "We were impressed with the results of the road reform implemented in New Zealand, at the time considered a world leader in this field," Alli said. The New Zealand model—which moved authority from a central government responsibility to one managed on a commercial basis, in which employees of the transit authority are not civil servants—appeared to be a very good model to guide reform in South Africa.

Following the 1996 adoption of the white paper and the decision to restructure the DOT, Maharaj managed to convince his colleagues at the political level that the change to an agency model was the correct option. "We faced opposition and skepticism with the proposed agency model at political and other levels. However, sound reasoning, based on the successful international experience from, especially New Zealand, prevailed and the proposed model was approved," he recalls. The concept was sold as part of the larger reforms being undertaken to redress the imbalances of the past. Informal meetings played an important role in convincing skeptics of the need for a paradigm shift to serve the country as a whole, especially previously underserved areas. Gordhan and Alli provided the technical leadership for implementation.

Two years after the adoption of the white paper, the government approved the establishment of SANRAL and promulgated the enabling legislation. Although SANRAL was established under its own founding legislation (Act No. 7 of 1998), it was also registered as a company under the Companies Act. Registration of the agency as a company enabled SANRAL to implement corporate standards of governance, accounting, and reporting, and the ability to raise capital based on the strength of its balance sheet while government was empowered to impose sanctions for breach of contract.

Operationalizing the Change

Following passage of the SANRAL-enabling legislation, the team—led by Alli, who was appointed chief executive officer (CEO) of SANRAL—implemented the required restructuring. The new legislation gave SANRAL responsibility for financing, management, control, planning, development, maintenance, and rehabilitation of the national road system. Alli was convinced that the provision and maintenance of roads is a business and that SANRAL should therefore be run as one.

Transfer of operational functions affected about 330 DOT employees. They faced four options:

1. Accept a voluntary retrenchment package.
2. Stay with the DOT, or seek a transfer (if a post is available) to another government department.
3. Become self-employed. The DOT provided a business management mentor and guaranteed contract work (on land surveys, design, and road monitoring and maintenance services, for example) at negotiated rates for a period of two years.
4. Resign from the DOT and join SANRAL. Salary adjustments equivalent to those awarded for civil servants were guaranteed for one year.

Alli and Gordhan handpicked a high-performing staff and convinced them to move to SANRAL. The process was a long one. Staff were aware that their benefits as civil servants would be terminated and that their future would be uncertain after the initial two-year contract. The stable government salary package would be replaced with a salary package including adjustments based on performance. Staff would be leaving the safe employment conditions of the public service for the risks (and rewards) of an agency run on commercial lines. Eventually, 91 people decided to join Alli.

Overcoming Challenges

Alli and his management team addressed several major challenges.

Narrowing the skills gap. SANRAL increased its staff complement, from the original 92 (including Alli himself) to about 277 in 2013. The larger workforce was needed to support the expanded road network, which grew from 7,200 kilometers in 1994 to 21,403 kilometers in 2014, and the changing nature of its business, from being a supplier of road infrastructure to being a manager/operator of road assets (SANRAL 2014a).

SANRAL is committed to achieving appropriate levels of representation for all designated groups at all grades. Doing so was difficult, however, given the shortage of the required skills in the South African labor market, especially among historically disadvantaged groups. To address the problem, SANRAL implemented a variety of skills development initiatives, including a scholarship program promoting mathematics and physical science for the last three years of high school and a scholarship program for civil engineering and related fields.

During the 2014 academic year, SANRAL enrolled 177 students in its scholarship program; 91 percent of them obtained distinctions in mathematics, and 85 percent achieved distinctions in physical science. Of the 20 students who graduated in December 2013, 16 were employed full time by SANRAL (SANRAL 2014a).

The agency also implemented a mix of measures to strengthen the capacity of recruited staff. It finances internal scholarships and actively supports staff participation in training programs that address the skills gaps within the organization. In 2013 SANRAL awarded 29 such scholarships and allowed 127 employees to attend specific training programs.

SANRAL recognizes the need for continued hands-on training after academic training has been completed. Toward that end, its flat organizational structure inculcates a culture of collective mentorship, individual responsibility, and empowerment while providing the opportunity for succession planning. It has been especially helpful in affording new employees the opportunity to contribute and learn. Having managers manage projects through the entire design, procurement, and implementation process has resulted in faster problem solving, shorter lag times, and full ownership of projects.

Establishing leadership structures. The enabling legislation provided the opportunity to establish a more hands-off relationship with government when compared with the now defunct Roads Board. SANRAL's board of directors consists of eight members. The minister of transport appoints seven of them: the chairperson, one member nominated by the minister of finance and representing the National Treasury, and five members with qualifications and experience related to national roads. The eighth member is the CEO of SANRAL. Important provisions to develop the arm's-length relationship between the new SANRAL and the minister and the Department of Transport were the signing of a compact or performance agreement between the two parties and the legal requirement that the chairman of the board cannot be a government official.

"Alli and his management team put in place a robust and reliable board secretariat function that consistently provided all information to board members in time. This was very helpful in building confidence between the board and the SANRAL management team in the early years," according to Andrew Donaldson, deputy director-general of the National Treasury. A transparent disclosure policy is also in place, with every annual report providing information on the number of board meetings and actual attendance.

The relationship between the sole shareholder (the minister of transport, representing the state) and the board is governed by a rolling three-year performance contract (known as a shareholder compact) between the minister and the board. The contract is mirrored in the contract between the board and the CEO. Staff members sign performance contracts that are assessed biannually.

Preventing corruption and fraud and enhancing transparency. Alli and Gordhan recognized that to attract private funding it was important that SANRAL should enjoy a strong reputation for the integrity and transparency of its business decision making. SANRAL implemented a fraud and corruption policy. "There is zero tolerance towards fraud and corruption. Any credible case will be investigated," says Alli. Business and investors welcomed this message.

SANRAL has a fraud hotline service, operated independently by Tip-Offs Anonymous, on which anyone within the organization or outside can anonymously report suspected fraud. SANRAL's 2014 annual report indicates that the agency investigated all fraud hotline reports. It also achieved 100 percent compliance with the requirements of the Public Finance Management Act on procurement and reduced the average impact of internally controllable risks.

The construction sector was rocked with allegations of collusion among major South African contractors in the award of contracts for the construction of stadiums for the FIFA World Cup of 2010. South Africa has constitutional and statutory requirements for fair and competitive procurement processes that led to the Competition Commission investigating the allegations. The Commission confirmed the alleged collusion, levied fines, and then referred the matter to the Competition Tribunal for finalization. The process allowed the whistleblower to be granted leniency. The proceedings were conducted under the Construction Fast Track Settlement Process (Competition Commission South Africa 2014).

This case has direct implications for SANRAL because the companies involved are beneficiaries of SANRAL contracts and concessions. Thirteen SANRAL projects spanning about eight years were affected. In line with its ethos of zero tolerance for fraud and corruption, SANRAL issued a formal complaint with the applicable law enforcement agency for criminal investigations. It was the only affected agency in South Africa to do so. SANRAL also conducted an exercise to estimate the damages suffered. Once it is completed, SANRAL will consider the prospects of a successful civil damages claim against the contractors concerned.

Reducing the maintenance and rehabilitation backlog. In 1994 the road sector faced the dual challenges of underinvestment and the need to upgrade the country's road network. SANRAL estimated that the cost of addressing the road maintenance backlog was more than three times the annual allocation from the National Treasury (Bennet 2011). The government budget deficit of 5.1 percent in 1994 reaffirmed the need to explore new models for managing the transport sector. Four strategies were particularly important.

The first strategy was adopting asset management as the basis for managing the network. "In the past, government did not use the principle of asset management to provide and maintain the national road network. We wanted to develop a management information system that would, based on the actual deterioration of the road network, provide sufficient information so that we can compile a credible annual budget that will allow us to maintain the road conditions at the optimum levels of service," said Alli. SANRAL developed a set of performance standards for the road network and reports on its performance against them in its annual reports. It uses the same performance standards to develop the annual budget proposal submitted to the National

Treasury for consideration and funding. These proposals usually include a sensitivity analysis showing the impact of different budgeting scenarios on these standards. Over the years, SANRAL has been able to show that additional allocations of funds have contributed to progress in road maintenance and improvement of pavement standards.

SANRAL trained staff to develop, implement, and manage the road asset management system in a way that provides reliable inputs for maintenance planning and budgeting. The system was implemented over time and is continuing to evolve. Data on road conditions are collected annually, and bridge condition data are collected every three years. SANRAL recently procured a specialized road condition survey vehicle that includes state-of-the-art technology used by only five similar agencies in the world. It is capable of conducting in-motion surveying of the entire network annually. The new system represents a major improvement over the earlier, much slower surveys, which required stationary testing (with the associated road safety risks). Overall performance is assessed using longer-term deterioration models that evaluate the costs and benefits of various technically viable interventions required to correct the identified faults and maintain the required service standards. These standards are based on specific performance criteria measuring road condition and road user comfort. Today SANRAL provides considered justification for its annual funding requests based on the analysis of the road asset management system data.

"One of the benefits of the longer-term planning and budgeting reports coming from this system is that Treasury could understand, in terms of simple service standards, how the road network is performing and how well SANRAL was applying the allocated funding," says Donaldson. "SANRAL's transparent approach to reporting performance in terms of these service standards helped in building a level of confidence that led to a gradual increase in funding allocation to SANRAL."

The second strategy was switching to performance-based contracting. SANRAL decided from the outset to outsource all road maintenance activities. The traditional approach of activity-based contracting was cumbersome to administer. A hybrid contract model, consisting of a mixture of activity- and performance-based payment items, was developed and refined over time. These contracts are applied for all routine maintenance and protection of the environment. This innovation has reduced SANRAL's contractual expenditures, as contractors provide roads that exceed the minimum service standards. Hybrid activity/performance-based contracting also reduces the technical inputs required during contract supervision.

The third strategy was developing a broader contracting base that includes small and medium-size enterprises (SMEs). After 1994 the government introduced policies to include all previously disadvantaged groups in all levels of the economy. SANRAL planned and implemented a very successful program to build and strengthen SMEs, especially companies owned by members of previously disadvantaged groups. Use of the hybrid performance-based contracting method exposed SMEs to a system that allowed mentoring and incentivized them to deliver services within specifications. SANRAL's annual report indicates that it contracted with 1,508 SMEs in 2014, including 1,137 black-owned businesses. Implementation of this program saw an increase in new entrants into the construction sector.

The fourth strategy was separation of funding streams. SANRAL also established two separate funding portfolios: nontoll roads and toll roads, with no cross-subsidization between the two types of roads. Toll roads are supposed to be self-financing; nontoll roads are funded from budgetary allocations made by the National Treasury.

Many countries, including New Zealand, earmark funding for roads through, among other mechanisms, a fuel levy. South Africa had dedicated a fuel levy that went to the Roads Fund, but it was abandoned in the 1980s when the fund accumulated large reserves alongside other government spending priorities. South Africa now has a fuel levy that contributes to the general government funding. The initial budget appropriation to SANRAL was equivalent to 4 cents per liter, but this was not an earmarked allocation. Alli and Gordhan considered the principle of budget allocations to be insufficient for longer-term roads, so the SANRAL Act included provisions for debt finance and cost recovery through tolls.

Over time, and with the development of the road asset management system, the need for relying on a fuel levy changed. The National Treasury allocation to nontoll roads became broadly based on actual requirements for maintenance and improvements, based on SANRAL's asset management system reports. The notion of funding nontoll road operations through fuel levy revenues was therefore discarded.

National Treasury allocations for nontoll roads have increased substantially since 2000. However, they have been offset by the higher costs of materials and the increase in road network length under SANRAL jurisdiction.

The principle of funding parts of the national roads through tolling is well established in South Africa—with the first tolls established in the 19th century, primarily to offset the costs of expensive mountain passes and other road links. More modern tolling operations were introduced in the 1980s. The policy on tolling was confirmed in the 1996 White Paper on transport policy. Adopting the "pay only when you use it" principle, the minister of transport authorized SANRAL to finance new toll roads largely through debt and not through budget allocations. It developed two options to fund its toll road portfolio: bond issues in the capital markets and concessioning. Overall borrowing limits are set annually by the National Treasury and approved by the shareholder. A portion of the debt raised is guaranteed by the government; the remainder is raised on the strength of SANRAL's balance sheet. Where roads are concessioned, the concessionaire is responsible for funding the project. It recovers its investment and operating costs through the revenue received from tolls.

SANRAL manages both its tolling operations and roadworks through performance-based contracts with private sector service providers. In 2014 about

3,128 kilometers (15 percent) of South Africa's road network was tolled. SANRAL financed about 59 percent of this network, with the rest financed by the private sector. Three private sector–financed concessions operate in South Africa; the N3 Toll Concession (Pty) Ltd (N3TC), the N1/N4 Bakwena Platinum Concession Consortium (BAKWENA), and the N4 Trans African Concession (TRAC), which operates the Maputo Development Corridor Highway. The TRAC contract was the first international concession traversing two countries, comprising tolling and road works in both South Africa and Mozambique.

SANRAL raises the funding required for its toll roads from capital markets by issuing bonds and taking out loans. In order to do so, it has to comply with internationally accepted accounting standards, including fully documented ownership of its road assets. Many of the road links transferred from the government did not have documentation showing that the land belonged to the state. Alli embarked on a program to identify and properly register all the assets transferred. This has been a lengthy and administratively challenging process, but it has also enabled economic value to be derived from sale or lease of land parcels in excess of requirements.

SANRAL's financial standing has come under stress in recent years because of delays and controversy associated with a major new tolling project, aimed at financing highway improvements in South Africa's economic heartland through an electronic open road tolling system. The negative impact on debt servicing of the delayed tolling of the Gauteng Freeway Improvement Project (GFIP) resulted in a ratings downgrade by Moody's (box 10.1). SANRAL revenue collections increased significantly after the start of toll collections on the GFIP in 2013. Moody's affirmed its Baa3-rating for SANRAL and changed its outlook from negative to stable in June 2014. As in many other countries, user charges to finance roads are unpopular and at the time of writing remain politically contentious.

Box 10.1 Impact of the Gauteng Freeway Improvement Project (GFIP)

The Gauteng Freeway Improvement Project (GFIP) comprises different phases to upgrade and implement a network that will eventually include 560 kilometers of freeway. It developed from the need to reduce congestion on the freeways around Gauteng, one of South Africa's nine provinces. Although the project was not a 2010 FIFA World Cup project, that event lent impetus to speed progress on the project.

From its inception in 2005, the project was based on the user-pay principle. SANRAL opted for an open-road tolling model. This innovative model consists of a multilane free-flow toll system using electronic toll collection that allows tolls to be charged without vehicles having to stop or slow down.

---

box continues next page

Box 10.1 Impact of the Gauteng Freeway Improvement Project (GFIP) *(continued)*

The first phase included the upgrading of 201 kilometers of the most congested freeways. It was to be completed in May 2010, just in time for the World Cup. Tolling was postponed until April 2011, after completion of all tolled sections.

The planned tolling cost structure created a public outcry. Motorists, taxi associations, and labor unions expressed concerns and disagreement. As a result of this social pressure, the minister of transport suspended the tariffs and appointed a task team to review the fee structure. The courts, including the highest court in the land, the Constitutional Court, also reviewed the issue, with the Constitutional Court twice finding in favor of SANRAL. However, there is still considerable opposition to road tolling on major urban networks. A 2014 Ipsos survey revealed that 34 percent of people were willing to pay, 27 percent were neutral, and 38 percent were unwilling to pay the tolls.[a]

This opposition led to the establishment, in 2014, of a Gauteng Provincial Government Advisory Panel on the socioeconomic impact of the Gauteng e-tolls by the province's premier. The Advisory Panel's report found that e-tolling benefits the economy and the people of the province in various ways, including a better-quality road system, reduced travel time, improved fuel efficiency, reduced vehicle operating costs, and improved logistics efficiencies for business. Premier Makhura subsequently announced that elements of the e-toll system would be reviewed to address questions of affordability, equity, fairness, administrative simplicity, and sustainability. The review process, chaired by Deputy President Ramaphosa, with participation from the Gauteng Province and the three affected metropolitan municipalities (Ekurhuleni, Johannesburg, and Tshwane), was completed with the e-tolling system intact but curtailed. Future expansion of the e-toll road network would be difficult to implement. (SAnews 2015b). Even after the publication of the review findings supporting the e-toll system, public opposition remains high and payment of tolls continues to be low.

The final chapter on the introduction of e-tolling and how public opposition might affect expansion of the system to other parts of the national road network has not been written. A lesson to be learned from the process is that politics play a significant role in decisions that affect road transport. As the Advisory Panel's report (Gauteng, Provincial Government 2014) noted,

> The NDOT and SANRAL seem to have ignored the central importance of politics. They seem to have viewed—wrongly as this impact assessment process shows—political issues as less important than the administrative battles fought over efficiency and economic growth. In fact, however, politics provide the real life and true meaning to the GFIP and the e-tolls. Without effective political participation, even the best transport administrative ideas will disappear and even enrage citizens.

The delayed implementation of the tolling systems had a negative impact on the financial situation of SANRAL, leading to a Moody's downgrade and some uncertainty about the future financing policy of national roads.

Source: SANRAL 2014a and diverse South African news channels.
a. Market research conducted in 2014 by Ipsos (http://www.ipsos.co.za).

Results Achieved

Under the leadership of Nazir Alli, SANRAL developed into a world-class road agency that dramatically improved the management of the national road network. Currently, SANRAL manages about 3 percent of the South African road network (table 10.1), although this accounts for a high proportion of long-distance freight and passenger traffic.

The asset management approach SANRAL adopted transformed the management of the national road network and led to a gradual transformation of the road construction and maintenance industry. Some of the major achievements are described below.

More than 95 percent of the roads SANRAL manages are in good to very good condition (up to 10 percent of a road network is often in poor condition), and 100 percent of its roads are under routine maintenance contracts. These success factors made SANRAL the preferred road network manager in South Africa. Because many provinces failed to maintain their road links in good condition, the government agreed to transfer some of these roads to the national road network. As a result, the national road network expanded over time with strong indications that it may expand to about 35,000 kilometers in the future (SANRAL 2014b). Provinces regularly ask SANRAL to provide technical assistance and help implement provincial road programs (Parliamentary Monitoring Group 2014).

The 2013/14 peer review by the Association of Southern African National Roads Agencies (ASANRA) examined the status of asset management at road agencies in Botswana, Lesotho, Malawi, Mozambique, Namibia, South Africa, Tanzania, Zambia, and Zimbabwe. It assessed performance against PAS 55:2008 (Institute of Asset Management, United Kingdom) standards, the international norm for good asset management practice at the time. (On January 15, 2014, these standards were replaced by ISO 55000 [International Organisation for Standardisation, Switzerland]; SANRAL has initiated preparations for an application for certification under the new standard.) Its review indicated that SANRAL's asset management meets PAS 55:2008 requirements for

Table 10.1 Management Responsibility for Paved and Gravel Roads in South Africa, 2014
Kilometers

Authority	Paved	Gravel	Total
SANRAL	21,403	0	21,403
Provinces (9)	47,348	226,273	273,621
Metropolitan authorities (8)	51,682	14,461	66,143
Municipalities	37,691	219,223	256,914
Estimated unproclaimed (public roads not formally gazetted by any authority)		131,919	131,919
Total	158,124	591,876	750,000

Source: SANRAL 2015.
Note: SANRAL = South African National Road Agency, Limited.

certification and that SANRAL is an international leader in asset management in the roads sector.

SANRAL's approach to rewarding performance and transforming the organization into one that better reflects South Africa's demographic led to very low staff turnover. It strengthens its capacity by "growing its own timber" through formal training at tertiary institutions and in-house training. SANRAL is not restricted to hiring based on an artificial organogram. It hires the skills it needs as and when required. In 2015 the Top Employers Institute, based in the Netherlands, recognized SANRAL as a top employer.

The introduction and rollout of performance-based maintenance contracting changed the business approach of contractors. In the past, the focus was on undertaking activity-based tasks. The new focus is on managing and maintaining roads at specific service standards, and with a special focus on improving safety and traffic management. Internationally, similar changes in contracting methodology resulted in cost savings of up to 30 percent compared with traditional contracting (Stankevich, Quereshi, and Queiroz 2005). Over time, SANRAL's practice of hiring SMEs, especially black-owned firms, will broaden the contracting base for the road sector, increasing competition and creating further opportunities for efficiency increases.

SANRAL's consistent application of road asset management reporting helped it win the trust of the National Treasury. As a result, allocations increased, allowing it to improve the condition of the national road network.

In addition, SANRAL has raised funding for toll roads comprising approximately 15 percent of the national road network through concessions and its own bond issues. Private sector involvement relieved the National Treasury of a significant funding requirement. However, opposition to the e-tolls of the GFIP may lead government to review its approach to cost recovery from road users, and to the appropriate balance between direct budget allocations from general revenue, dedicated fuel levy funding, license fees, and toll charges.

Conclusions: Success Factors, Challenges, and Lessons Learned

Several success factors and lessons learned account for SANRAL's success. First, political commitment to reform was strong. Mac Maharaj, the minister for transport at the time, drove the political sensitization and acted as the champion of the reform. He convinced his colleagues in the Cabinet of the important role of transport in the economy, getting them to designate transport as one of its five pillars for growing the economy, expanding trade and investment, and achieving social cohesion.

Second, Maharaj appointed a dedicated team to implement the institutional changes. Strong buy-in from the three key team members was key. Continuity was provided when Nazir Alli was appointed the first CEO of SANRAL. SANRAL's CEO has been in place since the agency's establishment. SANRAL's human resources policies foster morale within the agency and promote staff retention.

Third, SANRAL adopted a more business-like approach to managing roads. It introduced a pavement asset management framework and developed a staffing structure that responded to the identified requirements. However, managing roads in a more commercial manner does not remove political interest in the sector. The challenges of implementation of the GFIP show that politics and public opinion play very important roles in road management and financing. Agency management must allow for inclusive consultation procedures when considering any road infrastructure investment.

Fourth, SANRAL attracted private sector participation in its expanding toll road operations. Road users accepted this principle until the politically driven opposition to the e-toll system of the GFIP surfaced.

Still, some challenges remain. First, effective asset management needs to be expanded to the entire South African road network. The fact that provincial and local authorities have had more difficulty maintaining their road networks suggests that more road links need to be added to the national road network. Incorporating provincial roads—many of which are in very poor condition—into the national road network would put pressure on SANRAL's budget and the funding responsibility of the National Treasury. This approach may satisfy short-term needs, but it could be seen as inconsistent with the spirit of the Constitution, which assigns responsibility for these roads to the second- and third-tier authorities. The Constitution also obliges government to provide services efficiently and effectively, however. Shifting more roads into the national system while supporting provincial and local authorities in their road management responsibilities would help realize the government's vision to include all rural communities, especially previously disadvantaged ones, in the economy. International experience argues that all roads should be managed through appropriate asset management principles.

Second, the government needs to find a way to finance the provision and maintenance of road infrastructure. The controversy caused by the GFIP e-tolling system reduced the creditworthiness of SANRAL as a going concern. It has led to discussions of the national policy regarding toll roads and the user-pay principle and how to implement them in a more inclusive manner. There is a strong perception that a tolling system hurts the poor and low-income groups. Continuing opposition to the e-tolling system will result in a review of the current tolling policy. Opposition among road users should be addressed before South Africa embarks on other toll road projects. An earmarked fuel levy is a possible alternative, but it would at best be a proxy charge for road use and would need to be adapted, over time, to take account of vehicle technology change. Tolling may be fairer to the poor than a fuel levy. The technology exists to charge each vehicle per kilometer of road used, but implementation of such a system requires careful thought, given privacy concerns.

Third, land use issues need to be addressed in order to shorten travel times. The spatial development left over from the apartheid era places additional demands on parts of the transport network, resulting in longer travel times and higher transport costs for poorer people. SANRAL has an integral role to play in South Africa's adaptation to rising traffic volumes, urbanization, road congestion, growing long-distance trade and movements of people, and associated land use and traffic management policies. It is well placed to provide inputs on the transport infrastructure costs associated with any option the government would consider.

References

Bennet, Richard. 2011. "Increasing Transparency and Improving Project Management: South Africa's National Road Agency, 1998–2011." Innovations for Successful Societies Case Study, Princeton University, Princeton, NJ.

Competition Commission South Africa. 2014. "Statement on Competition Commission Meeting of 11 November 2014." Pretoria. http://www.compcom.co.za/wp-content/uploads/2014/09/Commission-statement-12-Nov-2014.pdf.

Gauteng, Provincial Government. 2014. *The Socio-economic Impact of the Gauteng Freeway Improvement Project and E-tolls Report.* Report of the advisory panel appointed by Gauteng Premier David Makhura. Johannesburg. http://www.gautengonline.gov.za.

Parliamentary Monitoring Group. 2014. Transport Budget Vote Speech by Minister of Transport Dipuo Peters at the Old Assembly Chambers, Parliament, Cape Town, July 15.

SAnews (South African Government News Agency). 2015a. "E-tolls Consultation to Continue." Press release, February 4. http://www.sanews.gov.za/south-africa/e-tolls-consultation-continue.

———. 2015b. "E-tolls Must Be Reviewed to Address Affordability: Report." January 15. http://www.sanews.gov.za/south-africa/e-tolls-must-be-reviewed-address-affordability-report.

SANRAL (South African National Road Agency, Limited). 2014a. *Annual Report.* Pretoria. www.nra.co.za.

———. 2014b. "Opening Remarks by Minister of Transport Dipuo Peters to the Advisory Panel on the Socio-economic Impact of the Gauteng E-tolls." Media release, November 4.

South Africa, DOT (Department of Transport). 1996. *White Paper on National Transport Policy.* Pretoria.

Stankevich, N., N. Quereshi, and C. Queiroz. 2005. "Performance-Based Contracting for Preservation and Improvement of Road Assets." Transport Note TN-27, World Bank, Washington, DC. Updated August 2009.

CHAPTER 11

Developing Renewable Energy through an Independent Power Producer Procurement Program

Joel Kolker

Introduction

South Africa has the largest energy sector in Sub-Saharan Africa. It produces more than half of the electricity on the subcontinent. The sector has made significant progress in overcoming the legacy of apartheid, nearly doubling the number of households with access to electricity between 2002 and 2013. By 2013, less than 15 percent of the population still lacked access (Statistics South Africa, 2014 data).

South Africa is the world's fifth-largest coal producer in the world. Not surprisingly, most of its power (70 percent) therefore comes from carbon. In 2009 South Africa was the world's 12th-worst carbon emitter and the largest emitter of carbon dioxide in Africa. To reduce its carbon footprint, the government embarked on a renewable energy program. The program's goal is to generate 20 percent of national capacity from renewable sources. The Renewable Energy Independent Power Producer Procurement Program (REIPPPP) has now completed five rounds of bidding to secure independent power producer agreements. Through the first five rounds,[1] over 90 transactions and private investment exceeding US$20 billion[2] and 6,300 megawatts (MW) of power were facilitated, making REIPPPP the largest independent power producer program in Africa. The first projects came online at the end of 2013. Private sector bidding

The author is the Lead Water and Sanitation Specialist at the World Bank's Water Global Practice. This chapter is based on "South Africa's Renewable Energy IPP Procurement Program: Success Factors and Lessons" (Eberhard, Kolker, and Leigland 2014) and has been revised to include updated information based on rounds 4 and 5 with the assistance of Karen Breytenbach, Sandra Coetzee, Gary Lloyd, and Paul Wroblicki from the REIPPPP unit. This chapter benefited from extensive interviews with current and former government officials, the private sector, and comments by the peer reviewers, including Luiz Maurer (International Finance Corporation), Karan Capoor (senior financial specialist in the World Bank Group's Energy and Extractives Global Practice), Mark Pickering (Globeleq), and Ros Thomas.

has increased in each round of bidding, prices have dropped, and transparency and competition have increased. By 2012, South Africa had become one of the top 10 countries in the world investing in renewable energy.

Eskom, the publicly owned national power utility, generates 96 percent of the country's electricity, owns and controls the national high-voltage transmission grid, and distributes about 60 percent of electricity directly to customers. Local authorities buy electricity in bulk from Eskom and distribute the balance. Direct electricity sales to mines and industry account for more than 40 percent of Eskom's distribution business.

In the 1970s, Eskom overestimated demand and embarked on a massive investment program, which continued into the 1980s, when it became apparent that the utility would have significant overcapacity. By the end of the 1990s, the country's electricity prices ranked among the lowest in the world. The utility had paid off the capital costs of much of its existing capacity, and customer prices were close to short-run marginal costs.

By 2004 demand for power was reaching the level of available supply. In response, Eskom initiated a $40 billion power plant construction program. A few years later, the National Energy Regulator of South Africa (NERSA) began allowing sharp upward adjustments in electricity tariffs, in an effort to sustain Eskom's financial viability.[3]

The formal planning system for the energy sector now mandates the Department of Energy (DOE) to produce an electricity plan called the Integrated Resource Plan. Based on this plan, the minister of energy issues periodic determinations regarding how much new power generation is needed and from which sources. NERSA can license new capacity only within the bounds set by these ministerial determinations. The most recent plan, updated in 2013, is for 2010–30.

In line with the Integrated Resource Plan, the government recognizes that independent power producers (IPPs) should be allowed to enhance the country's power-generating capacity.[4] Following the publication of the Energy Policy White Paper in 1998, the Cabinet approved a 70:30 split between Eskom and the private sector, and work commenced on the design of a competitive whole-sale power exchange. However, in 2004, with looming Eskom power shortages, the prospective wholesale market was abandoned in favor of the existing single-buyer model with Eskom the off-taker. IPPs were still expected to play a signifi-cant role in power generation; but the policy and regulatory framework for IPPs was not immediately put in place, and procurement programs run by Eskom for IPPs were mostly unsuccessful. No IPP contracts were signed except a handful of short-term power purchase agreements with industrial generators.

A dramatic turnaround occurred in 2011, as the result of a pioneering new power development program adopted by DOE that largely bypassed Eskom. The program, REIPPPP, has successfully channeled substantial private sector exper-tise and investment into grid-connected renewable energy at competitive prices.

In less than four years, more than 90 projects were awarded, the first of which are already online. Investments totaling $20 billion have been secured, and in excess of 6,300 MW of renewable power have been procured through five rounds of bidding. According to Ernst & Young's 2014 Renewable Energy Country Attractiveness Index, South Africa is one of the world's top 20 most attractive markets for renewable energy investments (and the only African state included in this list) (Ernst & Young 2014).

The Policy Challenge

REIPPPP represents the government of South Africa's dual policy objectives of rapidly bringing new energy sources online while minimizing the impact on climate change. The government began setting renewable energy targets in 2003, with the publication of a White Paper on Renewable Energy that envisioned reaching 10,000 gigawatt-hours (GWh) of renewable energy generation by 2013 (Department of Minerals and Energy 2003). The targets were not met.

The program was implemented against a background of institutional short-comings in the energy sector. Previous efforts to contract IPPs had been left to Eskom, based on instructions from the government.[5] All of them failed, perhaps because of a lack of capacity or, according to some critics, because of a fundamental lack of incentives for Eskom to weaken its monopoly on power generation.

The official renewable energy policy was not very effective in applying practical implementation strategies. Efforts to develop policies to mitigate climate change have had a much more profound impact. This outcome is surprising, because as a non-Annex I country under the Kyoto Protocol, South Africa is not required to reduce greenhouse gas emissions.[6] Nevertheless, the Department of Environmental Affairs commissioned research on long-term mitigation strategies. These strategies provided the basis for President Zuma to make a pledge at the Copenhagen Conference of Parties (COP) in 2009 that South Africa would reduce its carbon dioxide emissions by 34 percent below a business-as-usual scenario by 2020 and by 42 percent by 2025, provided the international community supported South Africa with financial aid and the transfer of appropriate technology. A subsequent National Climate Change Response White Paper, published in 2011, provided a wider band for emission caps (Department of Environmental Affairs 2011). At the COP17 meeting, in Durban in 2011, public and private sector stakeholder representatives agreed to 12 "commitments" aimed at achieving the government's goal of creating 300,000 new jobs in the "green economy" of South Africa by 2020.

South Africa's voluntary pledge in Copenhagen to reduce its carbon emissions from a business-as-usual scenario was the catalyst for new procurement strategies for renewable energy. South Africa first explored the option of renewable energy feed-in tariffs (REFITs). Globally, feed-in tariffs (FITs) have been the most widely used government support mechanism for accelerating private investment in renewable energy generation. They are meant to reflect the costs of producing particular kinds of energy, as determined by government analysis rather than through a competitive process. They are typically used to secure long-term supply contracts from renewable energy producers.

NERSA approved a REFIT policy in 2009. Tariffs were designed to cover generation costs plus a real after-tax return on equity of 17 percent and to be fully indexed for inflation. Considerable uncertainty about the nature of the procurement and licensing process remained. The legality of FITs within South Africa's public procurement framework was unclear, as was Eskom's intention to fully support the REFIT program.

In March 2011, NERSA introduced a new level of uncertainty with the surprise release of a consultation paper calling for even lower FITs, arguing that a number of parameters—such as exchange rates and the cost of debt—had changed. The new tariffs were 13 percent lower for concentrated solar, 25 percent lower for wind, and 41 percent lower for photovoltaic power. In addition, the capital component of the tariffs would no longer be fully indexed for inflation. NERSA did not change the required real return for equity investors of 17 percent (NERSA 2011).

More policy and regulatory uncertainty regarding REFIT was to come. Concerned that NERSA's FITs were still too high, DOE and the National Treasury commissioned a legal opinion that ultimately concluded that FITS amounted to noncompetitive procurement and were therefore prohibited by the government's public finance and procurement regulations.

The legal opinion provided an opportunity for DOE and the National Treasury to reconsider the government's approach. The fundamental goal of achieving large-scale renewable energy projects with private developers and financiers remained the same. However, the structure of the transactions, including the FITs, was to change significantly.

A series of informal consultations was held with developers, lawyers, and financial institutions throughout the first half of 2011. These meetings proved extremely important in allaying market concerns over the cancellation of the REFIT process and providing informal feedback from the private sector on design, legal, and technology issues. In essence, the meetings created a level of trust and indicated that the government remained committed to renewable IPPs, despite the uncertainties around the policy.

In August 2011, DOE announced that a competitive bidding process for renewable energy (REIPPPP) would be launched. Subsequently, NERSA terminated the REFIT program. Not a single megawatt of power had been signed since the launch of that program. A number of renewable energy project developers who had secured sites and initiated resource measurements and environmental impact assessments reacted with dismay to the abandonment of FITs. But it was these early developers who would later benefit from the first round of competitive bidding under REIPPPP.

Addressing the Policy Challenge

REIPPPP was different from REFIT not only because of the competitive nature of the bidding process but also because DOE took control of the effort, effectively shifting implementation from Eskom to DOE. DOE recognized that, like

Eskom, it had little institutional capacity to run a sophisticated, multiproject, multibillion-dollar international competitive bidding process for renewable energy. It therefore sought the assistance of the National Treasury's public-private partnership (PPP) unit to manage the process. A small team of technical staff from DOE and the PPP unit established a project office, known as the DOE IPP unit. It functioned outside the formal departmental structure of the national government to act as a facilitator for the REIPPPP process.

Policy Making

The REIPPPP team was led by a senior manager from the National Treasury PPP unit. She had worked there since its creation in 2000, helped establish Treasury's rigorous PPP project appraisal framework, and been involved with DOE's efforts to promote IPPs as early as 2007. Other legal and technical experts were also brought on board. They formed a small, tightknit team that was viewed favorably by both the public and the private sectors as a professional unit with a track record of expertise in closing PPP contracts and a reputation as problem solvers and facilitators rather than regulators. This kind of credibility allowed the unit to act effectively as a champion of the REIPPPP process.

Because the team was familiar with private sector infrastructure projects, as well as with most of the professionals involved in such projects in South Africa, the unit never exhibited the level of mistrust of private business that sometimes characterizes government efforts in South Africa. Dialogue with private sector counterparts on key REIPPPP design and implementation issues began almost immediately and continued throughout the process. High standards were set and maintained throughout the bidding process, including security arrangements and transparent procurement procedures. Documentation was extensive, high quality, and readily available on a specially designed program website.

Implementation

By the end of 2010, a team of consultants was on board and program design underway. When it became clear that the REFIT process would not proceed, the advisers recommended a new tender process, after reviewing international tender processes in Brazil, France, Germany, India, Spain, and elsewhere.

Design work and informal consultation with the private sector continued through the first half of 2011. In August of that year a Request for Proposals (RFP) was issued. It was followed by a compulsory bidders conference, held to address questions on bid requirements, documentation, power purchase agreements, and other issues. Some 300 organizations attended this conference. REIPPPP envisioned the procurement of 3,625 MW of power over a maximum of five tender rounds. Another 100 MW was reserved for projects below 5 MW, which were to be procured in a separate small projects IPP program. Caps were set on the total capacity for individual technologies; the largest allocations were for wind and photovoltaic power, with smaller amounts for concentrated solar, biomass, biogas, landfill gas, and hydropower. The rationale for these caps was to limit the supply to be bid out and therefore increase the level of competition among technologies and potential bidders.

Tenders for the different technologies were held simultaneously. Interested parties could bid for more than one project and more than one technology. Projects had to be larger than 1 MW, and an upper limit was set on bids for different technologies. Caps were also set on the price for each technology, at levels not dissimilar to NERSA's 2009 REFITs. Bids were due within three months of the release of the RFP, and financial close was to take place within six months of the announcement of preferred bidders.

From the bidders conference, it was clear that there was considerable interest in the market. One factor that impressed many private players was the effort made to meet most of the program's announced deadlines—something that stood in marked contrast to virtually all earlier IPP programs in the sector and clearly signaled to operators, investors, and advisers that this program was focused on results. An additional feature that gave the market confidence was the extensive use of private domestic and international advisers to design and help manage the program, review bids, and incorporate lessons learned into the program as it progressed through the bid stages.

All of these inputs depended on the availability of financial resources to pay for these experts, as well as offices, a website, various databases, and one of the most sophisticated, complicated bidding processes ever seen in Africa. The resources, which were provided by the National Treasury, were combined with technical assistance made available by bilateral donor agencies from Denmark, Germany, Spain, and the United Kingdom. The World Bank previously facilitated a $6 million grant from the Global Environment Facility (GEF) for advisory services under the Renewable Energy Market Transformation Project.

Overcoming Obstacles

Among REIPPPP bidders, the most controversial aspect of the program was its heavy reliance on nonprice factors in bid evaluation. These factors, organized in bid documents under the heading "economic development requirements," were designed to incentivize bidders to promote job growth, domestic industrialization, community development, and black economic empowerment with the objective of benefiting historically disadvantaged communities and businesses. Accounting for 30 percent of total bid value, economic and social development played a much larger role in the REIPPPP procurement process than nonprice criteria normally do under the government's preferential procurement policy.

These requirements were controversial for several reasons. Many international bidders felt that they were too demanding and played too substantial a role in bid valuation; domestic participants, backed by South African trade unions, thought the requirements were not demanding enough. Bidders of all kinds seem to have been confused by some of the criteria, especially criteria that called for local economic development plans to be part of the bids. No guidance on how such plans were to be prepared or how they would be evaluated was initially provided. In addition, as the process proceeded through five rounds of bidding, some of the economic development requirements became more onerous, seemingly in response to complaints by local stakeholders, rather than as a result of economic analysis or consultation with bidders.

Although some controversy about these requirements remains, it is clear that they helped generate political support for the program from politicians, investors, and the general public. By increasing the role of these factors to 30 percent of bid value, the program helped increase the visibility of economic development considerations and underscore their importance. The South African Parliament seems to have concluded that the economic development dimension of the program was successful, based on the commitments made during the five bid rounds.

Another potential obstacle was circumvented when a regulatory review determined that the REIPPPP would not be subject to National Treasury Regulation 16 for evaluating and approving PPPs. The PPP regulations are consistent with best practice in Organisation for Economic Co-operation and Development (OECD) countries, but they require a complicated, time-consuming, and expensive review process that must be implemented by expert consultants and officials. REIPPPP could never have rolled out so quickly if the PPP regulations had to have been followed for each transaction. The regulatory review found that the standard PPP approval process was not applicable to the REIPPPP because Eskom, which signs the power purchase agreements with private operators, is considered a state-owned enterprise rather than a government agency. Its purchase of power is therefore not subject to the National Treasury's PPP regulations.

Consensus Building

The promise of economic development benefits and rapid rollout of new generating capacity built support for the program among politicians and senior government officials. A major factor contributing to the widespread support for the program by the private sector was the global economic environment. The international renewable energy sector is highly competitive given the diversity of sources, the modular nature of most of the technologies, and the number of project developers. But for several years these industries had been experiencing global overcapacity and intense competition that resulted in very thin profit margins, if profits were generated at all. As a result, the industry continues to experience consolidation, the emergence of increasingly vertically integrated supply chains, and the steady movement of manufacturing firms into project development. Furthermore, at the outset of the bidding, renewable energy markets were in decline in Europe and developers were looking for new opportunities in emerging markets. All of these factors led to intense interest on the part of the global renewable energy industry in REIPPPP and growing levels of competition as the bidding progressed.

The quality and detail of the bid documentation, the clarity provided during the bidders conference, and the ongoing dialogue during the first half of 2011 seemed to alleviate some of the nervousness that had developed over the previous two years. Investors and operators particularly liked the initial structure of the pricing, as the REIPPPP tariff caps for round 1 were at levels similar to the earlier FITs. The integrity of the DOE IPP unit, combined with its reputation as problem solvers and dealmakers rather than regulators, also gave the market confidence and ultimately led to strong interest in the program.

Sequencing

The sequencing, or evolution, of the program was a key part of the multiround bid process. For the most part, the basic structure of the program has remained the same. Where adjustments have occurred, they were used to increase competition, transparency, and benefits under the economic development criteria.

The RFP was divided into three sections, detailing general requirements, qualification criteria, and evaluation criteria. The documents also included a standard power purchase agreement, an implementation agreement, and direct agreements. These agreements were nonnegotiable contracts developed after an extensive review of global best practices and consultations with numerous public and private sector actors. Although some bidders expressed reservations about the lack of flexibility to negotiate the terms of these agreements, most bidders were satisfied with the thoroughness and quality of the standard documents.

Bids were required to contain information on the project structure and the legal, land, environmental, financial, technical, and economic development qualifications. Bidders had to submit bank letters indicating that financing was locked in—a highly unusual way to outsource due diligence to the banks. This requirement effectively meant that lenders took on a larger share of project development risk. The arrangement dealt with one of the biggest problems with auctions: lowballing that results in renegotiation soon after closing.

Developers were expected to identify the sites and pay for early development costs. A modest registration fee was due at the outset of the bid process. Bid bonds or guarantees had to be posted. The guarantees were to be released once the projects came online or, if the bidder was unsuccessful, after the RFP evaluation stage.

The bid evaluation involved a two-step process. First, bidders had to satisfy certain minimum threshold requirements in six areas: environment, land, commercial and legal, economic development, financial, and technical. Bids that satisfied the threshold requirements then proceeded to the second step of evaluation, where bid prices counted for 70 percent of the total score. The remaining 30 percent was based on the economic development criteria.

Results Achieved

REIPPPP is the largest national IPP program ever attempted in Africa. In the first five bid rounds, 92 projects were awarded to the private sector (table 11.1). The first projects are already online. Private sector investments totaling $20 billion have been committed for projects that will generate in excess of 6,300 MW of renewable power. Prices dropped over the five bidding phases, with average solar photovoltaic tariffs decreasing 75 percent and tariffs for wind power falling 50 percent in nominal terms between round 1 and round 5. Most impressively,

Table 11.1 Results of First Five Rounds of the Renewable Energy Independent Power Producer Procurement Program (REIPPPP)

Item	Round 1 (Bid Window 1)	Round 2 (Bid Window 2)	Round 3 (Bid Window 3)	Round 4 (March 2014 CSP Round)	Round 5 (Bid Window 4)	Total
Number of projects awarded	28	19	17	2	26	92
Capacity awarded (MW)	1,425	1,040	1,4547	200	2,205	6,327
Total investment (millions of dollars)	5,974	3,534	4,504	1,739	4,439	20,190

Source: Presentations by the Department of Energy (DOE) and data provided by the DOE IPP unit.
Note: CSP = concentrated solar power; MW = megawatts. Data for rounds 1 and 2 is as at financial close; contracted capacity and investment amounts changed slightly from the time of bidding to the time of financial close. Investment data for bid round 1 were provided by the DOE IPP unit and differ slightly from data released in DOE presentations. Figures in rounds 1 to 3 were converted into dollars based on the exchange rate at the time the agreements were signed while the rates for rounds 4 and 5 were at the time of submission.

all of these achievements occurred over a three-and-a-half-year period. Improvements were also made in the economic development commitments, primarily benefiting rural communities. One investor characterized REIPPPP as "the most successful public-private partnership in Africa in the last 20 years."

The initial results of the first round of bidding were somewhat surprising to the DOE IPP unit. One official noted that the unit thought it might receive 12 bids and close 3 projects during the first round. Its biggest fear going into the process was that no bids would result in signed contracts. The thin global market, tight deadlines, earlier issues with REFIT, and the extensive qualification process were all factors that contributed to modest expectations.

In November 2011, 53 bids for 2,128 MW of power-generating capacity were received. The evaluation process took place over a four-week period. Preferred bidders were announced the next month, to coincide with the COP17 meeting in Durban. Twenty-eight preferred bidders were identified in the first round, offering 1,425 MW[7] for a total investment of $5.97 billion.[8]

A deadline of July 2012 was set for financial close and a deadline of the end of 2014 for the commercial operating date. These dates were later extended because the government took longer than expected to finalize its guarantees and because local banks, advisers, and other project partners were stretched to the limit with so many projects reaching closure simultaneously. This delay was the only significant one in implementing round 1 of the program.

Major contractual agreements were signed in November 2012, with most projects reaching full financial close within 10 days after conditions precedent were met. All the investments were closed on the same day in order to standardize and limit foreign exchange risk; doing so posed significant challenges to the banking system. Construction on all the projects in round 1 has commenced, with the first project coming online in November 2013.

Although bidders could not know for certain the total capacity that would be bid, they likely recognized that the tight deadlines and challenging threshold qualification criteria would result in less capacity being bid than was made available in round 1. Accordingly, the prices bid were largely unaffected by competitive limitations and only marginally below the caps specified in the RFPs. High initial transaction costs and possible policy uncertainty also affected prices.

Round 2 was announced in November 2011, using the same RFPs used in round 1, although the total amount of power to be procured was reduced to stimulate additional competition. The price caps remained at the same level, although the new RFP stated that the government expected prices to fall and was considering lowering the price caps in the third round.

A total of 79 bids were received in round 2, nearly a 50 percent increase over round 1 despite the significant drop in capacity offered. In March 2012, bids totaling 3,233 MW were received.[9] A team of local and international experts again evaluated the tenders. Fifty-one projects met the qualifying criteria. In May 2012, 19 preferred bidders were selected, offering 1,040 MW[10] of power. Wind and solar photovoltaic prices in the second round were much more competitive, falling 21.5 percent for wind and 40.4 percent for photovoltaic power (table 11.2). The price for concentrated solar fell 6.5 percent; there was little competition in small hydro, with only two qualifying bids.

According to government officials, the results of round 2—particularly the lower prices and better local content terms—saved the reputation of the program and suggested to some officials that competitive tenders might be a way to achieve significantly lower prices than FITs.

The procurement documents for round 3 were released in May 2013. They were based on the documents used in previous rounds, with further refinements.

Table 11.2 Average Bids in First Five Rounds of the Renewable Energy Independent Power Producer Procurement Program (REIPPPP)
Percent, except where otherwise indicated

Type of energy/bid change	Round 1 (Bid Window 1)	Round 2 (Bid Window 2)	Round 3 (Bid Window 3)	Round 4 (March 2014 CSP Round)	Round 5 (Bid Window 4)
Wind					
Price (South African cents/kilowatt)	114.3	89.7	65.6	—	57.5
Reduction from previous round		21.5	26.9	—	12.4
Total reduction from round 1			42.6	—	49.7
Solar photovoltaic					
Price (South African cents/kilowatt)	275.8	164.5	88.1	—	69.3
Reduction from previous round		40.4	46.4	—	21.4
Total reduction from round 1			68.1	—	74.9
Concentrated solar power					
Price (South African cents/kilowatt)	268.6	251.2	146.0[a]	136.4	—
Reduction from previous round		6.5	41.9	6.8	—
Total reduction from round 1			45.6	49.2	—

Source: Department of Energy presentations.
Note: CSP = concentrated solar power; — = not applicable. Prices are 2011 values.
a. The price structure for concentrated solar power in rounds 3 and 4 was different from rounds 1 and 2. It included a peak tariff of 270 percent of the base price.

The total capacity on offer was restricted to 1,473 MW, with individual capacity caps for different technologies. Price caps were adjusted downward (except for biomass and landfill gas) to stimulate the supply of projects. Once again bidders could offer fully or partially indexed prices.

In August 2013, 93 bids were received, totaling 6,023 MW. Seventeen preferred bidders were awarded in October 2013, for a total of 1,457 MW for a total investment of $4.504 billion. Prices fell again in round 3. The price of solar photovoltaic power fell 68 percent compared with round 1, and the price of wind energy dropped 42 percent. The price of concentrated solar power also declined, although round 3 had a new tariff system, so bid prices are not directly comparable with prices in rounds 1 and 2. As of June 2015, 15 of the 17 preferred bidders had signed their agreements and reached financial close. The remaining two were expected to finalize their agreements before September 2015.

In order to accommodate additional capacity from concentrated solar power projects, the DOE extended Bid Window 3 in order to have a special concentrated solar power round, round 4, at the end of March 2014. A total of three concentrated solar power bids were received and two preferred bidders were announced in December 2014 to provide 200 MW of generation capacity, with a total investment of $1.739 billion. The two projects are expected to reach financial close in the third quarter of 2015.

The most recent bidding, round 5 (also known as Bid Window 4), closed in August 2014; and a total of 77 bids for 5,805 MW of power were received and evaluated. In April 2015 there were 13 preferred bidders announced to provide 1,121 MW of generation capacity. Because of the growing shortage of electricity in the South African market, the large number of bid responses, and the highly competitive pricing provided by bidders in round 5, the DOE awarded another 13 preferred bidders in June 2015 to provide an additional 1,084 MW of generation capacity. Accordingly, 26 preferred bidders were awarded in total for round 5, providing 2,205 MW of generation capacity, with a total investment of $4.439 billion. The projects in round 5 are expected to reach financial close by the end of 2015.

As a result of the success of the REIPPPP, in April 2015, the Minister of Energy announced that her department will ask the regulator for an additional 6,300 MW under REIPPPP to maintain the momentum of the program. She also indicated that the DOE intends to hold an expedited round in order to procure an additional 1,800 MW from all renewable technologies. The procurement process is intended to be shortened and simplified to allow all unsuccessful bidders from previous rounds, and potentially new bidders, to submit bids for evaluation. The bid submission for this round is expected to begin October 2015 with the award of preferred bidders ideally made by the end of 2015.

The REIPPPP is expected to continue into the foreseeable future until all the capacity under the new determination has been successfully awarded. This should take place before 2020. The DOE has already indicated that it intends to redesign the procurement documents, following the award of the expedited round, for release in the second quarter of 2016. These procurement documents will be used to procure new projects in round 6 and beyond. Key aspects of the redesign are under consideration and may involve the local community involvement, local content, and industrialization regime as well as consideration of the constrained distribution and transmission systems.

Through five rounds of bidding, the results clearly exceeded the expectations of policy makers. The initial fear in round 1 was that there would be minimal interest. Even in round 2 there was a concern that prices would not drop substantially. Going forward, concerns remain about potential price increases. Nevertheless, debate about FITs versus competitive bidding in South Africa's renewable sector is clearly resolved for the foreseeable future. In fact, the chief procurement officer, a newly created position in the National Treasury, is examining the REIPPPP to determine how greater competition might be introduced in procurement elsewhere in the public sector.

Eskom's role in large-scale renewables has been limited to completing two plants financed by the World Bank, serving as the off-taker on the IPPs, and completing transmission lines. NERSA's role in setting tariffs remains unchanged, and DOE remains responsible for determining the mix of energy resources.

Conclusions: Success Factors, Challenges, and Lessons Learned

For a country as dependent as South Africa is on coal, and facing extraordinary development challenges, REIPPPP represented a striking break with the past. Numerous factors and lessons learned contributed to its success. One was high-level political support and the largely ad hoc institutional status of the DOE IPP unit, which acted at arm's length from DOE as a kind of dedicated project office. This arrangement allowed—and, to some extent, encouraged—an operating approach that emphasized problem solving to make the program successful rather than automatically following government operational policies and procedures that emphasized enforcement of rules. In addition, the unit was entrepreneurial in finding and accessing money to design and implement the program.

Second, several design features also contributed to the success of REIPPPP. Despite the higher initial cost of renewable energy, the program offered an expedited mechanism to roll out new power-generating capacity. Although it would take years for the large power projects planned by Eskom to begin generating power, REIPPPP was designed to roll out a significant amount of power in a very short time, using transparent procurement and implementation processes. REIPPPP also offered clear opportunities for developers to make profits. When the round 1 bid documents were released, developers saw what one called "REFIT-like" tariffs, meaning that the projects could potentially make equity returns close to 17 percent. In round 2, the competitive tendering seems to have helped tariffs fall sharply. The reduction was a major factor in the government's willingness to continue its support for REIPPPP. The nonnegotiable and standardized tender documents eliminated one of the main shortcomings of typical tender processes, which sometimes incentivize underbidding to win contracts followed by renegotiation in the hopes of securing more profitable deals. The sovereign guarantees provided by the Treasury, combined with South Africa's investment grade credit rating, also meant that no political risk insurance was needed, although it may be needed in the future. While REIPPPP's economic development requirements were controversial, they helped generate political support for the programs.

Third, an important lesson learned from REIPPPP is that, regardless of their size or location, private sponsors and investors in the renewable energy sector are seeking to invest in renewable power in emerging markets, especially when those markets adopt a business-friendly approach. If deals are reasonably profitable and key risks are mitigated in an acceptable manner, considerable private sector interest, expertise, and financing are likely. In many instances, a convincing case needs to be made repeatedly to justify the procurement of renewable energy. REIPPPP was preceded by several years of policy proposals and analytical work that supported mitigation of climate change. This effort, combined with the looming threat of power shortages and frustration with the earlier lack of action on IPPs, meant that REIPPPP was initially given the benefit of the doubt, even by critics of renewable energy costs.

Fourth, program champions helped drive successful programs. Professionals with credibility need to be able to interact convincingly with senior government officials, effectively explain and defend the program in meetings with stakeholders, deal with donors, select and manage consultants, communicate with the private sector, and manage a complicated procurement and contracting process. The champion does not necessarily need to be a senior government official. But he or she should be familiar with (and familiar to) senior officials, as well as someone with enough experience working with the private sector to be comfortable adopting the business-friendly approach mentioned above. This success factor is profoundly difficult to replicate.

Fifth, the need to identify the right design to suit the environment is also a key lesson from REIPPPP. The program illustrates this point by highlighting the evolution to competitive tenders from FIT regimes. REIPPPP's experience suggests that competitive tenders for renewable energy are potentially an attractive alternative to REFITs, because they may be able to keep tariffs under tighter competitive control. Finally, whether a FIT or a competitive tender is chosen, an effective, transparent, efficient procurement mechanism is required.

Nevertheless, there were challenges in the design and implementation of REIPPPP, and risks remain going forward. In terms of program management, the transactions costs were high for both the government and the bidders, certainly higher than for a traditional REFIT program. The most significant risk to the sustainable success of REIPPPP relates to transmission constraints and the related payments to the IPPs if Eskom's transmission planning lags or does not come to fruition. In these cases, Eskom as the off-taker will be liable for very significant deemed energy payments, even though no electricity would be fed into the grid.

There would also be a dramatic financial risk to the overall success of the REIPPPP program if the fiscal health of Eskom or the sovereign deteriorates, resulting in a further downgrade of either Eskom or South Africa's credit rating. A drop below investment grade would undermine the success of the program unless remedial actions were put into place.

Another test relates to one of the program's key success factors—its ad hoc character. The nondepartmental institutional setting, the off-budget funding, and the entrepreneurial attitude of the program team all facilitated performance and helped avoid the delays and indecision that crippled earlier attempts to develop IPPs in the power sector. This ad hoc character will inevitably give way to some kind of formalization, however, if only to guarantee a more secure source of funding and sustainability for the program. The challenge will be to proceed with institutionalization in a way that preserves as many of the program management success factors as possible.

A further potential challenge going forward is the possibility that the economic development activities, which target benefits to historically disadvantaged communities or businesses, will not be appropriately monitored or managed over the life of the contracts. Agencies responsible for monitoring local content performance have sometimes struggled to perform their tasks even in developed countries, despite sizable staffs (WTI Advisors 2013).

REIPPPP has also experienced some market-related challenges. For example, because of the huge demands on the local consulting industry, some firms were permitted to offer advisory services to the government, private bidders, and funders as long as they created adequate internal barriers within the firm to limit potential conflicts of interest. Some bidders complained that legal and financial firms were offering a "one-size-fits-all" service, which was not always appropriate for specific projects. In addition, the risk-averse character of South Africa's sophisticated commercial banking sector has meant that it has been limited in the extent to which it can support small and medium-size South African firms in gaining a foothold in the country's emerging renewable energy industry. Development finance institutions have played a larger role in financing these types of investors and operators.

Globally, the principal market-related risk affecting the changes instituted under the program is the volatility of private sector interest in such a program and the possibility of operators and investors backing away from new bid rounds the moment events suggest that their interests are better served elsewhere. If the global slowdown affecting the renewable energy industry experiences a turnaround and the industry begins to demonstrate renewed growth, global competition to attract investors and operators may increase. A related risk is that renewable energy prices may no longer continue to drop. Higher prices, or the opening up of large markets elsewhere, could affect the longer-term viability of South Africa's program.

Despite these challenges, there is little question that the five rounds of REIPPPP were successful and that the program provides a valuable opportunity to learn how to procure renewable energy projects quickly and effectively in emerging markets. Of course, not all of REIPPPP's success factors can be easily duplicated, particularly in low-income countries. Most African countries cannot mount a program of REIPPPP's size or one that includes a rolling, multiround bid process. No other African country has the kind of banking, legal, and other advisory resources that are readily available in South Africa (although services of this kind are available in other countries).

Many critical success factors—particularly transparency, consistency, and leadership—can be replicated. South Africa's program was able to create a true partnership that encouraged the flow of information and trust among government, donors, and the private sector. These factors are replicable in support of other projects and programs, regardless of the sector, location, size, or economic standing of the partners.

Notes

1. The five rounds includes the extended Bid Window 3, held in March 2014, to procure only concentrated solar power technology.

2. The exchange rate for rounds 1 to 3 is based on the dates the agreement were signed while the rate for rounds 4 and 5 is based on the rate at submission. All exchange rates are calculated from rand to USD at the time of financial close of the tranche.

3. Eskom is building two massive new coal-fired plants (Medupi and Kusile), each 4,800 megawatts (MW), as well as a new 1,300 MW pumped storage scheme (Ingula). It has also commenced its first procurement of renewable energy power—a 100 MW wind farm (Sere) and a 100 MW concentrated solar plant. Both projects were funded mainly by loans from the World Bank (which also partially funded the Medupi power station) and the African Development Bank.

4. In South Africa, IPPs are generally recognized as privately financed, newly constructed, or renovated generation plants supported by nonrecourse or limited recourse loans and backed by long-term power purchase agreements signed with Eskom, the country's single buyer of electricity.

5. One exception was an earlier effort by DOE to procure open-cycle diesel-fired turbines.

6. Under the terms of the Kyoto Treaty, Annex I countries that ratified it must have fulfilled their obligations regarding emission limitations established for the first commitment period (2008–12) by 2012. These commitments are listed in Annex B of the protocol. Non-Annex 1 countries, like South Africa, are not committed to these caps.

7. DOE presentations refer to a total capacity for round 1 of 1,416 MW as at the time of bidding; this was later updated by the IPP unit for figures at financial close, which totaled 1,425 MW.

8. DOE presentations refer to investment of R 47.792 billion in round 1 as of the time of bidding; this was later updated by the IPP unit for figures at financial close, which totaled R 49.326 billion.

9. The DOE announced a figure of 3,255 MW, but the DOE IPP unit database records 3,233 MW.

10. DOE presentations refer to a total capacity for round 2 of 1,044 MW as of the time of bidding; this was later updated by the IPP unit for figures at financial close, which totaled 1,040 MW.

References

Department of Environmental Affairs. 2011. *National Climate Change Response: White Paper.* Pretoria: Department of Environmental Affairs.

Department of Minerals and Energy. 2003. *White Paper on Renewable Energy.* Pretoria: Department of Minerals and Energy.

Eberhard, Anton, Joel Kolker, and James Leigland. 2014. "South Africa's Renewable Energy IPP Procurement Program: Success Factors and Lessons." Public Private Infrastructure Advisory Facility (PPIAF), Washington, DC.

EDF (Environmental Defense Fund). 2014. "South Africa: Environmental Policy Overview," The World's Carbon Markets: A Case Study Guide to Emissions Trading, March. http://www.ey.com/Publication/vwLUAssets/Renewable_Energy_Country _Attractiveness_Index_43/$FILE/RECAI%2043_March%202015.pdf.

Ernst & Young. 2014. "Country Focus: South Africa." *RECAI (Renewable Energy Country Attractiveness Index)* 40 (February): 28–29.

NERSA (National Energy Regulator of South Africa). 2011. *NERSA Consultation Paper: Review of Renewable Energy Feed-In Tariffs.* Pretoria: NERSA.

Paton, Carol. 2015. "Nene Lays Economic Problems at SA's Door." *Business Day*, April 17. http://www.bdlive.co.za/economy/2015/03/18/nene-lays-economic-problems -at-sas-door.

Statistics South Africa. http://www.statssa.gov.za/. Statistics South Africa, Pretoria.

WTI Advisors. 2013. "Local Content Requirements and the Green Economy." Paper prepared for the Ad Hoc Expert Group on Domestic Requirements and Support Measures in Green Sectors, Economic and Environmental Effectiveness and Implications for Trade, Geneva, June 13–14.

CHAPTER 12

The Making of the 1996 Constitution

Ivan Velev and Nonhlahla Zindela

Introduction

The adoption of the 1996 Constitution of South Africa is widely regarded as a watershed moment in constitutional jurisprudence.[1] It ended 300 years of minority domination, giving South Africans a new national identity defined by citizenship and civil and political equality. The Constitution has been praised as one of the most progressive constitutional frameworks in the world, reflecting the four generations of human rights,[2] the best international legal principles, and democratic institutions.

The 1996 Constitution was the outcome of an epic struggle for human dignity and social justice in the face of a repressive racist system, placing a strong emphasis on equal rights for all. It reflects the culmination of the "never again" principle by encoding two constitutional provisions: *founding values* and a *bill of rights*. These two constitutional features put "the people" as a sovereign in the center of the new system of government, founded on equality, human rights and freedoms, tolerance, universal suffrage, pluralistic democracy, and accountable and transparent governance. The rich global common law tradition as well as public and civil law, including human rights law, informed the constitutional design, which blended international law and other foreign legal rules with South Africa's own legal tradition.[3]

The 1996 Constitution ultimately gained the credibility and legitimacy needed to shape and consolidate South Africa and move the country forward after a long period of arrested economic and political development. The lessons from its creation are relevant today for the constitutional and policy reforms in many divided and conflict-stricken countries.

Ivan Velev is the Country Program Coordinator for the South Africa Country Management Unit at the World Bank, and Nonhlahla Zindela is a Senior Operations Officer in the same unit. This chapter benefited from extensive interviews with current and former government officials as well as from comments by peer reviewers Matthew Glasser and Zoe Kolovou (Lead Counsel in the Word Bank Group's Legal Department).

The Policy Challenge

The constitutional experience of South Africa as a modern nation since the 19th century was marked by nonmajoritarian constitutions, ethnic fragmentation, and conflict encouraged by a government whose policy was to divide the opposition, and, as a result, deepening violence. The trajectory of this historical experience reached a tipping point in the 1990s. Three main challenges had to be addressed in transitioning from apartheid to a new, modern democracy: building nationhood and constructing a new national identity, departing from the authoritarian constitutional tradition of the past, and defusing violence and deepening racial and ethnic reconciliation.

Separation versus Integrated Nationhood

The modern South African state, forged at the turn of the 20th century, was founded on reconciliation between Dutch and British settlers and premised on the exclusion and neglect of the black majority. This was further consolidated between 1948 and 1994, under the National Party's (NP's) rule, when colonial governance was transformed into a comprehensive system of racial laws and policies. The original constitution served as a key instrument for segregation and white domination.

Finding a working formula for negotiating national statehood was key to anchoring institutional change and a governance structure that would implement and protect the new constitution and nationhood. This formula had to integrate artificially established "homelands" and segregated local authorities into about 300 new nonracial governments. The main difficulty was setting up a governance structure that balanced centralization and federalization in order to escape the overlapping racial, ethnic, and linguistic divisions.

To address this legitimacy dilemma, a unique and inclusive process had to be devised to give validity to the constitutional design. As Justice Albie Sachs, formerly on the Constitutional Court of South Africa, put it: "building a new nationhood and citizenship was our main challenge." The only viable policy option available for attaining this goal was "through the acquisition of the rights of full and effective citizenship by all South Africans regardless of race."[4] Organizationally, the challenge was between a unionist and a decentralized state model.

Authoritarianism versus a Bill of Rights

South Africa's colonial and autocratic political history, rooted in the suppression of basic human rights, prevented South Africa from developing and entrenching earlier rules against government abuse. The democratic transitions in southern Europe's dictatorships (Greece, Portugal, and Spain) and the collapse of the Yugoslav and Soviet governance models during the 1980s indicated a decline of the central planning and etatistic prescriptions and influenced African National Congress (ANC) and South African Communist Party (SACP) internal debates. According to Justice Sachs, the South African Constitution does not exhibit any particular doctrine or judicial philosophy, except for the "never again" principle. However, reflecting this ideological shift, the ANC advanced two features—openness and a bill of rights—as key tenets. The human rights records in Yugoslavia and the Soviet Union and the debates among the European left at the time informed the internal ANC debate and reinforced beliefs that liberal democracy, and human rights protection, can bring radical societal transformation and a just and fair social order.[5]

The reform space for the introduction of a bill of rights opened gradually during the constitutional negotiations.[6] Initially, the NP government intended to create a more palatable reformed version of racial and ethnic separation.[7] Intended as limited democratization and a regime-enhancing measure, the Convention for a Democratic South Africa was soon overtaken by debates about majority rule (and its resistance), a bill of rights, and the scrapping of the apartheid system altogether. The challenge was to convince the white minority to commit to reform and accept the Bill of Rights and to convince the black majority that the Bill of Rights was not sealing white control over land and expropriated property. The likely solution had to ensure the protection of fundamental rights and square with both the debates about communitarian versus social justice rights and the debate about the unitary state.

Peace, Transitional Justice, and Reconciliation

The third main challenge for South Africa was how to come to terms with a repressive past and rectify not only the brutalities of the old regime but also the economic dispossession, so that victims and executioners could live together as citizens of the same country. The related dilemma was to make the parties focus on the future by having them agree about the past. This bridge between past and future had to unite the citizenry by agreeing on a collective memory for reconstitution into a new national identity.

Human rights violations and suffering had been acknowledged in the past in three ways: through amnesty, through prosecution under the criminal law, and through reconciliation and selective amnesty (Gross 2004).[8] In addition to honoring the victims and de-escalating the growing violent conflict during the multiparty negotiations, both sides were keen on achieving closure. The victims needed acknowledgment of gross human rights violations they had suffered and attendant reparations; the perpetrators sought pardon and reintegration.[9]

The process called on members of both sides to testify about their participation in acts of violence and atrocities. This part of the reconciliation process was contentious and toxic. Many observers found it abhorrent because of the moral equivalency it implied.

Addressing the Challenge

"The release of Mandela was the point of no return," recalls Roelf Meyer, the former NP chief negotiator who led the negotiations to end apartheid. After the ban on the ANC and other anti-apartheid political organizations was lifted,

Making It Happen • http://dx.doi.org/10.1596/978-1-4648-0768-8

in 1990, and the Convention for Democratic South Africa (CODESA) was convened in 1991, 19 political parties met for more than six months to work out arrangements for drafting and adopting the new constitution. CODESA launched the process of rescuing the country from the looming civil war through a "negotiated commitment to a fundamentally different constitutional order premised upon open and democratic government" (Motala and Ramaphosa 2002). CODESA set a very high objective. It sought not a reform of the old regime but an end to apartheid by addressing the transition from apartheid to a new nation-state, from authoritarianism to majoritarian liberal democracy, and from armed conflict to peace and reconciliation at the same time.

Implementation and Sequencing: Structure of the Negotiation Process

CODESA and its successor the Multi-Party Negotiation Process (MPNP) were not elected bodies, like the Constitutional Assembly that drafted the final Constitution. The apartheid Parliament was not representative of the country, and the "vision for the new constitution was not defined from the outset," according to Roelf Meyer. Creating laws under these parameters would not have provided the legitimacy needed to establish the Constitution as a founding document.

Solving this dilemma required devising an arrangement and leaving as much as possible for the elected body to decide. CODESA endorsed a unique implementation pathway consisting of structured negotiations leading to adoption of constitutional principles; free elections for the Constitutional Assembly and the interim Government of National Unity; an interim constitution prepared by the Convention; a final constitution adopted by the Constitutional Assembly; and review and certification of the Constitution.

At the core of this construct was a two-stage constitutional transition that produced first an interim and then a final Constitution. This construct, which looked complex and tenuous, allowed for making course corrections, broadening the public debate at each step, building common ground, and mobilizing support.

The structure of the negotiations took longer to emerge. It can be divided into three phases: latent, formal, and settlement. During the *latent phase* (before 1989)—later known as "talks about talks"—the ANC and the NP negotiated ground rules and agreed broadly on the process. Throughout this stage, the NP sought to remain the "party of power," controlling all key government institutions. The NP pursued trilateral negotiations (with both the ANC and the Inkatha Freedom Party [IFP]). In contrast, the ANC's initial negotiation strategy was to adopt a constitution through a democratically elected assembly.[10] The latent phase was marked by two agreements (the Groote Schuur Minute and the Pretoria Minute).[11] During informal exchanges accompanying these agreements, negotiators established a degree of trust that helped set the stage for formal negotiations.

During the *formal stage* (1989–92), also known as CODESA, the main parties undertook unilateral steps by opening direct talks about win-win gains. In a joint declaration, the parties articulated the common binding goal: establishing multiracial democracy in South Africa.[12] The buildup of trust allowed the parties to move beyond "tit for tat" strategies and create cooperative opportunities for mutually acceptable solutions; however, the process broke down when the ANC withdrew from the negotiations in response to the NP demand of veto power[13] and created a gridlock. The ANC resumed mass action. During this period some of the worst clashes and most brutal acts of violence were committed, including the Bisho and Boipatong massacres. "Violence created urgency to find a political solution. This was a turning point leading to paradigm shift on the NP side to accept equality as a principle of engagement with other parties and as fundamental civil right," Roelf Meyer said.

During the *settlement phase* (1992–96), both parties put mutual interest above brinkmanship. Their efforts helped de-escalate the violence and reach power-sharing arrangements. The Bisho and Boipatong massacres resulted in a reversal in the dependency roles between ANC and NP. In the event, a taste of violence was enough to forestall full-scale civil war. Glimpsing the abyss of full-blown civil war, the NP changed position. According to the recollections of Roelf Meyer, the violence changed the calculus of consent, and the NP was determined to make a deal with the ANC to avert a national tragedy. The main factor, though, as Roelf Meyer recalls, was "the breakdown in the negotiations that forced us to find a way forward. That led to the question how we really want the future South Africa to look like and the consequential shift to accepting individual rights on an equal basis as the cornerstone of our constitution."

All parties saw their power less in terms of domination and more in terms of mutual dependence. Finding alternative arrangements to accommodate interests, compromises, and working commitments became new ways of gaining power, after the realization that neither side can immediately defeat the other in violent confrontation. Despite the mobilization and ethnic violence,[14] this period was marked by a two-track (bilateral and multilateral) formal negotiation. After the collapse of the CODESA I negotiations, the chief negotiators, Cyril Ramaphosa for the ANC and Roelf Meyer for the NP, opened direct talks involving only the two parties. In a series of secret meetings, they worked out an agreement that led to the signing of a Record of Understanding between De Klerk and Mandela at their 1992 summit. The breakthrough that enabled the negotiations to proceed included the election of a Constitutional Assembly and the forming of an interim government of national unity. These bilateral talks enabled resumption of multiparty negotiations under a modified procedural arrangement that became known as the Multiparty Negotiation Forum (MPNF).

The MPNF was a more effective mechanism than CODESA. It created compromise-seeking and deadlock-breaking mechanisms, such as technical committees, and branched organizational structures, allowing more routes and opportunities for escaping impasses.[15] The technical committees were not involved in political matters. They acted as a deadlock-breaking channel. A not-for-profit, nonpartisan body was hired to provide overall administration (during the CODESA negotiations, management had been partisan). A small shuttle group of "trouble-shooters"— consisting of Mac Maharaj, Ben Ngubane, and Fanie van der Merwe—was tasked to keep the overall process on track; they acted very effectively as advisers and strategists. This group's credibility and skill allowed it to facilitate agreements. Where no consensus was possible, the group turned to Cyril Ramaphosa and Roelf Meyer as chief negotiators. If they failed to agree, the issue was escalated to Mandela and De Klerk. According to Mac Maharaj, "This three-tier paired mechanism, with De Klerk and Mandela on the top, proved very effective. If we had to go to Mandela, however, the first question he would ask was: 'do we have an agreement on majority rule?'"

On November 16, 1993, Mandela and De Klerk reached a last-minute package agreement to complete the interim Constitution (known as the "six-pack agreement"). On November 18, the MPNF approved the interim Constitution and it was voted into a law by the old (apartheid) Parliament, paving the way for the first democratic elections in South Africa, which took place April 27, 1994. Following certification by the Constitutional Court of South Africa, on December 10, 1996—International Human Rights Day—President Mandela signed the new Constitution of the Republic of South Africa, at a symbolic ceremony in Sharpeville.

Overcoming Obstacles: Principles, Compromise, and "Sufficient Consensus"

"Drafting an interim constitution enabled experimental learning and agreeing on the constitutional principles that guided the drafting of the constitution by the Constitutional Assembly," Roelf Meyer said. In the final compromise, which led to breaking the impasse and adopting first the interim and later the final Constitution, both parties "obtained their goals without sacrificing principle" (Motala and Ramaphosa 2002) by creating original decision-making procedures and deadlock-breaking mechanisms.

The 34 initial constitutional principles served a dual role, providing the multistage drafting process with increased democratic representation and thus establishing legitimacy (the ANC demand). The adoption of the principles calmed the fears of the minority about "being engulfed by a black majority," something that was achieved through sunset clauses (which included civil service contracts during transition), amnesty considerations, and the establishment of the government of national unity. The principles served as a bridge between two constitutional regimes. The principles themselves were far from being a coherent set; they held internal tensions and contradictions, reflecting the ideologies and aspirations of very different political parties. Some of the most apparent tensions were between social rights and color-blind liberty, exclusion and democracy, meritocracy and equality, government accountability and fragmentation of state authority, and judicial review and democracy.

In addition to the constitutional design principles, some procedural understandings and values took precedence during the constitutional drafting process (Ebrahim 1998), including the following:

- *Participation*, so that all South Africans would identify with the national goal (Sachs 1996)

- *Inclusiveness*, which ensured that the voices of all political actors would be heard in the Constitutional Assembly and within civil society[16]
- *Solicitation* of the ordinary people's views through radio, TV, and the Internet and other means to reach rural and poor communities without connectivity[17]
- *Transparency* (opening the procedures and hearings of the Constitutional Assembly to the public)
- *Consensus* about the final version of the Constitution
- *Accommodation* (not narrow bargaining but identifying with the needs of the other)
- *Virtuous leadership*, anchored in the *ubuntu* principle ("goodness of the other"), loaded by other values, such as public good, solidarity, respect, dignity, civility, and transparency to facilitate common ground and agreement.[18]

The new democratic constitution required not only jurisprudential innovation but also cooperative behavior for striking a compromise. The most notable agreements, which delivered the final deal, included the following:

- *Protection of minority parties*. Constitutional Principle XIV demanded the participation of the minority political parties as a trade-off within the unitary national legal framework, where "not [the dictate of] majorities but consensus shapes the new constitution."
- *Transitional confidence-building mechanisms*. The sunset clauses, which included extension of civil service contracts during transition, together with amnesty and the government of national unity, led to the agreement on interim institutional arrangements, including the creation of independent transitional bodies, such as the Electoral Commission and the Transitional Executive Commission, for observing fair treatment during the run-up to the first democratic elections, while the NP still controlled the Cabinet (Motala and Ramaphosa 2002).[19]
- *Supermajority for adopting the final constitution*. A parliamentary majority to adopt the final constitution was set at 66 percent. In return for this concession, the ANC obtained a deadlock-breaking provision for calling a referendum if the 66 percent majority could not be obtained.
- *Constitutional court with a veto over the final constitution*. The Constitutional Court of South Africa was an important assurance about the supremacy of the Constitution as distinct from untrammeled majority rule in a system in which Parliament rules supreme. In a unique precedent, a nonelected body determined the constitutionality of the document based on an agreed ex ante principle as supra-law ("solemn pact"), and it became the ultimate arbiter on the legality of all statutes and actions.
- *Establishment of nine provinces with provincial and local government powers*. The NP and IFP had demanded the creation of broader regional autonomy with significant devolution of powers. This move represented a compromise.
- *Possible establishment of a Volksstaat*.[20] A written constitutional provision left open the possibility of creating an Afrikaner homeland after the elections,

Making It Happen • http://dx.doi.org/10.1596/978-1-4648-0768-8

with defined "ethnic" boundaries.[21] If the Afrikaner parties could not reach an agreement, the fallback option was passage of the bill of rights. This arrangement secured the Freedom Front's support for the Interim Constitution and the first free elections. In the end, the Afrikaner community did not reach consensus about where to establish a Volksstaat and the default (a bill of rights) prevailed.

The two major parties agreed to work through bilateral channels (formal and informal) and a two-party consensus first, before engaging smaller parties in the decision process. This "sufficient consensus" approach served as a lever for forcing the hand of other parties for collective action. This single procedural tool could, to a large extent, be credited with the success of the MPNF compared with the ineffectiveness of CODESA, which operated with a rotating chairman, had no single negotiating body, and gave all parties veto power over the final decision. The sufficient consensus, according to Pravin Gordhan, was applied sparingly, and "ANC and NP used it only twice—to determine the date of the elections, and endorse the Interim Constitution."

Results Achieved

Good institutions are predictors for long-run growth. A robust constitutionalism is one of the preconditions of such stable ex post institutions, striking a delicate balance between commitments to rules and outcomes.[22] The 1996 Constitution symbolizes and embodies this balance. The compromises that led to the adoption of the 1996 Constitution still experience an overwhelming acceptance and a broad-based support. The 1996 Constitution laid the foundation for keeping the country "together" as opposed to living "apart."

The main result of this process was achieving united nationhood, rebuilt through constitutionalism, based on consistent equality and not domination. Dismantling apartheid by establishing a new constitutional order achieved a triple transition—from racially and ethnically fragmented pieces to a consolidated unitary state; from entrenched past authoritarian tradition to a democratic form of government rooted in a new set of values—liberty, tolerance, and social justice; and from a potential civil war to peace and reconciliation. In order to implement change and address these complex challenges, an inclusive negotiation and transition process was adopted, which ensured equal representation and consolidation of ethnic, racial, and gender divisions. The process used to achieve these goals became an organic part of what the Constitution stands for as a fundamental law: departure from the past legal and political tradition framed mainly by elites and minority interests.

One key outcome of the constitution-making process was particularly important: the fact that the Constitution did not result from the white-controlled legislature. The new Constitution was certified against values and principles owned and shared by most political groups, small and large.

The Constitution safeguards the sustainability of this comprehensive and fundamental departure from the past in three ways: (i) it protects rights and freedoms through a strongly entrenched bill of rights,[23] including socioeconomic rights (also known as "second-generation rights"[24]); (ii) it includes an institutional architecture in which the Constitutional Court is tasked with judicial review to protect the supremacy of the constitutional provisions; and (iii) it creates special institutions established to protect democratic governance.[25]

The key feature of the 1996 Constitution—and the cornerstone of South Africa's democracy—is the Bill of Rights. It not only spelled out for the first time that all South Africans have equal rights but it also obliged the state to "respect, protect, promote, and fulfill" these rights with special provisions and institutions, known as "Chapter 9 institutions." According to Thuli Madonsela, the Public Protector of South Africa, "the purpose of Chapter 9 institutions is to restore trust in the key South African institutions and to ensure that never again will the state be captured by an unaccountable elite and a failing human nature, acting in its own interest and not in the interest of the people."

The Constitution averted both economic collapse and civil war. Through threats and blame, push and pull, violence and cooperation, the constitutional negotiations ended in a peaceful finish, despite the fact that the two main opponents had sought to defeat each other.[26]

South Africa developed an uncommon parallel justice institution.[27] By establishing Truth and Reconciliation Commissions (TRCs), running concurrently with the constitutional negotiations, both parties defused the intensity and incidence of violence and threats of violence. Reconciliation created a more favorable environment for reaching compromises during the negotiations. Most perpetrators, however, were granted amnesty and went unpunished, leaving the victims without meaningful compensation or closure. In redressing the wrongs of the past, South Africa chose to fill the gap with another *ubuntu* principle ("forgive but do not forget") instead of redistributing assets and social rights upfront to compensate for property and economic dispossession.

Efforts to undo past economic, spatial, and social deprivation in order to repair race relations have been challenging. Twenty years of democracy and economic growth have not eradicated persistent inequality or significantly narrowed the poverty gap. One achievement of the new Constitution has taken root, nonetheless. According to the 2014 report of the Reconciliation Barometer Survey,[28] racial prejudice has been declining since 2003, and interracial contact has increased, particularly regarding marriage, neighborhoods, and schools (Wale 2013). Although white racial prejudice is declining, class inequality still follows racial lines.

The constitutional transformation started from a very narrow reform space as attempted NP "apartheid perestroika" with an intent for limited reform and rearrangement of surface components of the old regime. During the transition, the breakdown of negotiations, punctuated by mobilization and violence, forced the hand of all parties to open the negotiation space wider and accept *majority rule*, a *unitary state*, and a *bill of rights* granting equal citizenship to all.

In the process, all parties outgrew their initial partisan reluctance to find an acceptable agreement. In the dramatic story about choosing between living together or dying by trying to separate, all parties had to give up something sacrosanct. The NP had to accept majority rule, the IFP had to accept a unitary state, and the ANC had to embrace devolution of power and democratic checks in which the Constitution rather than Parliament reigns supreme. By doing so, these players created a new civic space in South Africa that did not exist before.

Conclusions: Success Factors, Challenges, and Lessons Learned

The significance of the 1996 Constitution is not only in creating a new identity and new *polity* "for all people in South Africa" but also in the fact that its success and importance are marked by introducing a new *way* of approaching constitution making as a *virtuous circle*. The South African experience that produced a distinctive construct to escape the trap of legal deficit at the design stage also sequenced and phased the process with unique elements, including convening and multiparty mechanism and "sufficient consensus" threshold; prior agreement on constitutional principles; drafting an interim Constitution by the (nonelected) Convention; holding of general elections to generate qualified parliamentary majority; processing of the final Constitution through the Constitutional Assembly, with broad public participation; and certification of the Constitution by the Constitutional Court, to confirm that it reflected the prior principles.

As pointed out earlier, one of the main procedural challenges facing South Africa's constitution making was ensuring *acceptance* of the final outcome of the negotiated agreement by all parties. This was accomplished by two means: (i) by establishing constitutional principles, balancing minority and majority rights, against which the Constitution can be validated, and (ii) by making the Bill of Rights the heart of the Constitution as protection of all citizens' rights, regardless of their race, status, ethnicity, or gender. This provided *accommodation* and countered the fear of the white minority by entrenching the participation of the minority parties in the democratic process. According to Justice Sachs, "The Bill of Rights gave assurance to the black majority, through justiciable social and economic rights, that it is not a protective concession to the whites, but an emancipation document addressing historical social injustice."

According to Mac Maharaj, the negotiation process failed to make early attempts "and may have started 10 years too late, while many opportunities may have been missed, after the irreparable damage caused by the violence of the 1980s." Despite the delay, by and large, it was a superior outcome for all parties compared to the counterfactual of collapsing social order and civil war. The ANC achieved majority rule. The NP did not have a better alternative to the negotiated agreement than the Bill of Rights.

Some compromises did not prove viable. The regional government structures—the nine provinces—which were largely an accommodation of the

NP federalist aspiration to counter the proposals for a black unitary government, ended up legislating a tension between two principles—*unitary* and a *federal* (provincial) governance (see also Motala and Ramaphosa 2002).

Post-revolutionary periods always raise questions about just how much change actually occurred. Critics on the right note that the ANC is the new party of power and complain that it constrains structural policy making downstream out of self-interest. Critics on the left decry the fact that, in an attempt to address the minority's fears, negotiators let the white elite retain economic power and perpetuate stark inequality and deep social divisions.

Nonetheless, the 1996 Constitution holds a hidden balance that guarantees the long view. In this delicate balance both parties found their competing moral convictions and anxieties to be accommodated only in a long-run approach. Being a framework grounded in principles and not a power balance, and by establishing a majority by the disadvantaged, it prevents deep structural reforms with high social costs; while at the same time providing a broad framework within which meaningful social transformation can occur.

What is undeniable, however, is that the new Constitution gave an *identity* and a whole *new life* to a previously fragmented country and a promise to become a truly organic nation. The second-generation (socioeconomic) rights and a fair social order remain for now a deferred *progressive* and inspirational goal. Affirmative approaches like the Black Economic Empowerment (BEE) are distributive justice strategies to partially undo the historical injustice of exclusion, rectified through restitution of political and economic rights. However, more fundamentally, the new "citizenship" that the Constitution advanced is a precondition and motivation to pursue social fairness for all by putting constitutional claims on the state for inclusive policy decision making and for better serving the needs of the bottom percentiles of the population (South Africa, National Planning Commission 2012).

There are nine striking lessons from the South African constitution-making process:

First, *establish critical pathway and progression.* It is essential to construct a virtuous path with a trajectory and progression to break the vicious circle of legitimacy deficit at the start. The South African experience gave birth to a five-step transition with two constitution-drafting stages.

Second, *favor acceptance over domination in establishing a legitimate process.* Agree on a type of a Rawlsian "initial position" on what is a just outcome for the new social contract. Include all parties. The ownership over the process establishes ex post stability and ownership of the outcomes. In the case of South Africa, the initial 34 constitutional principles served this purpose (Haysom 2002).

Third, *acknowledge the opponent's hierarchy of basic needs.* Formulate options for accommodating the adversary's anxieties. Understand the other side's hierarchy of needs and consider how they can be addressed. Make clear the binding constraints of the parties, and outline the space for trade-offs and deal breakers. Mandela's proposal to create an Afrikaner homeland is a good example.

Making It Happen • http://dx.doi.org/10.1596/978-1-4648-0768-8

Fourth, *solve cooperatively the prisoner's dilemma*. A total win creates a shaky democracy, as Madonsela notes. Decide if you prefer a defeated opponent or a partner; a defeated opponent cannot sell to its constituency a signed agreement; therefore, strengthen the hand of your opponent to remain a credible player, advises Meyer (see also Haysom 2002).

Fifth, *bring in the best international knowledge*. South Africa drew on the constitutions of two previous waves of liberation, especially India and Namibia, the Universal Declaration of Human Rights (Haysom 2002), and the Canadian, German, Irish, and U.S. experiences. No other country before South Africa has tapped into the rich legal and cultural knowledge of so many foreign legal systems to draw ideas and precedent about constitutional designs.

Sixth, *ensure team diversity*. Build a balanced team that includes both generalists and technicians.[29] Writing a constitution requires a wide spectrum of skills during the drafting process—those not only of lawyers but also of economists, historians, sociologists, anthropologists, and linguists. The text needs to be free of legalistic formulations and of racial, ethnic, religious, and gender prejudice (Murray 2001).

Seventh, *assume a mobilization–de-escalation cycle*. Without compromises and concessions the opponent's base will be left with the impression that their party's participation is not justified and can revert to mobilization and hostilities; one needs to make a means/end distinction between "power" and "interests" and "position" and "interests," as Meyer said.

Eighth, *control the environment, and enter negotiations only with credible parties and commitments*. Frame negotiations as cooperative and not as a distributive game; distributive negotiations undermine trust. According to Maharaj, it is crucial to work out consensus and tie-breaking mechanisms—that is, when to decide by unanimity and when to apply "sufficient consensus," or fractional majority; such procedural tools will prevent noncooperative small players from exercising a veto and derailing the process.

Ninth, *work with multitrack negotiations channels* and "switch tracks when an impasse is reached" remarks Maharaj. When CODESA stalled, the ANC and NP opened a direct two-party negotiation channel, before later returning to multiparty negotiations. Use third-party mediators, for example, in the case when IFP was brought to the table and to participate in the elections.

Sharing the South African experience can inform deep reforms and transitions in postconflict countries, or in countries with intensive internal racial, ethnic, and linguistic divides. The South African experience can fit well countries with a deep split between a large dominant majority and many small groups aspiring to equality, fundamental rights, and democratic governance. Another application of South Africa's experience can be in countries with significant territorial fragmentation in pursuit of balanced central versus local authority. Many lessons from South Africa have already informed and helped constitutional reforms and postconflict transitions in Afghanistan, Central Asian countries, Indonesia, Iraq, Kenya, South Sudan, Sri Lanka, and Ukraine. Experts from the negotiations teams in South Africa have provided advice to Liberia, Libya,

Nepal, the Philippines, Sierra Leone, Myanmar, South Sudan, Sudan, Tunisia, and Zimbabwe.

According to Madonsela, the South African constitutional experience needs to be studied by the new generations of South Africans as a source of inspiration for the "many rich lessons about how to engage from the position of moral strength and will for change." It is a great success story about how putting limits on authority opened space for social self-organization, citizens' energy, and a lateral common vision about a new desirable future, compared to the narrow partisan loyalties. This experience can still teach lessons about accountability, contestability of decision making, and partnerships to hold the state accountable on its delivery promise for good governance.

No constitution is ever finished, and the pursuit of the core ideals it enshrines is a protracted process. The desire for shared knowledge about how to build nationhood, create shared vision, negotiate a social contract, and reestablish faith in the goodness of the "other" remains a perpetual need.

Notes

1. The Constitutional Court approved the final Constitution on December 4, 1996. The Constitution came into effect on February 4, 1997.

2. First-generation rights encompass civil and political rights. Second-generation rights deal with entitlements to housing, health, education, and health care and other social and economic rights. Third-generation rights, also known as "solidarity rights," include the right to peace, a healthy environment, and development. Fourth-generation rights are considered to include gender and communication. Third- and particularly fourth-generation rights are under debate in international law, and not yet fully recognized. First-generation rights are largely considered "negative rights" (that is, protections are needed to ensure against their infringement). Second-, third-, and fourth-generation rights are "positive rights." They place a duty on the state to provide (see Sachs 2009).

3. The legal system in apartheid South Africa was a mix of Roman-Dutch law and elements of English law. During the apartheid, South Africa had little interest in international or comparative law.

4. In *August v. Electoral Commission and Others 1999*, Justice Sachs ruled that, if the state can deprive a prisoner of a right to vote, "In a country of great disparities of wealth and power it declares that whoever we are, whether rich or poor, exalted or disgraced, we all belong to the same democratic South African nation; that our destinies are intertwined in a single interactive polity.... Universal adult suffrage on a common voter's roll is one of the foundational values of our constitutional order" (Sachs 2009, 122).

5. ANC's historical positions in support of freedom, rights, and a democratic form of governance were formulated in three framing documents: the 1942 African Claims document, the 1955 Freedom Charter, and the Constitutional Principles for a Democratic South Africa of the 1980s.

6. The first version of a bill of rights in South Africa was the Freedom Charter, adopted by the Congress of the People at Kliptown on June 26, 1955.

7. De Klerk attempted to reform the apartheid system by restoring South African citizenship, involving black communities in decision making, offering full black ownership, and providing uniform identity documents (Burdzik and van Wyk 1987).

8. Many countries in Latin America and Southern and Eastern Europe pursued hybrid approaches of transitional justice (Popovski and Serrano 2012).

9. According to Mac Maharaj, the NP sought a guaranteed amnesty for the security forces and the army in order to ensure a peaceful and orderly transition.

10. The ANC established the objectives of the negotiated settlement in the Harare Declaration, adopted by the Organization of African Unity in 1989.

11. In these agreements, the NP accepted the ANC demands formulated in the Harare Declaration and agreed to release all political prisoners. The ANC committed to suspend the armed liberation struggle.

12. The convention broke down the main objective into committee work organized around five issues: political freedoms, constitutional principles, transitional government, homelands reintegration, and the time frame for the transition.

13. The NP strategy sought veto powers, which also according to Roelf Meyer "aimed to preserve NP's superiority in the negotiations" by raising the ceiling for required majorities to 70 percent for a regular decision of the Constitutional Assembly and 75 percent for decisions on the bill of rights (Motala and Ramaphosa 2002).

14. After violent clashes between the IFP and the ANC and the descent into a civil war, Mandela and IFP leader Mangosuthu Buthelezi called for international mediation over the status of KwaZulu-Natal; soon afterward, eight IFP marchers were killed and 84 injured outside the ANC's headquarters. The Afrikaner Resistance Movement (AWB) commandos sent to protect Bophuthatswana's leader were killed on camera. The IFP decided to take part in the election at the very last moment, after mediators brokered an agreement.

15. The MPNF structure included a negotiation council, a planning committee, seven technical committees, and two commissions.

16. An example of the inclusive spirit of the Constitution is its recognition of 11 official and 4 unofficial languages, together with "all languages commonly used by communities in South Africa," including languages used for religious purposes (see Chapter I, "Founding Provisions", Section 6 (5b) of the 1996 Constitution of South Africa).

17. More than 7 million copies of the Constitution were distributed, in all 11 languages (see the website of the Constitutional Court of South Africa at http://www .constitutionalcourt.org.za/site/theconstitution/history.htm).

18. Mandela once remarked that "historical enemies succeeded in negotiating a peaceful transition from apartheid to democracy exactly because we were prepared to accept the inherent capacity for goodness in the other."

19. In November 1992, the ANC National Executive Committee adopted a strategy paper ("Strategic Perspectives") that reflected the shift in its position toward compromise and offered these concessions.

20. The debate behind this compromise was about the choice between federalism and unitary nationhood or between consociationalism advancing a federated state to entrench group rights versus liberal citizenship (bill of rights). Under a consociationalist agenda, the NP and IFP tried belligerently to advance federalist proposals, ranging from confederation to territorial federation and racial federalization. The unitary state proposals, offered by the ANC, were anchored in the supremacy of the Constitution and the Bill of Rights, drawn from the experience of other liberal democracies for establishing a single polity with effective checks against excessive state powers (from interview with Albie Sachs; see also Sachs 1997).

21. The creation of a Boer homeland would have been unacceptable to the ANC and almost inevitably have led to armed conflict. General Viljoen could have mobilized a force of 50,000 men. A committee of retired generals with local provincial branches had been established. Mandela's instinct averted a devastating scenario by offering the general a constitutional option, which Viljoen took.

22. The established constitutional literature insists that constitutions should be the high-level framing documents committing everyone to rules rather than outcomes. Policies should be dealing with the latter.

23. See Chapter 2 of the Constitution; only a 75 percent supermajority can amend the Bill of Rights.

24. The justification for socioeconomic rights rests on the Universal Declaration of Human Rights (1949), the liberation struggle legacy, and the need to "redress patterns of disadvantage," according to Justice Sachs.

25. Chapter 2, Section 7(2), and Chapter 9 of the Constitution create independent institutions to support and protect the system of democratic governance (the South Africa Human Rights Commission; the Electoral Commission; the Commission for the Promotion and Protection of the Rights of Cultural, Religious and Linguistic Communities; the Commission for Gender Equality; the Auditor General; and the Public Protector).

26. According to Mac Maharaj, General Viljoen had set up camps in Angola for detaining the ANC leadership after introduction of martial law to preempt the first democratic elections.

27. About 30 countries in Latin America and Eastern Europe attempted different "transitional justice" approaches. Many countries introduced punitive solutions, from criminalization of perpetrators to lustration and limitation of political rights and civil rights. South Africa chose reconciliation over justice (see Popovski and Serrano 2012; and Hayner 2010).

28. Survey conducted regularly by Institute for Justice and Reconciliation, http://www.ijr.org.za/political-analysis-SARB.php.

29. According to Justice Sachs, the father of South Africa's Bill of Rights, the ANC proposals and later versions of the Constitution drew heavily on the Universal Declaration of Human Rights (1948); the European Convention for the Protection of Human Rights and Fundamental Freedoms (1950); the International Covenant on Economic, Social and Cultural Rights (1966); and the International Covenant on Civil and Political Rights (1966). Inspiration also came from national sources, including South Africa Freedom Charter, Canada's Charter of Rights and Freedoms, and the German Basic Law. See also Sarkin's (1998) analysis, on the effects of constitutional borrowings on the drafting of the South African Constitution.

References

Burdzik, Jean, and Dawid van Wyk. 1987. "Apartheid Legislation, 1976–1986." *Acta Juridica* 1987: 119–64.

Ebrahim, Hassen. 1998. *The Soul of a Nation: Constitution-Making in South Africa*. Oxford: Oxford University Press.

Gross, Aeyal M. 2004. "The Constitution, Reconciliation and Transitional Justice: Lessons from South Africa and Israel." *Stanford Journal of International Law* 40: 47–104.

Making It Happen • http://dx.doi.org/10.1596/978-1-4648-0768-8

Hayner, Priscilla. 2010. *Unspeakable Truths: Transitional Justice and the Challenge of Truth Commissions.* New York: Routledge.

Haysom, Nicholas. 2002. "Forty-One Lessons from the South African Negotiations." *Track Two* 11 (3): 35–44.

Motala, Ziyad, and Cyril Ramaphosa. 2002. *Constitutional Law: Analysis of Cases.* Oxford: Oxford University Press.

Murray, Christina. 2001. "A Constitutional Beginning: Making South Africa's Final Constitution." *UAEL Law Review* 23: 809–823.

Popovski, Vesselin, and Monica Serrano. 2012. *After Oppressions: Transitional Justice in Latin America and Eastern Europe.* Tokyo: United Nations University Press.

Sachs, Albie. 1996. "Constitutional Developments in South Africa." *International Law and Politics* 28: 695–709.

———. 1997. "The Creation of South Africa's Constitution." *New York Law School Law Review* 41: 669–701.

———. 2009. *The Strange Alchemy of Life and Law.* Oxford: Oxford University Press.

Sarkin, Jeremy. 1998. "The Effect of Constitutional Borrowings on the Drafting of South Africa's Bill of Rights and Interpretation of Human Rights Provisions." *University of Pennsylvania Journal of Constitutional Law* 1: 176–20.

South Africa, National Planning Commission. 2012. National Development Plan 2030: Our Future—Make It Work. Pretoria. http://www.gov.za/issues/national-development -plan-2030.

Wale, Kim. 2013. Confronting Exclusion: Time for Radical Reconciliation—SA Reconciliation Survey: 2013 Report. Cape Town: Institute for Justice and Reconciliation.

Conclusions: Lessons on Policy Making and Implementation

Introduction

South Africa has been on a remarkable transformational journey since the dawn of democracy in the country in 1994. The country has embarked upon multiple social, economic, and political transformations to help improve the lives of its people. The deep-rooted challenges of high poverty, inequality, and structural unemployment required public interventions in a broad array of economic sectors. It also required providing better access to, and quality of, social services to previously underserved population groups. In all cases, this required building new inclusive institutions, or strengthening existing ones, in ways that reflected the needs of the majority of the population.

The twelve case studies of institutional reforms presented in this book demonstrate not only the *why* and *what* of these changes but also, more important, *how* South Africa has developed policies, management systems, delivery mechanisms, and capacities that have had notable success in improving public service delivery. This is about developing inclusive institutions in a constantly changing and challenging political environment. Although substantial challenges still remain across a broad range of areas, these case studies highlight selected areas where the development of inclusive institutions for service delivery has been a reality and a hallmark of government action.

Each chapter provides an analysis of the policy-making and implementation process, drawing important lessons about how policies were made, how consensus was built, how obstacles were overcome, how implementation took place, and how inclusive institutions were developed. This chapter presents the eight cross-cutting lessons that were critical to the success of the reforms studied, as well as the challenges and risks inherent in the progress to date.

This book is about South Africa's story. The challenges the country faced—in building a budget and intergovernmental fiscal system, improving access to economic and social services, and providing support to the poor and the marginalized—are all needs that are common to other countries in the region and beyond. Although the experiences reflected in this book are unique to South Africa, the cross-cutting lessons derived from them are universal. These lessons are about the "how-to" of developing effective and inclusive institutions for service delivery, which might be relevant for other countries engaged in reforms on similar issues.

The South African story is very much about holistic approaches to institutional reforms and getting the basics right. It is about creating virtuous cycles of change that can drive the political economy processes. It is about using the existing reform space and, by creating quick wins, expanding this reform space to pave the ground for further reform. However, there is no unique path or magic solution to institutional reforms. On the contrary, the South African experiences confirm the value of key reform ingredients that need to be well combined and adjusted to the reform context to reach the intended reform outcomes. Nevertheless, there are various nuances to the South African experience—as seen in the way it exploited its unique reform space/opportunity, expanded it, adopted pragmatic decision making, built upon existing capabilities, and provided appropriate incentives for institutional reform. Some of the reforms could take place given the leadership of historic figures like Nelson Mandela and others and the unique reform space of the post-apartheid years. However, the key message for other countries is that the fundamentals of institutional reform matter, both for policy making and for policy implementation, as the following success factors underline.

Key Success Factors in Policy Making

Commitment to a Common National Goal

After the 1994 elections, there was a unique historic moment in South Africa. A common sense of purpose drove all the stakeholders: to develop a new South Africa that would work for its citizens. The government and the economy had to respond to the needs of all the people. The first democratically elected president, Nelson Mandela, embodied a common national vision and goal that people across boundaries were willing to commit to and make sacrifices for. There was a sense of a special moment around this common national goal of nation building, of developing a "rainbow nation" that serves one and all. The needs were immense, poverty and inequality needed to be addressed immediately, and the call to public action was clear.

Political support was strong, popular support was broad, and expectations were high. The type of institutional reforms needed to achieve the national goals required creating incentives, systems, structures, and capacities and transforming the mind-set of public officials to create a culture of service, in which people came first. Such a focus on the national goal of a new, inclusive South Africa meant putting past barriers behind, moving beyond ideology and party lines to agree on pragmatic solutions. It also meant showing willingness to make sacrifices for the common good.

Making It Happen • http://dx.doi.org/10.1596/978-1-4648-0768-8

The new Constitution was, perhaps, the best expression of the commitment to a common national goal. In fact, it became the foundation for far-reaching reforms. First, the constitution-making process itself was a good example of how the principles of inclusiveness, consensus building, and pragmatism were applied. Second, it had a strong rights-based approach, enshrining key economic and social rights. The institutional reforms discussed in this book implemented many aspects of these rights, such as on access to social services and social grants. Third, the Constitution provided for a new system of government, establishing three spheres of government with concurrent powers in many areas. Fourth, the accountability framework also derives from the Constitution, as reflected in the separation of powers of the executive, legislative, and judicial systems with a clear system of checks and balances. It also provides for the establishment of specific institutions such as the Public Protector, the National Prosecuting Authority, the Auditor General, and the Competition Commission, all important elements of the accountability system. Although the legal framework governing these agencies is well designed, the key challenge since 1994 has been the development, work, and impact of these new accountability institutions, ensuring their independence and effectiveness and, more broadly, translating accountability into practice.

Transformational Leadership

Transformational, strong, inclusive, and broad-based leadership at all levels mattered. Strong leadership was exercised not only by politicians but also by officials at all levels, showing a clear vision, technical expertise, and the drive to make reforms happen. Common to the stories in this book is the historic leadership initially provided by President Nelson Mandela, who showed the need for transformational reforms that would be inclusive and provide economic and social opportunities for all. His vision and his pragmatic and reconciliatory approach were fundamental to bringing together people and helping break down racial, economic, social, and other boundaries. Former minister of transport Mac Maharaj recalls Nelson Mandela's advice not to question the integrity of others, to control the environment, and to establish personal credibility in negotiations. It may not always have been the direct guidance from President Mandela that prompted the reforms, but it was his call for principled, fair, and measured approaches that made the difference. Even his writings from prison, for instance, on the principle of majority rule to be reconciled with white minority demands for structured guarantees shaped the mind-set of the African National Congress (ANC) leaders tasked with the drafting of the Constitution.

President's Nelson Mandela's leadership was complemented by the political leadership of ministers, agency heads, provincial leaders, and other senior policy makers. Many of the people interviewed for this book were reform champions: leaders and facilitators who empowered others and drove change to make public services accessible to and work for all citizens. This is evident in how former minister Trevor Manuel developed an inclusive process for the budget formulation process and the integration of new provinces into the national fiscal system. His leadership style was consultative, inclusive, and empowering.

Making It Happen • http://dx.doi.org/10.1596/978-1-4648-0768-8

Recognizing that the three spheres of government enshrined in the Constitution had concurrent powers in many areas, he reached out to the new provincial leaders, treating them as equals and earning their trust. Doing so created immense buy-in across the spheres to the new intergovernmental system. He lent considerable political authority to the reform process, making bold decisions to implement the Medium-Term Expenditure Framework in his first year as minister, and using his position to champion the reforms needed to cement the system.

Leadership styles were different across the chapters, but these differences were fundamental to respond to the respective organizational needs. Former minister of public administration Zola Skweyiya talks about the persuasive approach needed to overcome the difficulties in getting cabinet consensus on a new and comprehensive social grants system, crucial for addressing the common goal of reducing poverty and inequality. Former director-general of social development Vusi Madonsela recalls former minister Skweyiya taking senior managers to poor areas so as "to look poverty in the eye" and to motivate them to accelerate reform implementation. When it came to reforming the tax system, the leadership style of former commissioner of the South African Revenue Service (SARS) Pravin Gordhan was critical in its organizational transformation. His ability to attract qualified people with integrity, and empower them, was among the most important factors in the organization's turnaround. He had a hands-on leadership style, with a focus on problem solving. He personally walked the floor to countless offices to see firsthand what worked and what didn't, setting an example of how things needed to be done. Former minister of home affairs Dlamini-Zuma took a proactive approach and personally led the implementation of the national ID system, and became the public face of the reforms of her department. The strong leadership of the minister of health, Motsoaledi, as evidenced by his ability to engage with civil society and key political leaders to mobilize public support for the nationwide HIV/AIDS testing and counseling campaign, was fundamental to the revitalization of the public health sector and the success of the HIV/AIDS program. The statistical system and the roads agencies developed as centers of excellence because of the sustained leadership of their heads, Pali Lehohla, the statistician general for Statistics South Africa (Statistics SA) and Nazir Alli, the chief executive officer of the South African National Roads Agency Limited (SANRAL).

But it would be a mistake to think that the leadership that mattered was always from the top. An enabling and empowering environment helped technical teams to exercise leadership and take institutional reforms forward. For instance, in the case of performance monitoring and evaluation (M&E), the system was a political creation but was developed by a technically strong and committed team of individuals, under a leadership that gave them broad room for maneuver to create new systems. They built alliances for support, both within the then Department of Performance Monitoring and Evaluation (DPME) and across departments, in order to make progress. The political leadership supported them, but it was the technical team that actually drove forward the change. In the National Treasury, key players such as Andrew Donaldson and Ismail Momoniat were fundamental to the new intergovernmental fiscal framework and the Public Financial Management Act. They combined a longer-term vision, pragmatism, strong technical expertise, and a collaborative approach to drive change.

Consensus Building

Devoting time, money, and effort to developing and strengthening consensus was central to developing broad support for institutional change. Perhaps the process of constitution making was the ultimate in developing a broad consensus on the foundations for the new state. The practice was to seek full consensus among all the parties through discussion until agreement was reached. In some cases, the process took a lot of time, but it also helped build trust, and ensured that all options were explored and analyzed and the most suitable position of that moment in time could be found. In very rare cases, such as for determining the date for the elections and for adopting the interim constitution, a "sufficient consensus" strategy was used, which declared consensus achieved if the principal actors were in agreement on a proposal. According to the coleader of the constitution-making process, Roelf Meyer, the "inclusive nature of the process was key to developing the trust and social relationships" that included the creative use of both formal and informal processes of consultations. There were the formal structures of different constitutional committees, which managed large group deliberations. But there were also informal "retreats" and meetings among key members that were equally important. There was a lot of focus on teatime and creating time for people to engage informally to build trust and facilitate compromises. Meyer recalls a fly-fishing trip with his then colead from the ANC and now current deputy president of South Africa Cyril Ramaphosa and the importance of the communication channels established between them that lasted for three months while the negotiations came to a complete halt in 1992. Both contributed to building mutual trust and respect.

Consensus building became a defining feature of the success stories for several reasons. First, there was the recognition that an inclusive approach was key to creating a broad support for the reform initiatives. Inclusiveness was key. There was also a need to build bridges across different political and economic perspectives and for agreement on the *what* and *how* of the key institutional reforms. For example, the White Paper on Transport Policy included extensive consultations with more than 300 organizations and people from the transport industry, government, and academia. In the case of the South African Social Security Agency (SASSA), there were differences and disagreement on the scale, effect, and sustainability of the social grant system within the Cabinet. Creating representative technical committees and building coalitions outside government, with faith-based organizations and nongovernmental organizations (NGOs), helped build greater consensus within government. Communication was key. At the Department of Home Affairs, one challenge was how to gain public trust. Adopting an internal and external communications plan for engagement with management, staff, and the public was essential to achieving buy-in and changing perceptions about the department. This effort included giving feedback to staff, acknowledging good work, and providing media briefings on progress.

Second, there was an enduring belief in negotiated outcomes. There was an understanding borne out of the struggle movement and the negotiations for a peaceful solution that, as former minister Mac Maharaj put it, "the strongest thing is to listen to the other side, so as to unpack their fears and concerns." Constructive engagement, listening to others, building on their proposals, and jointly working out common proposals were key elements of the consensus-building strategy. Negotiating and understanding each other's demands was also an important step in consolidating the reform at SARS. More than 80 percent of the agency's workforce was unionized at the time of the reforms. The unions could have blocked the reform effort. But a strong culture of negotiation meant that management and the unions talked through the issues for eight months to craft an agreement for moving forward. The resulting Siyakha Protocol developed a shared strategy and made it possible to overhaul the agency. Unions and agency officials held a joint "road show" at their regional offices to ensure employees and managers understood the details of the changes they had agreed to.

Third, there was a clear recognition that consensus building was needed to ensure sustainability and protect against policy reversals. The performance M&E system built consensus around the importance of measuring performance to improve public policy outcomes. Top-down imposition would not have worked. What was needed was a persuasive approach to obtain sector buy-in and make the reform last. High-level engagements with ministers, deputy ministers, and directors-general on a collective or individual basis helped create greater support and openly address concerns at the department level. National and international workshops, trainings, how-to clinics, and other events helped create greater interest, enthusiasm, and support for the system and strengthen technical capacity to enhance demand for the different tools by DPME. Moving from a culture of compliance to one of continuous learning and improvement helped confirm that the system did not seek to control departments but rather to give them the tools to continuously enhance their own performance.

Finally, creating consensus across the three spheres of government was critical because the Constitution provides concurrent powers on many issues. For former finance minister Trevor Manuel the creation of "Team Finance" brought together the Members of the Executive Council (MECs) of finance from the provinces (representing different political parties) with the National Treasury. This process provided an inclusive platform that is now institutionalized as the Budget Council for the national budget as well as the revenue and expenditure sharing arrangements. Once matters were resolved between the MECs and the minister and their staff in Team Finance, winning the political support in the cabinet system was easier. Trevor Manuel explains how open discussion, consultation grounded in data, and a focus on problem solving fostered "common purpose and trust, helping overcome potential political obstacles."

Learning from International Experiences

Despite the unique nature of the South African post-apartheid environment, policy makers drew heavily on international experience to inform their decisions and undertook an analysis of the issues and different national and international options before taking decisions. The government recognized that drawing on good international practices, and adapting them to the country's needs, was essential for development.

Examples abound of how international experiences on what worked and what did not influenced the institutional design and implementation mechanisms of South African institutions. For instance, the National Treasury subjected all local work on the intergovernmental system to international peer review. This not only built local capacity but also resulted in a judicious mix between local and international, civil society, and government expertise. Peer reviews by international consultants were also used to resolve methodological disputes in different statistical outputs produced by Statistics SA, ensuring that the products not only were credible domestically but also met international standards. Likewise, in analyzing different international organizational models, New Zealand strongly influenced the establishment of SANRAL. Although the agency model was replicated in several areas, "not all were successful, demonstrating that no one-size-fits-all model works," according to Mac Maharaj. The design and structure of SASSA was modeled after the Australian social grants payment agency. The development of SARS drew upon the Swedish experience, as former commissioner Pravin Gordhan recalls. The national evaluation system followed an evidence-based analysis of national needs and built on the experiences of Chile, Colombia, Mexico, and other countries. In the constitution-making process, "the notion of cooperative governance was borrowed from the Canadians and the fundamental principles of the state in the Constitution were inspired by the Directive Principles of the Indian Constitution," notes Roelf Meyer. The constitutional choice for a unitary state emerged after a review of several federal state and other models, including Australia, India, the United Kingdom, and the United States, which led policy makers to conclude that federalism posed strong risks for fragmentation.

Global trends toward transparent budgets, new public management approaches, performance monitoring, and greater accountability also helped shape the reform agenda. The design of the M&E system was also enriched by international good practices. Instead of reinventing the wheel, the DPME team felt it wanted to learn as much as possible from other countries before designing its system. International visits were undertaken to more than ten countries to analyze their national M&E systems and to learn both from their successes and explicitly also from their failures. Study tours were well prepared and followed up and helped avoid much more expensive mistakes in design and implementation and thus proved to be a very strategic investment. DPME continues to play a strong role in international exchanges in building on what others have done, and it was able to access good practices, adjust them to the local context, and proceed rapidly in the design of new systems.

Making It Happen • http://dx.doi.org/10.1596/978-1-4648-0768-8

The international trend toward greater transparency helped make transparency a key reform ingredient that became a model for other countries, for example by including service delivery and performance-oriented information in the budget process, increasing the budget coverage and comprehensiveness, and introducing medium-term budgeting. International expertise, such as from the International Monetary Fund (IMF), the Austrian government, and top foreign universities, was drawn on to help design the budget system and the intergovernmental framework. The new budget system was to be among the top-performing systems worldwide, and building on other countries' experiences helped ensure a technically solid design, allowing South Africa to regularly achieve top ranks in the Open Budget Index. Statistics SA has become an institution that creates and promotes transparent and high-quality information and features products that are recognized globally. It plays an important regional role in improving statistical systems in Africa, leading the Reference Regional Strategic Framework for Statistical Capacity Building and the Africa Symposia for Statistical Development.

Key Success Factors in Policy Implementation

Promoting Inclusive Institution Building

Inclusive institution building emphasized two main points: first, creating new inclusive institutions, and, second, ensuring inclusive staffing.

First, the organizational changes were key in several reform cases highlighted in the book, most notably on the intergovernmental framework (Financial and Fiscal Commission [FFC]), tax administration (SARS), performance M&E (DPME), social grants (SASSA), biodiversity (South African National Biodiversity Institute [SANBI]), and national roads (SANRAL), among others. Policy makers realized that, in order to push through the intended reforms, the current institutional setup was insufficient. In some cases, there was a need for more informal new institutions that could lead the reforms, such as the informal Team Finance and FFC, to bring forward the reforms. In other cases, creating new institutions helped to start from scratch without the resistance to reform that might be found in some of the existing institutions. In other cases, an institution that was at arms length or more private sector inspired (SANRAL) could be better placed to attract funding and maintain certain autonomy, and was therefore seen as the more appropriate organizational form. Likewise, the creation of SANBI allowed for a more community-focused approach while including a greater focus on income generation through its commercial activities. New mandates, structures, and organizational forms helped generate a sense of reform and of urgency. They also provided greater reform flexibility. More strategic decisions could be taken for the new institutions, more strategic mandates and roles could be envisaged, and different types of new service delivery models could be designed, with less resistance to change. The new institutions formalized reform objectives and gave policy makers the foundation, tools, and structures to accelerate the necessary reforms. They also deepened the reform momentum and were able to attract new staff, ready to roll up their sleeves to take on new responsibilities for the good of their country. As different as all these institutions were, they all became vehicles for reform, the shell in which all other factors (leadership, consensus building, staff, policy, and politics, to name a few) were combined, differently in each of the cases, allowing policy makers to carry out more ambitious reforms, such as in the case of SASSA and DPME.

Second, people were key to the design and implementation of policies. As part of the constitution-making process, South Africa made the political decision and provided sufficient funding to attract new staff and maintain continuity of key existing staff in the public sector. This was done with the explicit goal of avoiding large layoffs and political polarization. The challenge was to keep the veteran staff who had strong knowledge about the institution and the area of expertise, yet to make institutions more inclusive and bring in a new cadre of staff often with less experience. For former commissioner Pravin Gordhan, the transformation of SARs was achieved by twinning younger black officials with senior managers to provide on-the-job training. A more diverse workforce was brought in, with opportunities for promotion to management. This strategy transformed the racial structure of the agency. For Statistics SA head Pali Lehohla, an overarching goal guiding the transformation of Statistics SA was retaining senior skilled individuals and attracting and training new staff with the critical skills needed for the agency.

The choice of new staff was very important to former transport minister Mac Maharaj as he sought to transform the transport department. He undertook "a detailed mapping and scoping of talent, to develop a professional core, and select managers with people management skills." The emphasis was "not to let politics overwhelm professionalism." Many departments, such as Home Affairs, created in-house training courses to train new incoming staff. Some, such as SANRAL, worked with universities to create specialized courses for students to enhance the pool of potential recruits and to encourage technical training at universities, such as a mandatory specialized MBA course for senior provincial managers offered by the University of Witwatersrand.

The quality of management also needed to be fundamentally strengthened. Managers and staff were not used to operating as a team. At the Department of Home Affairs, management met only at the deputy director-general and higher level. Regular meetings needed to be instituted, including with provincial managers so as to create a sense of shared purpose. Trevor Manuel instituted biweekly meetings with his management staff so they could air problems. Ms. Dlamini-Zuma refers to the "first 500," a meeting for the top 500 managers, to discuss common issues and promote interaction between regional and national managers. She also encouraged performance, ranking offices according to performance and promoting exchanges between the best and worst performers.

DPME recruited strong technical staff who were often trained in house and on the job. It provided leadership positions to help build a new cadre of management from in-house positions. Incentives included opportunities for staff to further develop their skills, for instance, access to further education and training; financial and nonfinancial incentives for good performance; and disincentives for poor performance (perform or move, a soft application of the "up-or-out" principle). A specialized unit set up for capacity-building purposes has designed a capacity-building strategy, conducts workshops and trainings, and has created a community of practice.

Transforming staffing also meant creating a sense of identity, an attractive corporate culture, and a sense of pride in work. This was noticeable across the board, in areas such as statistics, tax administration, roads, and budget management and in national identification documents. The professionalization of SARS and the improved work conditions transformed it into an employer of choice. SARS was quite creative in establishing a new corporate culture. It used communication and mass mobilization skills acquired during the previous two decades and applied them to institutional reforms. The management culture—in fact, the entire corporate culture—was changed. This was illustrated by a move from an inward- to an outward-looking institution, with a more client-centric culture. Service delivery improvements included establishing relationship managers for key sectors, creating call centers with a high first-time resolution rate of complaints, and the increased use of information technology (IT) tools, such as e-filing and e-payments.

Creating Virtuous Cycles with "Quick Wins"

In a climate of having achieved the impossible and a spirit of euphoria for the possible, policy makers had to respond quickly to the long-denied needs of the population. It all started from leadership and the sense of national purpose (see figure C.1). The new leaders were driven by a sense of urgency. This came from a desire to respond to the dire needs of the people who had suffered for so long and for whom the fruits of their sacrifices had to show in improved living conditions. But many of the leaders themselves had come from humble backgrounds and had suffered incarceration and torture during the apartheid era. This reinforced the deeply felt need for immediate action to undertake fundamental organizational changes in key institutions. Strategy development was important, but so was the need to be pragmatic and avoid getting caught up in ideological battles. The focus was on implementation and quick results, which were essential to reinforce the political support and fuel the momentum for change. In effect, success was in creating a virtuous cycle of change with "quick wins."

A sense of urgency in addressing the needs of the population drove the changes. In the case of social grants, for former minister Zola Skweyiya, time was of the essence in developing an effective social grant system because poverty was deep and the poor had a constitutional right to receive support. Regarding national roads, former transport minister Mac Maharaj reflects on how the urgent need for setting up a specialized road agency and putting it on a commercial footing was driven by the long distances that many poor black workers had to cover on a daily basis and the debilitating effect these commutes had on their lives and finances. The acute poverty and inequality, especially in the townships, had to be addressed as a matter of urgency. Similarly, for former home affairs minister Dlamini-Zuma, delays in getting identification were denying citizens'

Figure C.1 Creating a Virtuous Cycle of Change

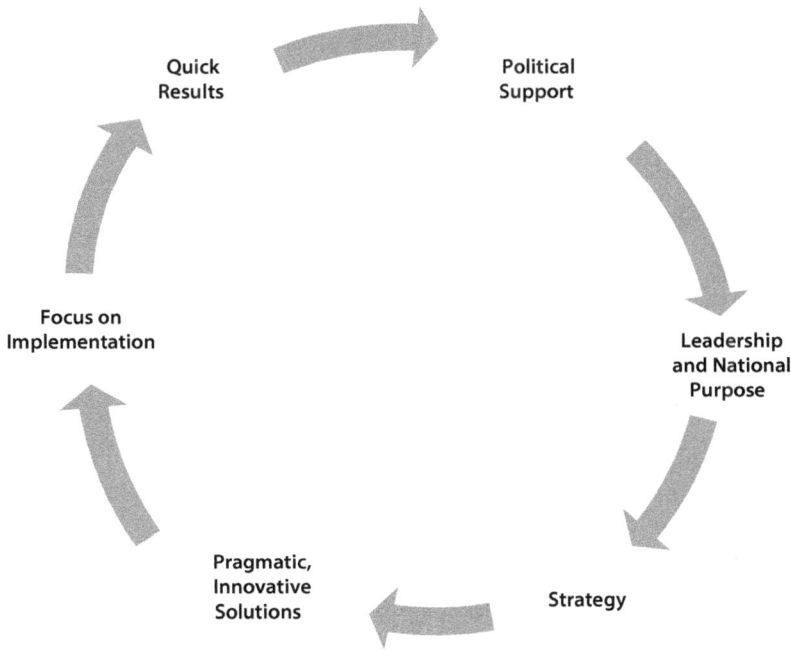

access to pensions and social grants and often forcing them into destitution and even suicide. She recalls how she once camped out in a department office just to make sure that the services were provided to a suffering citizen.

Adopting Pragmatic, Flexible, and Innovative Approaches

The adoption of flexible approaches to reform implementation proved to be a main factor in moving forward with reforms and overcoming obstacles. The case studies clearly highlight the adoption of pragmatic solutions. Notwithstanding the ideological past of many of the policy makers, the solutions adopted and implemented reflected the urgency of addressing the problems of the people and learning from whatever works. There was a need to come together as a nation and design and implement those policies that would achieve quick results. The goal was not to design the perfect, academic model but to come up with practical, effective solutions that responded to citizens' needs and could also generate broad support. For example, in the fight against HIV/AIDS, pragmatic solutions such as the antiretroviral treatment (ART) ended up triumphing over more ideological approaches.

In most cases, an experimental, innovative, learning, and adaptive approach was adopted. The flexible approach to reforms provided scope for improvements to develop over time in light of actual experience. Instead of a rigid legal framework establishing DPME, a more flexible cabinet decision was sought that would allow the young institution to grow and evolve according to future needs.

DPME's management arrangements were set up in a flexible way, promoting further evolution of thematic areas, effective collaboration between units, and staff mobility between units and the creation of new units and tools as the need emerged.

The ability to manage dynamically was also a key factor of success for SASSA, which regularly redesigned its business processes and systems to address obstacles effectively. Sometimes, innovative management practices were a result of creative energy, for example, through the independent initiatives of the branch managers or technical staff. As Minister Pravin Gordhan said, "You drive from the top in terms of intent and example, but most organizations will have activists if you give them the space to pick up that and add their own variations." Once a good practice was set, it spread throughout the institution and people began to innovate in their own way. This happened in SARS's front offices, where small innovations on greater client orientation (for example, a different way of organizing queues or simply serving hot coffee to people waiting outside an office on a cold morning) had a great impact.

Flexible approaches were also about learning from failures. The story behind these cases is not always just about immediate "success" but also about too many different failures that generated a wealth of experiences to redesign the reform path. The failures allowed rethinking both policy design options and implementations options, and were often a necessary process that helped pave the way to the achievement of the reform outcomes. They were thus a crucial element of the "how-to" of reform. The success of the ART program was the result of years of failing to roll it out and effectively reach people. The majority rule and the bill of rights granting equal citizenship to all in the constitutional reform were results of several different failed attempts to reach consensus. Failures have transformed all stakeholders along the reform process—leaders, institutions, staff, and citizens—and, instead of discouraging them, gave them new ideas to make things happen. And finally, as pointed out in each chapter, there are still important challenges on the way forward in many reform areas that in some cases actually risk undermining the success achieved so far (for example, SARS).

Strengthening Transparency and Accountability

The objectives of transparency and accountability were central features of the transition to democracy. They are recognized in the new Constitution that started to change the structure, distribution of power, and management of public resources in South Africa. The principles of transparency and accountability have guided the National Treasury in formulating the laws, practices, and procedures that govern public finance, resulting in a more transparent and credible budget process. The creation of a cutting-edge performance M&E system was an important step toward enhancing the quality of public services in key areas by using tools and information to enhance accountability across government. Although the production of information (in terms of both the budget process and institutional performance) has been fruitful, the use of this information to ensure system accountability is still a major challenge.

Making It Happen • http://dx.doi.org/10.1596/978-1-4648-0768-8

As many chapters showed, simple and clear accountability arrangements were key to getting things done. First, a main element was clear decision-making structures in the respective organizations and the enforcement of decisions. The Public Finance Management Act was a huge step forward in promoting accountability of the intergovernmental fiscal system. Its premise was to "let managers in all spheres manage but hold them to account" in the words of Ismail Momoniat, deputy director-general of the National Treasury. The act shifted responsibility for the management and use of resources from the center to managers in spending departments and agencies of each sphere. It set out who in the spheres was responsible for putting in place processes and procedures, what these should achieve, and how these results should be reported and monitored. Enforcement was as important to ensure accountability. Momoniat recounts that in the early days "people were scared of the sanctions and took them very seriously. If you did not deliver, there was trouble."

Second, the problem of massive corruption had to be addressed urgently. The Department of Home Affairs was beset with fraud. Nurses worked with crime syndicates to register false births in order to enable access to grants, and officials colluded to issue false IDs to fraudulently access pensions and other payments. Officials would take turns going on leave and pass on their computer user codes to others in the syndicate to do fraudulent work. Similarly, at Johannesburg's international airport, criminal syndicates would smuggle foreigners into the country. The creation of a special investigative unit in Home Affairs, the restriction of access by the use of finger print identification tools, the use of technology, and very public arrests and indictments helped. At the airport, a group of 300 immigration officials were replaced by trained defense forces staff, and the enforcement of the immigration system was systematized to prevent abuses. Former minister Dlamini-Zuma recounts how many observers thought that this could not be done, but that with strong political will the government was able to address this problem proactively. Preventive anticorruption communication and demonstrable cases of consequences sent a very strong signal to everyone that corruption was unacceptable. SANRAL implemented a fraud and corruption policy with the objective of protecting its revenue, assets, and reputation, including an independently operated fraud hotline service operated by Tip-Offs Anonymous. Although corruption is still a major concern across institutions, these mechanisms have set examples of how to reduce opportunities for corruption if there is accountability—in this case, political will and technical know-how to do so.

Third, the use of IT systems to fight corruption was very important. Online applications for passports and the easy and real-time registration of births by connecting hospital registration to Home Affairs registration of newborns helped reduce opportunities for corruption. At SARS, IT systems, such as electronic tax declarations and other tools for administrative simplification, helped reduce corruption between officials and taxpayers. When the Department of Home Affairs was struggling with capacity challenges, SARS provided IT support that helped it to address the challenges and introduce new tools.

Making It Happen • http://dx.doi.org/10.1596/978-1-4648-0768-8

Increased information sharing was another reform element promoting transparency. The role of the media was central to promote such transparency policies, on the basis of broad public consensus. Much of the negotiations on the constitution were conducted under the public gaze, with immediate reporting in the media. Policy makers often appeared on the news to discuss the reform status and received feedback from citizens. Former home affairs minister Dlamini-Zuma recalls that her Cabinet colleagues and department staff were surprised when she decided to appear on a monthly call-in radio show to listen to the concerns of the citizens, involve them in providing solutions, and explain what the government was trying to do. These activities helped build trust and move toward a more responsive, constructive engagement with citizens. The media also played an important role in increasing consensus on the reform of social grants. By sharing information about the incidence and depth of poverty around the country, and on reform plans and progress in implementing them, the media helped make the point for the need for reform. In terms of parliamentary transparency, Minister Pravin Gordhan notes how the openness of parliamentary committee meetings was agreed upon as the rule, not the exception.

Risks to Sustainability

The institutional reforms documented in this book have been transformational. This book has covered only a selected number of case studies. There are other successful areas as well as many failures and shortcomings, which have not been documented here. The basic hallmark of the experience documented is the creation of inclusive institutions, which have improved public service. Some have taken more time than others, but they have all developed with the active lead of the state and the participation of its citizenry.

While a lot has been achieved in the areas documented in this book, there are risks to their sustainability that need to be managed lest they undermine the gains to date. There are two main sources of risks.

First, there is the risk of complacency. Institutional reforms have to be an ongoing dynamic process, endogenous to the changing environment in order to stay relevant to the changing needs of society. For instance, although budget transparency has been achieved, further reforms are needed to ensure budget efficiency to achieve the desired outcomes. A continued focus on implementation and on maintaining the pragmatic, flexible, innovative approach to institutional change is needed. Complacency risks stagnation, capture by vested interests, and ultimately decay in the change process.

Second is the risk of the perceived weaknesses in the systems of accountability. Policies, systems, and tools for greater government performance to deliver economic and social goods have been created. The institutional reforms have helped bring much information to the public eye and enhance transparency. How this information is actually used for greater internal and external accountability, to ensure that the institutions and systems created can have the desired impact, is essential to get the full benefits from these changes. Accountability means that there have to be clear consequences for poor service delivery, the abuse of authority, and the misuse of funds and corruption, which would, over time, corrode the institutional gains made. Transparency is critical to the pursuit of accountability but not sufficient by itself to ensure it. The key question then is how this transparency dividend can be turned into an accountability dividend. This is a key risk and challenge for the institutions discussed in this book.

The Final Word

South Africa's history has been unique. So has been the development trajectory since the birth of the new democracy in 1994. This is still a very new democracy by global standards and one that is still evolving. So is the South African experience then replicable in other countries?

The answer to this question is an irrevocable yes—but with due adaptation to country-specific situations. The challenges the country faced in providing social support to the poor and the marginalized, developing an effective system for tax administration, preserving its precious biodiversity, strengthening its statistical and budgetary systems, developing its road network, providing for a unified intergovernmental fiscal system, and, above all, anchoring the state in a solid constitutional system are all needs that are common to the comity of nations.

The eight cross-cutting lessons derived in this book are unique to South Africa and yet universal. These lessons are about the how-to of developing institutions of excellence, not only in the design of public policies but also in their delivery. The precise design features of institutions a particular country may wish to develop may be different, as may be the links with other institutions and the sequencing of implementation; but the overall thesis of putting "people first" and using it to drive the creation of inclusive institutions is applicable to all.

But South Africa's experience documented here speaks not only to the rest of the world but also to the South Africa of today, which is still struggling to improve public services for its citizens, especially the poor, in many critical areas. There are many other challenges that are beyond the focus of this book, including inequality, unemployment, and social sector outcomes. The lessons from yesteryear also hark to the policy makers of today, and bring valuable wisdom and experience that can help create the South Africa that is true to the aspirations of all its citizens.

Making It Happen • http://dx.doi.org/10.1596/978-1-4648-0768-8

Environmental Benefits Statement

The World Bank Group is committed to reducing its environmental footprint. In support of this commitment, the Publishing and Knowledge Division leverages electronic publishing options and print-on-demand technology, which is located in regional hubs worldwide. Together, these initiatives enable print runs to be lowered and shipping distances decreased, resulting in reduced paper consumption, chemical use, greenhouse gas emissions, and waste.

The Publishing and Knowledge Division follows the recommended standards for paper use set by the Green Press Initiative. The majority of our books are printed on Forest Stewardship Council (FSC)–certified paper, with nearly all containing 50–100 percent recycled content. The recycled fiber in our book paper is either unbleached or bleached using totally chlorine-free (TCF), processed chlorine-free (PCF), or enhanced elemental chlorine-free (EECF) processes.

More information about the Bank's environmental philosophy can be found at http://www.worldbank.org/corporateresponsibility.

green
press
INITIATIVE

www.ingramcontent.com/pod-product-compliance
Lightning Source LLC
Chambersburg PA
CBHW080417270326
41929CB00018B/3058